W9-AWC-552

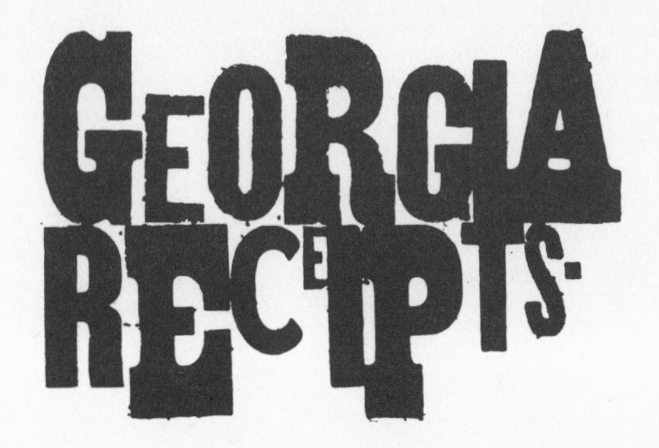


a guide to superlative Southern cuisine

Compiled and edited by
Glenn McCullough

for

The Georgia Press Association

Published By
Hallux, Inc.

GEORGIA RECEIPTS



Library of Congress Catalog Card Number: 74-158351

Manufactured In The United States of America

Published By
The Georgia Press Association
1075 Spring N. W.
Atlanta, Ga. 30309

Publication Supervision By
Hallux, Inc.
Publishers of Books
Peachtree Center Sta. (56214)
Atlanta, Ga. 30343

## Acknowledgments

To the many newspaper folk, their friends, their readers, who so graciously shared their favorite family receipts, we express our sincere appreciation.

A special thanks to Mrs. Sam Griffin of the Bainbridge *Post-Searchlight,* who conceived the idea of publishing such a cookbook after having received so many excellent receipts at the women's breakfast session, during a convention of the Georgia Press Association.

To Ben Green Cooper of Cobb County, who provided wood type from his shop for the cover and title pages.

To Ken Kendrick of the Phoenix in Underground Atlanta, for providing both wood type and press proofs of the various title pages.

To Hartmut Paul for the title page photography.

To Nancy Cucich for her assistance in layout and design.

To the GPA staff for its untiring efforts in preparing the manuscript and proofing.

To Wilton Hall, Jr. for his patience and help and for constantly extending our deadlines.

And finally, to Shirley, my wife, for nagging me to meet deadlines.

G. M.

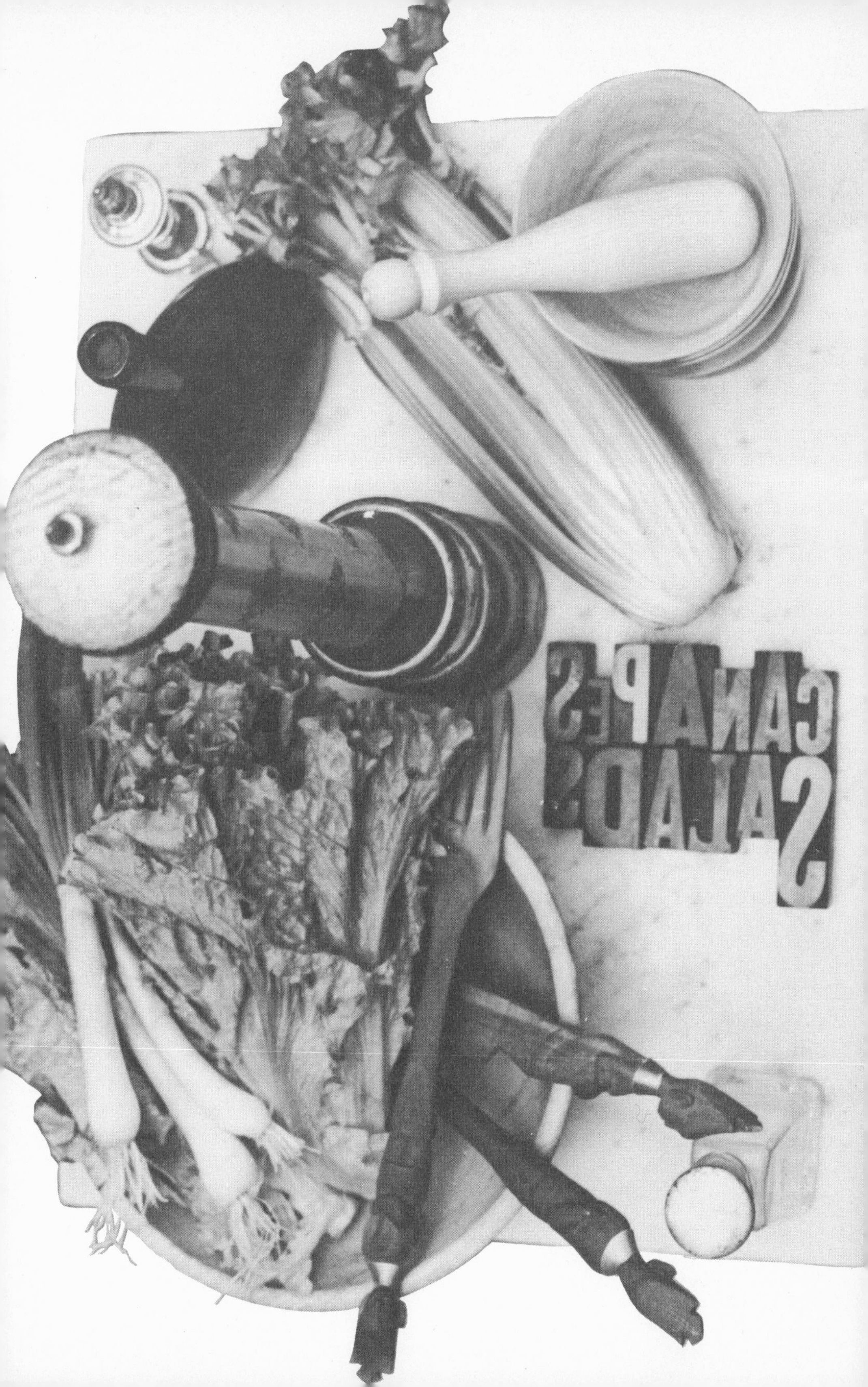
CANAPES
SALADS

## Cheese Blintzes

*Glenn McCullough*

Blintzes

1 cup flour
1/2 teaspoon salt
4 eggs
1 cup milk
real butter
patience

Filling

1 pound dry cottage cheese
1 egg yolk
1 tablespoon melted butter
1 tablespoon sugar
pinch of salt

*Blintzes:* Sift flour and salt together. Beat eggs, then add milk and beat some more. Now, gradually add flour to eggs, taking care to stir constantly to avoid lumps. The best bet is to place the whole mixture in a blender and set on mix. Lightly coat a small (6-inch) iron skillet with butter and place over moderate to high heat. Pour about 1/2 cup of mixture into skillet and let it remain a short while (until it has time to stick) then pour the excess back into the blender or container. Let the coating cook until blisters appear and the edges break away from the iron. Now, even though the middle of the blintze may be still moist, dump it out on a wooden board by sharply striking the board with the inverted skillet. Repeat the process until all the batter is used up, re-greasing the skillet about every third time around. Now, set the blintzes aside and prepare the filling.

*Filling:* Combine all ingredients and place a tablespoon in the center of each blintze – brown side. Raise the bottom flap to cover the filling, overlapping that with the top flap and tucking in the sides like a little blanket. Fry in a generous amount of real butter until golden brown on each side. Serve hot with applesauce, blueberries (simmered with a little flour and sugar), strawberry jam or peach preserves and a generous topping of sour cream. All this is a great deal of trouble and requires constant attention for an extended period, but the results make it all worth it.

### Chili Cheese Ball

1 small package cream cheese
1/2 pound sharp cheese
garlic, grated
chili powder
1/4 cup pecans, ground
olives
1/2 tablespoon cream to make consistency to roll

Mix ingredients except chili powder. Roll on waxed paper that has been "floured" with chili powder. Chill and slice. Serve with crackers.

### Cheese Diable

3/4 pound Philadelphia brand cheese
1 tablespoon Tabasco sauce
4 pickled walnuts, finely chopped
1/2 pound Roquefort cheese
2 ounces butter
1 tablespoon Worcestershire sauce
sweet cream

Combine ingredients except cream. Moisten with sweet cream and mix to a smooth consistency. Serve with crackers.

### Cheese Roll

1 package Old English cheese
1 wedge Roquefort cheese
chopped parsley
3 packages cream cheese
chopped pecans
garlic

Rub bowl well with garlic. Mix cheeses together and form roll. Roll in chopped pecans and chopped parsley. Set in ice box to harden. Slice.

### Date-Cheese Balls

1 box dates
pecans, halves or broken
cheese straw dough

Put nuts in dates. Roll dates completely in cheese dough. Place on cookie sheet and cook for 30 minutes in a very slow oven (250 degrees). Let cool. Store in tin. Will keep a week or longer.

### Cheese Fondue

2 cloves garlic
12 tablespoons flour
6 cups half and half
6 cups Cheddar cheese, shredded
3 loaves French bread
12 tablespoons oleo
8 teaspoons mustard, prepared
9 cups Swiss cheese, shredded

Rub inside of saucepan with garlic. Melt butter; blend in flour and mustard. Add half and half, Cheddar cheese and Swiss cheese. Pour into chafing dish.

### Brandied Cheese Balls

1 pound sharp cheese
3 tablespoons mayonnaise
2 ounces good brandy or bourbon
2 dashes bitters
salt to taste
red pepper, dash or two

Let the cheese stand at room temperature for several hours, then put through meat grinder. Cream this thoroughly with other ingredients. Chill before rolling into small balls. Touch on one side with paprika or sprig of green. Store in ice box until ready to use.

## Chicken Toasties

*Julia Dyar*

1 cup cooked chicken, diced
1/2 teaspoon curry powder
soft butter or margarine
paprika
1 tablespoon celery, minced
1/2 cup mayonnaise
1/2 teaspoon onion salt
14 slices fresh white bread, soft and easy to roll

The day before serving, combine chicken, mayonnaise, onion salt, curry powder and minced celery until creamy. Trim crusts from bread. Butter each slice lightly, then spread 1 tablespoon of mixture over each. Sprinkle with paprika. Roll up, jelly-roll fashion, wrap in waxed paper and refrigerate.

Just before serving, slice each roll crosswise into 6 or 7 slices. Toast under broiler on each side. Makes 7 or 8 dozen.

## Shrimp Paste

8 packages cream cheese
1 1/2 pounds shrimp, cooked
1 large bottle Durkees dressing
onion juice to taste
1 teaspoon prepared mustard
1 teaspoon red pepper
lemon juice to taste
1 medium-size bottle stuffed olives, chopped

Mix ingredients in order of cream cheese, shrimp, dressing, olives, mustard, pepper and lemon and onion juice. Let stand in refrigerator until firm. Slice thin and serve on cocktail crackers or small squares of toast. Serves 40 to 50.

## Curried Tuna Toasties

1 can chunk style tuna,
  (1 cup)
1/2 teaspoon curry powder
soft butter or margarine
1/2 cup mayonnaise
1/2 teaspoon onion salt
14 slices fresh white bread,
  soft and easy to roll

The day before serving, combine tuna, mayonnaise, onion salt and curry powder until creamy. Trim crusts from bread. Butter each slice lightly, then spread 1 tablespoon of mixture over each. Sprinkle with paprika. Roll up, jelly-roll fashion, wrap in waxed paper and refrigerate.

Just before serving, slice each roll crosswise into 6 or 7 slices. Toast under broiler on each side. Makes 7 or 8 dozen.

## Creme Vichyssoise

6 leeks (white part only)
2 medium onions
1/4 pound butter
3/4 pound white potatoes
chives
2 quarts chicken stock
1 cup sweet cream
salt
white pepper

Chop onions and leeks fine, then cook slowly in 1/4 pound butter. Do not brown, just cook until soft, then add stock and potatoes (peeled and cut into small pieces). Add salt and pepper to taste and cook until potatoes are done. Put through a very fine strainer. Add cream. Chill thoroughly. When serving, sprinkle finely chopped chives on top. Serves 6 to 8.

## Egg Roll

1/2 cup water
2 eggs, beaten
1/2 cup flour, sifted
1/2 cup shrimp, cooked
1/2 cup bamboo shoots
1/2 teaspoon pepper
2 teaspoons oil
1/3 cup water chestnuts
1 tablespoon scallions, diced
1 tablespoon celery, sliced
1 teaspoon salt
1/2 cup pork or beef, cooked
1 teaspoon Enhance, msg

Beat eggs, water and salt. Add flour gradually. Grease chafing dish pancake pan. Heat and pour in thin layer of batter. Cook 1 minute and cool on towel. Repeat for all. Combine rest of ingredients for filling. Place 1 tablespoon of mixture on each cooled pancake. Roll, tucking in edges. Moisten edges with batter and press. Chill 20 minutes. Fry in deep hot fat. Drain.

## Cheese Roll

1 pound American cheese, grated
1 package cream cheese
1/4 teaspoon sugar
1/4 teaspoon salt
bud garlic
1/8 teaspoon cayenne pepper
dash paprika
8 stuffed olives, finely chopped
1/4 cup pecans, finely chopped

Rub mixing bowl with bud garlic and cream remaining ingredients well. Divide mixture into 3 parts, make into 3 rolls and wrap separately in wax paper. Place in refrigerator overnight. Keeps for several days.

### Guacomole

*Glenn McCullough*

3 large ripe avocados
juice of 1 lime
1 teaspoon salt
1/2 teaspoon garlic powder
  or 1 clove garlic, crushed
1/2 cup sour cream
1 small onion, chopped
  fine
2 tablespoons olive oil
green hot peppers (to taste)
Tabasco sauce

Peel and mash avocados in bowl and sprinkle with lime juice. Add salt, peppers, Tabasco, garlic, onion, oil and sour cream. Mix well, preferably in blender. The amount of Tabasco should vary with the number of green peppers used. If green peppers are unavailable, be generous with the sauce, otherwise a few dashes are sufficient to impart a distinguished taste. This makes an excellent dip for corn chips.

### Smoky Egg Dip

12 hard cooked, diced eggs
2 1/2 teaspoons liquid
  smoke seasoning
3/4 cup sour cream
1 tablespoon wine vinegar
3 teaspoons brown mustard
2 teaspoons Worcestershire
  sauce
4 drops hot sauce
1 teaspoon salt
1/2 teaspoon pepper
1/2 teaspoon onion salt

Combine all ingredients and beat until smooth. Refrigerate. About 30 minutes before serving, remove from refrigerator; pile into chilled bowl. Serve with raw cauliflowerettes, crackers, celery and carrot strips.

### Pickled Watermelon Rind

3 pounds prepared watermelon rind
2 pounds sugar
2 cups white vinegar
6 3-inch cinnamon sticks
2 tablespoons whole cloves
2 tablespoons whole allspice

Use rind from firm, not overripe watermelon. Trim outer green skin and pink flesh allowing a thin line of pink to show. Cut into 1 1/2 X 1 X 3/4 pieces. Soak overnight in salt water (3 tablespoons salt per quart of water); drain. Cover with fresh water and cook until tender; drain. Heat sugar and vinegar to boiling. Add spices tied in cheesecloth bag. Add rind. Cook, uncovered, until transparent, about 45 minutes. Remove spice bag. Simmer while quickly packing 1 hot sterilized jar at a time. Fill to within 1/8-inch from top. Be sure vinegar solution covers rind. Seal each jar at once. Makes 3 pints.

### White Cherry Salad

1 can large white cherries
pecan halves
cream cheese
1 envelope gelatin
1/2 cup cold water
1 cup juice from cherries
sugar
mayonnaise

Seed cherries and stuff with pecan halves and cream cheese. Put stuffed cherries in individual molds. Soak gelatin in cold water for 3 minutes then add fruit juice which has been heated and sweetened to taste. When partly set pour over cherries and chill. Turn out on lettuce leaves and top with mayonnaise.

### Tiny Tim Appetizers

red cocktail tomatoes
anchovy or tuna, crab or
green olive
cream cheese, softened
Tabasco

Slice off stem and remove pulp of red cocktail tomatoes. Discard the slice and pulp. Stuff the shells with cream cheese and anchovy or with tuna, crab and chopped green olive, blended with cream cheese and a drop or two of Tabasco. (Use the shells filled with horse-radish and serve with roast beef, corned beef, etc.)

### Mushroom Tempters

mushrooms, finely chopped
butter
1 tablespoon flour
little minced onion
garlic salt
1 tablespoon cream

Saute mushrooms with minced onion in butter, seasoned with garlic salt. Stir in flour and cream. Make bite-sized sandwiches, brush with melted butter and place under broiler until golden. Serve hot.

### Cucumber Soup

4 cups cream sauce
salt
1/2 cup cream
3 cucumbers
pepper
2 teaspoons bitters

Add peeled and thinly sliced cucumbers to cream sauce. Cook slowly until soft and transparent, then rub through a sieve. Reheat, season with salt and pepper and add cream and bitters. Serves 6.

### Stuffed Cucumber

1 cucumber, pared
chives or capers
cream cheese

Remove center from cucumber with apple corer and stuff firmly with cream cheese, seasoned with chives or capers. Chill. Slice 1/4-inch thick.

### Deviled Ham Canapes

deviled ham, canned
1/2 small onion, grated
stuffed green olive
1 tablespoon horse-radish
coarse black pepper

Blend deviled ham with horse-radish and 1/2 grated onion per can. Season to taste with coarse black pepper. Spread on bases and top with thin slice of stuffed green olive.

### Canape Bases

These may be simple crispy crackers, Melba toast, miniature cream puffs, small biscuits, sliced cucumber, zucchini or summer squash, dill pickle slices or thin, round, star, crescent cut toast.

### Bacon-Blanketed Appetizers

Roll 1/2 strip bacon around any of an almost infinite number of foods and broil for about five minutes, or until bacon is done. Place in chafing dish so warmth is held for party self-serving.

Suggested foods for blanketing: large green stuffed olive; frozen crab puffs; raw oyster; pineapple chunk; cooked mushroom; cooked shrimp; cooked chicken liver; Vienna sausage; cubed Bologna, etc.

### Fried Artichoke

8 tiny artichoke hearts
2 eggs
olive oil
1 teaspoon oregano
pepper, freshly ground
1 cup bread crumbs
1 tablespoon parsley, chopped
salt

Season artichoke hearts. Beat eggs, combine parsley with crumbs. Dip canned artichokes in egg, then in crumbs. Heat 1 inch of olive oil in chafing dish pan over direct flame until smoking. Fry artichokes in hot oil until brown. Drain on absorbent paper. Serve hot with toothpicks.

### Tomato Aspic

1 tablespoon gelatin
2 tablespoons water
2 tablespoons vinegar
2 cups tomato juice
1/8 teaspoon pepper
1 bay leaf
1 onion, sliced
1 teaspoon sugar
1 teaspoon salt
few celery leaves

Soften plain gelatin in cold water and vinegar. Simmer tomato juice with seasonings for 15 minutes. Strain over gelatin, stir until dissolved. Pour into molds and chill until set.

### Cheese Slaw

*Aline Burgess*

1 small cabbage
1/4 cup onion, diced
1 small green pepper, diced
1/2 cup cream cheese
1/3 teaspoon salt
1/2 cup sugar
1/2 cup mayonnaise

Combine cabbage, salt, onion, sugar, pepper and mayonnaise. Chill 1/2 hour, then add cheese. Serve on lettuce with water cress or paprika.

## Sherry Cheese Stuffed Celery

12 heart celery stalks
3 ounces Roquefort cheese
1/2 teaspoon Worcestershire sauce
3 ounces cream cheese
4 tablespoons sherry wine
1 tablespoon cream

Mash the cream cheese smooth with a fork, add the cream and beat smooth. Crush the Roquefort cheese and add with the sherry and Worcestershire sauce. Pile roughly, but neatly, into the celery stalks. Decorate with paprika or a row of capers. Chill before serving.

## Pepper Relish

12 green sweet peppers
8 large onions
2 teaspoons white mustard seed
12 red sweet peppers
2 cups granulated sugar
1 quart vinegar

Grind pepper and onions. Cover with boiling water, drain and cover with boiling water again. Let come to a boil, stand 10 minutes and drain again. Add the salt, vinegar and mustard seed. Boil 15 or 20 minutes. Seal in hot, sterilized jars.

## Ham & Sweet Rolls

4 sweet potatoes, cooked
1/2 cup brown sugar
2 tablespoons water
1/2 cup pineapple juice
4 tablespoons butter
4 thin slices ham, precooked

Combine sugar, water and butter in chafing dish pan over direct flame. Cook until it becomes thick and syrupy. Add potatoes and glaze. Remove potatoes with large spoon and place on slice of ham. Roll and secure with toothpicks. Return to syrup and heat through. Serve hot.

## Super Stuffed Celery

### Olive Nut Filling

3 ounces soft cream cheese
4 stuffed olives, diced
1 tablespoon mayonnaise
10 almonds, blanched and minced

Mix all ingredients and fill celery stalks 2 or 3 inches long. Refrigerate for 1 hour before serving.

### Ham and Cheese

2 tablespoons blue cheese
3 ounces soft cream cheese
1 small green pepper, diced
2 1/4 ounces deviled ham, canned

Mix all ingredients and stuff celery stalks. Chill well. Cut into bite-size pieces.

### Sardine – Pickle

1/2 cup sardines, mashed without oil
1 tiny onion, grated
1 tablespoon lemon juice
2 tablespoons pickles, chopped
pinch salt
2 tablespoons mayonnaise

Mix all ingredients and fill celery. Chill well before serving. Cut into bite-size pieces.

### Sharp Pineapple

3 ounces soft cream cheese
1/4 cup pineapple, crushed
1 teaspoon horse-radish

Drain pineapple and mix with remaining ingredients. Stuff celery, place together in pairs with filling touching and roll tightly in waxed paper. Chill well. Cut into 1/2-inch slices.

## Baby Pizzas

toast
onions, thinly sliced
ripe olives, sliced
pepper
grated gouda
tomatoes, thinly sliced
anchovies
salt
basil

On toast round, place thin slice of tomato and cover with thin slice of onion, piece of anchovy and slice of ripe olive. Season with salt, pepper and basil. Top with grated gouda and place under broiler until cheese begins to bubble. Serve hot.

## Tequenos

4 cups sifted flour
1/4 teaspoon powdered thyme
1/8 teaspoon white pepper
1 cup shredded wheat cereal (crushed to 1/2 cup)
3/4 pound very sharp cheddar, cut into 2 1/2 X 1/2 X 1/4-inch strips
1 1/4 teaspoons salt
1/4 teaspoon powdered marjoram
1 egg, beaten
1/2 cup soft butter
1 cup warm milk
oil for deep fat frying

Heat fat to 400 degrees. Sift flour and seasonings together and stir in crushed cereal. Add egg, butter and milk and mix until smooth. Knead several times on floured board and divide into three equal parts. Roll and stretch until very thin. Cut into strips 2 X 1/2 inch. Wrap tightly around cheese in spiral form, overlapping slightly to cover and completely seal the cheese. Fry a minute or until golden brown. Drain on absorbent paper. Makes about 50. They may be frozen after wrapping and sealing cheese, then thawed at least an hour at room temperature before frying.

## Canape Lorenzo

*Ben Green Cooper*
*The Jefferson Davis Receipt Book*

1 medium shallot, chopped
1 tablespoon flour
1 pound crab meat
cayenne pepper
1/4 pound butter
red pepper
white pepper
2 ounces butter
1 pint cream
salt
bread
1/2 pound Parmesan cheese, grated

Chop shallot and fry lightly without coloring in 2 ounces of butter; add flour and wet with a pint of cream. Add crab meat, salt and cayenne pepper; leave on the fire until it has just begun to bubble. Cut slices of bread 1/4-inch thick and trim in any shape desired, either round, oval or square. Toast only one side of the bread, place ingredients on the toasted side and cover them with a layer 1/8-inch thick of butter prepared from 1/4 pound butter and Parmesan cheese, well minced together and seasoned with red and white pepper. Put canapes on buttered dish and color in the oven.

## Tartar Cream Sauce

1/4 cup mayonnaise or salad dressing
1 tablespoon onion, finely chopped
2/3 cup evaporated milk
2 tablespoons pickle relish, drained

Mix all ingredients in a 1-quart saucepan. Stir over medium heat to thicken. Do not boil. May be served hot or cold.

### Spiced Pickled Shrimp

2 pounds shrimp
4 tablespoons olive oil
2 tablespoons tarragon vinegar
1/2 teaspoon salt
1/2 teaspoon dry mustard
1/2 teaspoon sugar, powdered
6 small white onions
lemon juice
handful of pickling spices
bay leaves
cayenne

In a crock, put a layer of boiled shrimp, a layer of bay leaves (about 5 to a layer) and a layer of very thinly sliced onions. Alternate until all shrimp are used. Make a French dressing of the other ingredients and pour over the shrimp. Cover and put in the refrigerator for 24 hours. Stir occasionally and if needed add more salt and lemon juice. Serve with toothpicks in a bowl over ice or as a salad with lettuce.

### Shrimp Aspic Salad

1 package Knox gelatin
1 can condensed tomato soup, heated
1 cup mayonnaise
2 cans shrimp, or same amount fresh shrimp, boiled
1/2 cup cold water
1 large cake Philadelphia cream cheese
1 cup celery, chopped
onion
salt to taste

Dissolve gelatin in cold water and add soup. Mash the cheese and add mayonnaise. Pour soup over cheese and mayonnaise. Add celery and shrimp; also add little onion and salt to taste. Put in greased mold or individual molds.

### Cranberry Salad

1 package orange jello
1 medium orange, unpeeled
2 tablespoons sugar
1 3/4 cups hot water
2 cups raw cranberries
1/4 cup chopped nuts

Grind together orange and cranberries. Combine with remaining ingredients. Add celery and apples to taste if desired.

### Avocado Dip

1 avocado, large
1 teaspoon grated onion juice
few drops Tabasco
2 teaspoons lemon juice
4 tablespoons mayonnaise
salt to taste

Split a large avocado lengthwise and remove stone. Scoop out the meat and mash it with a fork until perfectly smooth. Add lemon juice, onion juice, mayonnaise, Tabasco and salt to taste. Blend the mixture thoroughly, then pile it into one of the avocado shells.

### Clam Canape

1 tall can clams, minced
dash salt
dash pepper
bread rounds, toasted
2/3 small package cream cheese
dash Tabasco or horse-radish sauce

Drain and mash clams; add cheese and seasonings. Toast bread rounds on one side. Put clam mixture on other side and place under broiler for about 2 minutes.

## Pickled Shrimp

2 pounds shrimp
1/4 cup pickling spices, mixed and tied in bag
3/4 cup white vinegar
2 teaspoons celery seed
Tabasco sauce
celery tops
boiling salt water
1 cup salad oil
1/4 teaspoon black pepper
1 teaspoon salt
1 large onion, chopped

Cook shrimp, handful of celery tops and pickling spices in boiling salted water until shrimp is done. Drain and cool in running cold water. Shell and remove veins.

Mix salad oil, white vinegar, black pepper, celery seed, salt and a few drops of Tabasco sauce. Pour over shrimp which has been arranged in layers with chopped onion. Cover and chill thoroughly. Shrimp will keep a week in the refrigerator.

## Beet Chutney

2 number-2 cans beets, diced
juice of 1 lemon
rind of 1 lemon, grated
rind of 1 orange, grated
6 tablespoons vinegar
2 tablespoons cornstarch
1/2 box raisins
1/2 stick butter
juice of 1 orange
juice from beets
1 cup sugar
2 teaspoons allspice

Add allspice, vinegar, sugar and cornstarch to beet juice. Cook juice mixture until thickened. Add remaining ingredients except beets and cook until thickened. Pour mixture over beets. May be served hot or cold. Serves 12. Keeps well for several days if refrigerated.

## Barbecue Sauce

1 quart meat stock
1 tablespoon prepared mustard
1/2 cup tomato or chili sauce
1 cup onion, minced
salt
1 cup vinegar
2 tablespoons Worcestershire sauce
1/2 lemon rind and juice
1 clove garlic
1/2 cup butter
pepper

Combine all ingredients.

## Hollandaise Sauce

3 tablespoons butter
paprika
2 tablespoons flour (scant)
1 cup hot water
2 egg yolks, beaten
salt
2 tablespoons lemon juice
1 teaspoon lemon rind, grated
red pepper to taste

Put butter in double boiler and add flour. Gradually add hot water, and remaining ingredients.

## Souffle Sauce

3 tablespoons flour
1 cup milk
3 tablespoons butter

Mix flour in butter after it has been melted. Add milk and cook until thick and smooth.

## Bearnaise Sauce

3 tablespoons tarragon vinegar
1 teaspoon shallots, finely chopped
4 peppercorns, crushed
tarragon leaves
1 tablespoon cold water
4 egg yolks
1/2 cup butter
salt to taste
1 teaspoon minced fresh tarragon, or 1/4 teaspoon dried

In small saucepan, combine tarragon vinegar, shallots, peppercorns and a few tarragon leaves. Simmer until liquid is reduced to half. Strain; add cold water.

Beat egg yolks in top of double boiler (not over water). Add herb liquid. Have butter at room temperature. A tablespoon at a time, add 3 tablespoons of the butter to the egg yolks, stirring until smooth after each addition.

Place egg yolk mixture over hot, not boiling, water. Cook and stir until butter melts and sauce thickens. Continue adding remaining butter, in small amounts, stirring constantly.

Remove from heat. Salt to taste and add minced fresh tarragon or crushed, dried tarragon. Makes 1 cup.

## Creamy Dill Sauce

1/2 cup dairy sour cream
1/4 teaspoon dried dillweed
1/4 cup mayonnaise or salad dressing

Combine ingredients and let stand at room temperature 1 hour before serving. Makes 3/4 cup.

**Cocktail Dip**

*Kay Jarvis, Food Editor*
*San Diego Evening Tribune*

1 pound Monterey Jack, Muenster or American cheese, grated
1 can (10 ounces) white sauce

Combine white sauce and cheese and place in shallow casserole. Let melt in 325-degree oven, mixing as it melts. Place over warmer. Serve as a dip with corn chips.

**Dill Dip**

1 3-ounce package cream cheese
1 tablespoon finely chopped stuffed green olives
1 teaspoon grated onion
1/4 teaspoon dried dill weed
dash salt
1 to 2 tablespoons light cream

Soften cream cheese and add olives, onion, dill weed and salt. Stir in light cream until of dipping consistency. Chill. Serve with zucchini or celery sticks, or cauliflowerets as appetizer or relish. Makes about 2/3 cup.

**Chutney Cheese Spread**

2 3-ounce packages cream cheese, softened
1 cup shredded sharp natural cheddar cheese
2 tablespoons dry sherry
1/2 teaspoon curry powder
1/4 teaspoon salt
1/4 cup finely chopped chutney
1 tablespoon finely snipped chives or green onion tops

Combine cheeses, sherry, curry and salt; blend well. Stir in chutney; chill. Turn into dish; top with chives. Serve as appetizer or dessert. Makes 1 2/3 cups.

### Barbecue Sauce

2 1/4 cups catsup
2 1/2 tablespoons
Worcestershire sauce
3/4 teaspoon cayenne pepper
3/4 teaspoon chili powder
1/2 cup tarragon vinegar
1 cup salt pork liquor
1 cup sugar
6 - 8 cloves garlic, scored
1 tablespoon minced onion

Make salt pork liquor by boiling 2 strips (1 1/2 X 5 X 1/8-inches) salt pork in 1 1/2 cups water for about 5 minutes. Drain off 1 cup liquor. Then, combine with remaining ingredients in saucepan. Bring to boil and remove pieces of garlic. Makes about 1 quart.

### Remoulade Sauce

*Julia Dyar*

2 hard boiled egg yolks
1 teaspoon dry mustard
1 tablespoon vinegar
dash cayenne pepper
1 medium onion, grated
2 tablespoons olive oil
1/8 teaspoon salt

Sieve egg yolks. Blend in onion, mustard, oil, vinegar, salt and cayenne. Makes about 3/4 cup sauce.

### Pear Relish

8 or 12 red bell peppers
1 peck of pears
6 large onions
2 pounds sugar
1 tablespoon salt
5 cups vinegar
1 tablespoon allspice

Grind all ingredients in food chopper and add vinegar. Boil 30 minutes.

## Anchovy Spread

1 can anchovy filets
1 onion, grated
1 cake cream cheese
1 tablespoon Worcestershire sauce
2 tablespoons lemon juice

Mix well and use as a spread.

## Cheese Balls

*Julia Dyar*

4 pounds sharp New York State cheese (grated fine)
3 big bars Philadelphia cream cheese, softened
1 1/2 cups chopped nuts
garlic salt to taste
little salt
2 tablespoons mayonnaise
paprika or chili powder

Mix cream cheese and New York cheese. Combine garlic salt, salt and mayonnaise and add to cheese mixture. Mix in chopped nuts. Roll in balls and sprinkle with paprika or chili powder. Chill.

## Cheese and Tomato Curry

3 tablespoons butter
3/4 cup milk
3/4 cup tomatoes, canned and drained
1/2 teaspoon salt
1 1/2 teaspoons curry powder
3 tablespoons flour
2 cups cheese, grated
1/2 teaspoon dry mustard

Mix flour with a small amount of milk, making a smooth paste. Add remaining ingredients and cook in a double boiler until thick. Serve with crackers or French Bread.

### Avocado Cream

1 avocado
2 tablespoons lemon juice
1/2 cup pineapple juice
1 cup sour cream
1 teaspoon sugar
1/4 teaspoon celery salt
pinch, monosodium glutamate
1/4 teaspoon salt

Peel and mash avocado with fork or puree in blender, working in lemon juice while processing. Beat in pineapple juice, sour cream and other ingredients. Makes about 2 cups.

### Quiche Lorraine

*Allen Selby*

2 boxes pie crust mix
2 pints heavy whipping cream
pepper
nutmeg
1 pound Swiss or Gruyere cheese
5 eggs
salt
cayenne pepper
6 slices bacon
Quiche dish, large or regular

Preheat oven to 425 degrees.

Make a double mixture of a boxed pie crust. Mix as directed and form into ball. Place in refrigerator and chill.

Meanwhile, in large bowl add 5 eggs to heavy cream, salt, pepper, cayenne pepper and nutmeg. Whisk very well and let sit. Fry bacon until crispy, then chop finely. Grate cheese and set aside.

Take out ball of dough. Sprinkle flour on a large surface and roll dough very thin. Place in pie plate, large or regular quiche dish. Sprinkle bacon and some cheese in crust. Add egg and cream mixture, then rest of grated cheese. Place in oven at 425 degrees for 15 minutes; turn oven down to 350 degrees and bake for 30 more minutes. Let cool and serve.

### Tomato – Cheese Eggs

3 eggs
1/2 pound cheese, cubed
1 pint tomatoes, cooked and strained
1 tablespoon butter
2 teaspoons onion, chopped
salt
pepper
dash of cayenne
buttered thin toast

Cook the onion in butter until soft. Add the tomatoes and cook for 3 minutes. Stir in the cheese and add the seasoning and eggs. Stir until thick and serve on toast.

### Bacon-Mushroom Rarebit

6 large mushrooms, sliced
2 tablespoons butter
6 slices brown toast, buttered
6 eggs, fried or poached
12 slices bacon, cooked crisp
paprika
3 cups Welsh rarebit

Sauté the sliced mushrooms in butter and arrange on the buttered toast. Cover with very hot Welsh rarebit. Serve the egg on top, sprinkled with paprika. Lay the bacon on top.

### Welsh Rarebit

2 tablespoons butter
2 1/2 tablespoons flour
1/2 teaspoon salt
pepper to taste
1/2 teaspoon dry mustard
1/2 cup beer
2 cups milk
2 teaspoons Worcestershire sauce
2 cups New York cheese, finely chopped

Melt the butter in top of double boiler, add dry ingredients and cook until smooth. Slowly add the milk, stirring constantly. Add the cheese and when the mixture is smooth, add the beer and Worcestershire sauce. Serve at once on buttered toast.

## Mushroom Eggs

6 eggs, beaten
1 number-2 can condensed mushroom soup
2 tablespoons butter
salt
pepper
1/2 cup mushrooms, chopped, with liquid from can

Mix beaten eggs, soup, mushrooms and liquid in which they were canned and season with salt and pepper. Melt the butter in a skillet and when hot pour in the mixture. Scramble until eggs are cooked. Serve in patty shells or on buttered toast. Very good with bacon or ham.

## Onion – Almond Omelet

3 eggs
1/4 cup mushrooms, cooked
2 tablespoons onion, grated
1/16 teaspoon pepper
1/4 teaspoon salt
1/4 cup almonds, blanched and and halved

Beat the eggs and stir in all of the ingredients. Cook as other omelets.

## Burgundy Poached Eggs

4 eggs
2 tablespoons onion, chopped
4 toasted English muffin halves
1 1/2 cups Burgundy wine
salt
pepper

Place wine and onions in chafing dish pan with seasonings. Bring to just below boiling point and slip eggs into liquid. Remove from flame, cover and place over hot water pan filled with boiling water to keep hot. When well set remove from liquid with slotted spoon and serve on buttered muffins.

## Eggs Benedict

4 eggs
4 slices ham
2 tablespoons ripe olives, chopped
4 English muffins, split and toasted
hollandaise sauce

Poach eggs in water which has been brought to boil. Fry ham until edges curl. Place ham on toasted muffins, top with poached egg and cover with hollandaise sauce. Sprinkle with chopped olives.

## Hollandaise Sauce

*Julia Dyar*

1 tablespoon lemon juice
1 tablespoon tarragon vinegar
4 egg yolks
1 cup sweet butter
1 teaspoon salt
1/8 teaspoon white pepper
pinch cayenne
1 teaspoon hot water

Mix together egg yolks, lemon juice, vinegar and water in the top of a double boiler. Stir over barely simmering water until thick. Slowly add butter by teaspoonful, beating vigorously. The sauce will not separate unless cooked too long, stirred too little or allowed to become too hot. Remove when all butter is used and the sauce is thick and smooth. Beat briskly for a few minutes and add the salt and pepper. Should the mixture curdle, remove from fire and beat in 2 tablespoons hot water or cream.

## Mushroom Salad

1/2 cup chopped fresh onion
1/4 cup chopped celery
1/2 cup sour cream
1/4 cup mayonnaise
2 tablespoons fresh lemon juice
1 tablespoon chopped fresh parsley
1 teaspoon salt
1 teaspoon horseradish
1 teaspoon prepared mustard
1/4 teaspoon dried leaf oregano
1/8 teaspoon pepper
1 pound fresh mushrooms, thinly sliced
salad greens

Mix together all ingredients except mushrooms and salad greens. Place mushrooms in bowl; add onion-celery mixture and mix well. Chill at least 2 hours. Serve on salad greens. Makes 6 to 8 servings.

## Full a Beans Salad

*Glenn McCullough*

1 can Blue Lake green beans
1 can yellow beans
1 can lima beans
1 can kidney beans
1 medium sized onion
1 Bell pepper
1/2 cup sugar
1/2 cup tarragon vinegar
1/2 cup salad oil
1/2 teaspoon dry mustard
1/2 teaspoon celery seed
some chopped fresh parsley
1/2 teaspoon basil

Drain beans. Slice onion and pepper very thin and combine with beans in bowl. In another bowl, combine remaining ingredients and dribble over contents of first bowl. Marinate, covered, overnight, stirring a couple of times at intervals. When ready to serve, stir again and drain. Serves about 12.

### Pickle, Pineapple Nut Salad

*Mrs. Dupree (Margie) Jordan*

1 large can pineapple, diced
8 small sweet pickles
1 cup water
1/2 cup sugar
1/3 cup vinegar from pickles
2 envelopes plain gelatin
1 cup pecans, chopped

Simmer 1/2 cup water, sugar and pickle vinegar for 5 minutes. Soak gelatin in remaining 1/2 cup water. Cut pickles and nuts and mix with pineapple. Combine cooked mixture with gelatin and add fruits when cool. Place in molds.

### Marinated Vegetables

*Jere N. Moore*

1 number-303 can English peas
1 number-303 can French beans
1 bell pepper, chopped
2 small onions, cut up
1/2 cup water
2 small sliced cucumbers, unpeeled
1 cup chopped celery
1 cup vinegar
3/4 cup sugar
1/2 cup oil
salt to taste

Combine vegetables. Mix liquids and bring to boil. Remove from heat and cool. Pour over vegetables at least 36 hours before serving. (The longer the better.)

### Kraut Relish

*Beatrice Parker*

1 number-2 1/2 can chopped Kraut, drained
1 2-ounce pimento, chopped
1 cup diced onions
1/2 cup diced bell pepper
1/2 cup sugar
1/2 cup vinegar

Dissolve sugar in vinegar and pour over remaining ingredients. Marinate overnight. Improves with age.

### White Fruit Salad

1 number-2 can crushed pineapple, drained
1 envelope plain gelatin
1 jar white cherries
1/2 cup almonds, chopped
6 tablespoons mayonnaise
2 tablespoons confectioners sugar
1/4 cup small marshmallows
3/4 cup heavy cream, whipped
few maraschino cherries

Oil mold with salad oil. Save juice from fruit and water to make 2 1/4 cups. Soak gelatin in 1/4 cup fruit juice. Heat 1 cup fruit juice. Whip heavy cream while gelatin is soaking. Mix softened gelatin and marshmallows in remaining 1 cup hot fruit juice. Cool. Add fruit, nuts, mayonnaise and whipped cream. Place in oiled mold and chill until set. Serve on bed of curly leaf lettuce.

### Molded Three-Fruit Salad

2 3-ounce packages cream cheese, softened
1 cup mayonnaise or salad dressing
1/4 cup lemon juice
1/4 teaspoon salt
2 cups canned pineapple tidbits, drained
1/4 cup sugar
2 cups diced orange sections, drained
1 cup chopped maraschino cherries
1 cup quartered Royal Anne cherries
1 cup coarsely chopped pecans
2 cups whipping cream

Blend cream cheese, mayonnaise, lemon juice, salt and sugar. Lightly mix in fruits and pecans. Whip cream; fold into fruit mixture. Pour into lightly oiled 3-quart mold. Cover top with foil; freeze.

When ready to serve, unmold and garnish with additional whipped cream and maraschino cherries or fresh strawberries. Makes 16 servings.

## Sour Cream Salad

*Mrs. Claud Bagwell*

1 can peeled apricots
1 can pineapple chunks
1 can free-stone peaches
1 can Bartlett pears
1 package miniature marshmallows
1/2 pint commercial sour cream

Drain fruit and save liquid. Chop into large bowl and add marshmallows. Mix enough fruit liquid with sour cream so that it will pour easily over fruit and marshmallows. (Usually about 1/4 cup is sufficient.) Chill, overnight if possible, and serve. Be sure all ingredients are mixed well.

## Apricot Salad

*Julia Dyar*

Salad

2 packages peach jello
1 large can crushed pineapple (drain and save juice)
1 medium can apricots
1 cup small marshmallows
1 cup nuts
2 cups hot water

Sauce

1/2 cup sugar
1 tablespoon flour
1/2 cup pineapple juice
1 whole egg, beaten
2 tablespoons butter
1 package Dream Whip or Cool Whip

*Salad:* Mix jello with hot water and 1 cup marshmallows. When cool, add 2 cups of pineapple and apricot juice (use enough water to make 2 cups). (Save 1/2 cup pineapple juice for sauce).

*Sauce:* Melt butter and combine with other ingredients. Let sauce thicken and cool, then prepare and add 1 package Dream Whip or Cool Whip.

### Frozen Fruit Salad

1 tablespoon lemon juice
1/2 teaspoon salt
2 tablespoons mayonnaise
2 3-ounce packages cream cheese
2 tablespoons crushed pineapple
1/2 cup Maraschino cherries, cut in quarters
1/2 cup white cherries, sliced
1/2 cup nuts, chopped
1 cup cream, whipped

Add lemon juice and salt to mayonnaise and stir into cheese. Mix with pineapple, cherries and nuts and fold in cream. Turn into trays and freeze about 3 hours. Serves about 10 or 12.

### Waldorf Salad

*Julia Dyar*

2 large apples, peeled and diced
lemon juice
2 tablespoons light brown sugar
parmesan cheese
1/4 cup chopped walnuts or pecans
1/2 cup diced celery
2 large tablespoons mayonnaise

Pour lemon juice over diced apples. Mix apples, celery and nuts. Stir in brown sugar. Add mayonnaise and chill. Before serving add several tablespoons of parmesan cheese.

### Creamy Celery Seed Dressing

1/2 cup mayonnaise
1 tablespoon lemon juice
1/4 teaspoon paprika
1/4 cup honey
1/2 teaspoon celery seed

Combine ingredients and blend well. Makes about 2/3 cup.

### Chicken Salad

2 1/2 cups diced, cooked chicken
1 cup finely chopped celery
1 cup halved green seedless grapes
1 teaspoon salt
1/2 cup mayonnaise
1/2 cup sliced, toasted almonds
2 tablespoons snipped fresh parsley
1/2 cup sour cream
1 tablespoon lemon juice

Combine all ingredients and chill. Serve on crisp lettuce. Garnish with cranberry sauce, if desired.

### Tuna Loaf Salad

*Laura Conway*

salt and pepper, to taste
1 cup broth (or water)
4 cups chicken or tuna
2 cups chopped celery
6 hard-boiled eggs
1/2 green pepper
2 tablespoons chopped olives
1 cup mayonnaise
1/2 teaspoon paprika
2 envelopes gelatin

Soften gelatin in broth. Combine all ingredients in broth and put in pans or molds, greased with oil or mayonnaise. Serves 8 to 10. (Chill until ready to serve).

### Frozen Salad

*Laura Whorton*

1/2 pint sour cream
1 small can crushed pineapple
3/4 cup sugar
1 small can maraschino cherries

Mix ingredients together and freeze.

## Hot Potato Salad

6 slices bacon
1 cup chopped onion
2 tablespoons flour
2 tablespoons sugar
6 medium potatoes
1 1/2 teaspoons salt
1/2 teaspoon celery seed
3/4 cup water
1/3 cup vinegar
dash of pepper

Boil the potatoes in their jackets, peel and slice thinly. Fry bacon in skillet slowly until crisp and drain on paper. Saute the onions until golden in the bacon fat and blend in other ingredients, except water and vinegar. Cook over low heat, stirring until smooth and bubbly. Remove and stir in water and vinegar. Bring to boil, stirring constantly. Boil for a minute and carefully stir in potatoes and crumbled bacon. Remove from heat and cover until ready to serve.

## Crab Salad Parfait

*Shirley McCullough*

1 package lime flavored gelatin
1 cup hot water
1/2 cup cold water
1 1/2 tablespoons wine vinegar
1/3 cup salad dressing
3/4 cup cottage cheese
1/4 teaspoon salt
1 cup chopped raw spinach
1/3 cup finely diced celery
1 tablespoon chopped green onion
1 tablespoon chopped pimento
1 can flaked crab (6 1/2 ounces)

Dissolve gelatin in hot water and add cold water, vinegar, salad dressing and salt. With rotary beater blend it well and refrigerate until partially set. Whip until fluffy and fold in remaining ingredients and pour into mold. Place in refrigerator until set. When ready to serve garnish with black and green olives. Serves about 6.

## Cucumber Salad

*Mrs. Gerri Smith Sadler*

2 large cucumbers
1 large onion
1/2 cup apple vinegar
1/2 cup water
1 teaspoon salt
2 tablespoons sugar

Pare and slice cucumbers and onion thinly. Place in bowl. Heat remaining ingredients to boiling point and pour over cucumbers and onion. Chill in refrigerator until ready to serve. Serves 4 to 6.

## Fluffy Honey Dressing

2 eggs
1/2 cup honey
1/4 cup lemon juice, freshly squeezed
2 tablespoons frozen orange juice concentrate
1/8 teaspoon salt
1/2 cup whipping cream, whipped
2 teaspoons grated lemon peel

In small saucepan, beat eggs, stir in honey, lemon juice, orange juice concentrate and salt. Cook over low heat, stirring constantly, until thickened. Cool; fold in whipped cream and lemon peel. Serve with fresh fruit. Makes 2 cups.

## Chef's Special Dressing

pinch tarragon
pinch thyme
pinch basil leaves
2 tablespoons vinegar
1/2 teaspoon salt
1/3 cup olive oil
1 tablespoon Dijon-style mustard
1/2 teaspoon ground pepper
1 clove garlic, crushed

Soak tarragon, thyme and basil leaves in vinegar for 1 hour. Dissolve salt in seasoned vinegar and add remaining ingredients. Shake well. Use with greens.

### Wilted Spinach Salad

*Shirley McCullough*

1 pound crisp fresh spinach, washed, dried and chilled
4 or 5 slices bacon
2 teaspoons brown sugar
1/4 cup sliced green onions
1/4 teaspoon salt
1 1/2 tablespoons vinegar
1/8 teaspoon dry mustard
dash of paprika

Break spinach coarsely into a bowl. Cook bacon in iron skillet over medium-low heat until crisp. Remove bacon, allow to cool, then crumble. Add sugar, green onions, salt, crumbled bacon, vinegar, mustard and paprika to the skillet. Bring to boil and immediately remove from heat. Pour the hot dressing over the spinach and toss lightly just before serving. Serves 4.

### Fresh Spinach Salad

1/2 pound crisp fresh spinach, washed, dried and torn
1 small thinly sliced onion
pepper
1/4 cup diced celery
4 hard boiled eggs, sliced
salt

Toss all ingredients lightly.

### Lemon Dressing

1 tablespoon salad oil
2 tablespoons flour
1/2 cup water
1/2 teaspoon salt
egg yolk
1/2 teaspoon dry mustard
1/4 teaspoon paprika
2 tablespoons lemon juice
1/2 cup salad oil

Mix 1 tablespoon salad oil, flour and water and bring to a boil. Boil one minute, stirring constantly. Remove from heat and blend in remaining ingredients. Beat until smooth. Cool before serving.

## Frozen Fruit Salad

*Julia Dyar*

1 package sour cream
1 small bottle red cherries, drained
1 small bottle green cherries, drained
juice of 3 lemons (or more) or 2 1/2 tablespoons lemon juice
1/2 teaspoon salt
1 cup sugar
1 cup crushed pineapple, drained
2 bananas, chopped
1 cup English walnuts, chopped, or almonds blanched and slivered

Combine all ingredients and freeze.

## Congealed Salad

*Beatrice Parker*

2 packages strawberry jello
1 number-2 can crushed pineapple
2 ripe bananas, mashed
1 pint strawberries, thawed and mashed
1/2 pint sour cream

Prepare jello with 2 cups water and combine with all ingredients except sour cream. Pour 1/2 of mixture into large serving dish. When firm, cover with sour cream and add remaining 1/2 mixture.

## Fruit Salad

*Frances Long*

1 can pineapple chunks
1 can mandarin oranges
1 can coconut
1 package orange jello
1 package miniature marshmallows
1 carton sour cream

Bring 1 cup of water to boil and stir in jello and marshmallows. Stir until marshmallows are melted and add other ingredients. Pour into mold and refrigerate until firm.

### Black Cherry Salad

1 number-2 1/2 can Bing cherries
1 cup almonds, blanched and chopped
1 package gelatin, cherry flavored
8 olives, chopped
liquid from cherries

Pour hot water over gelatin. When dissolved add cherry juice with enough hot water to make 2 cups liquid. Chill until it begins to harden. Add cherries, almonds and olives. Pour into mold and allow to set. Serve on crisp lettuce with mayonnaise.

### Welsh Rarebit

1 tablespoon butter
1 pound sharp Cheddar cheese, grated
dash of salt
bread
1 cup beer
2 egg yolks
1/4 cup milk
Worcestershire sauce
paprika

Place butter and beer (stale beer is fine) in a chafing dish or double boiler. When warm, place cheese in boiler and melt without rushing, stirring with patience until smooth. Add egg yolks which have been intermingled with milk, salt and two or three generous shakes of Worcestershire sauce. Stir into the mixture until thickened and serve on slices of bread, the downsides of which have been toasted. Sprinkle with paprika. Excellent with celery, olives or salted nuts.

## Frozen Cranberry Cream Salad

*Julia Dyar*

1 16-ounce can jellied cranberry sauce
3 tablespoons lemon juice
1 cup heavy cream, whipped
1/4 cup mayonnaise
1 teaspoon sugar
1/2 teaspoon vanilla
1 cup walnuts or pecans

Crush cranberry sauce with fork and add lemon juice. Pour into paper cups or refrigerator trays. Chop nuts, combine with remaining ingredients and spread over cranberry mixture. Freeze. Unmold on crisp lettuce.

## Fruit Salad Loaf

1 number-2 can pineapple tidbits
orange juice
4 envelopes plain gelatin
1 1/2 cups water
1/4 cup sugar
1/2 cup lemon juice
1/4 teaspoon salt
2 3-ounce packages cream cheese
1 cup mayonnaise
2 oranges, peeled and diced
2 avocados, peeled and diced

Drain pineapple thoroughly; add sufficient orange juice to pineapple juice to make 2 cups liquid. Allow gelatin to soak in 1 cup of water. Combine fruit juices and remaining water, sugar and salt. Bring to a boil and use to dissolve gelatin. Cool slightly. Blend cream cheese and mayonnaise. Mix thoroughly with gelatin. (It will probably take an egg beater to do a good job). Chill until syrupy. Fold in pineapple, oranges and avocado. Pour into loaf pan which has been brushed with salad oil. Chill until firm. Unmold on crisp salad greens. Makes 8 to 10 servings.

### Newberg Spread

1/4 cup butter
1/2 teaspoon salt
1/4 teaspoon paprika
dash of Tabasco
egg yolk, beaten
lemon juice
2 tablespoons flour
1/4 teaspoon black pepper, coarse
3/4 cup coffee cream
1 cup flaked lobster, crab, chopped shrimp or fish

Melt butter in saucepan and add flour, salt, black pepper, paprika and dash or two of Tabasco. Slowly add coffee cream, stirring until it boils. Boil a minute and stir some of it into the egg yolk. Blend egg mixture into the remaining mixture in saucepan, along with lobster, crab, shrimp or fish and a little lemon juice. Cool.

### Roquefort Cheese Dressing

1 package Roquefort cheese, medium size
1 large package cream cheese
1 bouillon cube
1 tablespoon vinegar
1/2 teaspoon onion salt
1/2 cup cream
1/2 cup mayonnaise
1/2 cup water

Dissolve bouillon cube in 1/2 cup water. Add with cream to both cheeses and remaining ingredients. Add mayonnaise, if desired.

### Cheese Puffs

1 cup sharp cheese, grated
1/4 cup soft butter
1/2 cup flour, sifted
1/4 teaspoon salt
1/2 teaspoon paprika
24 stuffed olives or dates

Blend cheese with butter. Stir in flour, salt and paprika. Mix well. Wrap teaspoon of dough around each olive or date, covering it completely. Refrigerate for 1 hour. Bake puffs at 400 degrees for 10 to 15 minutes. Serve warm.

### Cole Slaw

1 medium head cabbage, shredded
1 large onion, chopped
3/4 cup Wesson oil
3/4 cup vinegar
7/8 cup sugar
1 tablespoon sugar
1 tablespoon celery seed
1 tablespoon prepared mustard

In large mixing bowl mix together cabbage, onion and 7/8 cup sugar. In small saucepan mix the other ingredients. Boil for 2 minutes then pour hot over cabbage mixture. Chill for several hours or overnight before serving.

### Yum Yum Salad

2 tablespoons Knox gelatin
1 number-2 can pineapple, crushed
1 cup cheese, grated
1/2 cup cold water
1 cup sugar
juice of 1 or 2 lemons
1/2 pint whipped cream

Soak gelatin in cold water for 10 minutes. Place pineapple in boiler and heat; add sugar, lemon juice and hot gelatin. Let set until cool. Add cheese and cream which has been whipped. Mix well and place in refrigerator. Serves 12.

### Compote of Fruit with Champagne

1 cup orange sections
1/2 cup fresh pears, sliced
1 cup pineapple, diced
1/2 cup bing cherries
champagne
sugar to taste

Mix this or any combination of fruits and serve very cold in tall dessert glass or champagne glass. This may be used as a first course or for dessert.

### Spinach Dressing

1 egg
4 tablespoons sour cream
1/4 cup vinegar
1 scant tablespoon ham drippings
4 tablespoons sugar

Beat whole egg. Have vinegar hot and not too strong. Mix all ingredients, cook and serve over spinach. Garnish with hard cooked eggs.

### Spiced Peach Salad

1 cup peach juice, canned
1/2 cup sugar
3 small sticks cinnamon
2 cups peaches, sliced
1/4 cup vinegar
12 cloves, whole
1 package gelatin, orange flavored

Combine ingredients except peaches and bring to a boil. Strain syrup and add enough water to make 2 cups liquid. Dissolve gelatin in hot liquid and chill. When slightly firm, fold in sliced peaches.

### Ginger Ale Salad

1/2 cup water
1/4 cup orange juice
2 packages gelatin
1 cup pecans, broken
1 orange rind, grated
1/2 cup sugar
2 teaspoons lemon juice
1 cup gingerale
1 large can pineapple, crushed

Drain juice off pineapple. Dissolve sugar in pineapple juice, add lemon and orange juice; put on stove and bring to boil. Pour over gelatin; let cool. Add pineapple, orange rind, nuts and ginger ale. Place in refrigerator to congeal.

## Honey Dressing

2/3 cup sugar
1 teaspoon dry mustard
1 teaspoon paprika
1/4 teaspoon salt
1 teaspoon celery seed
1/3 cup strained honey
5 tablespoons vinegar
1 tablespoon lemon juice
1 teaspoon onion, grated
1 cup salad oil

Mix dry ingredients, add honey, vinegar, lemon juice and onion. Add oil slowly, beating constantly at high speed with electric mixer. Makes 2 cups dressing.

## Pineapple Salad

1 package lemon jello
2 cups pineapple, crushed
15 marshmallows
salad dressing
1 cup hot water
1/2 pound cheese, grated
1 cup whipping cream

Cut the marshmallows in half and let stand with the drained, crushed pineapple for two hours or longer. Dissolve the jello in the hot water. Whip the cream. When the jello begins to thicken fold in the pineapple and marshmallows, cheese, and last the whipped cream. Refrigerate to become firm. Serve with a salad dressing.

## Chef's Salad Dressing for Fruit

1 cup mayonnaise
3 tablespoons sour cream
1 teaspoon sugar
2 teaspoons fruit juice, fresh fruit or pineapple juice

Blend or whip ingredients together. Makes enough dressing for 6 or 8 salads.

## Broccoli Congealed Salad

1/2 package frozen broccoli, cooked
1 package gelatin, unflavored
dash Worcestershire sauce
pepper
dash paprika
2 hard-boiled eggs, grated
1 can consommé
3/4 cup mayonnaise
dash Tabasco
salt
juice of 2 lemons

Cook 1/2 package of broccoli until tender, then chop. Heat to boiling all but 1/4 cup of consommé, adding 1/4 cup consommé to gelatin. Add this mixture to hot consommé. After cooling consommé, beat in mayonnaise, Tabasco, Worcestershire sauce, paprika and lemon juice. Then add eggs and broccoli. Salt and pepper. Serves 8. Congeals quickly.

## English Pea Salad

1 number-2 can small English peas
1/4 bell pepper, chopped
parsley, if desired
2 tablespoons mayonnaise
1 apple
1/2 cup celery, diced
3 boiled eggs
1 small onion, diced
endive
salt to taste

Drain peas, chop eggs, apple, celery, pepper, parsley and onion. Mix well with mayonnaise. Serve on lettuce.

## Cherry – Pineapple Salad

*Julia Dyar*

1 large (number 2) can sour cherries, pitted and drained
juice from cherries
1 envelope plain gelatin
grated rind of 1 lemon (1 teaspoon)
grated rind of 1 orange (1 teaspoon)
1/4 cup cold water
1/2 teaspoon almond extract
1 large can pineapple, crushed
juice from pineapple
1/2 cup pecans, chopped
1 package gelatin, lemon flavored
juice of 1 lemon
juice of 1 orange
1/2 cup sugar (less for tart flavor)
red food coloring

Soften plain gelatin in cold water. Mix sugar, lemon flavored gelatin, juice from cherries, orange and lemon juice and bring to a boil over medium heat. Remove from heat and add 1/2 teaspoon almond extract and several drops red food coloring. Combine with softened gelatin and stir until completely dissolved. Cool. Mix together cherries, pineapple, pineapple juice, nuts and grated rinds. Turn into cooled gelatin; mix. Pour into molds and refrigerate until firm. Serves 10 to 12.

## Dressing

1 cup mayonnaise
1/4 teaspoon mustard
2 tablespoons whipped cream
1 1/2 teaspoons lemon juice
1/4 cup pineapple juice, drained from 2 cups crushed pineapple

Blend ingredients. Good on pineapple salad.

## Sausage Pineapple Kabob

1 pound brown & serve sausages
1 can pineapple chunks
1 cup pineapple juice

Heat pineapple juice in chafing dish pan over direct flame. Cut sausages into cubes. Spear a sausage cube and a pineapple chunk on toothpicks and heat in juice. Serve hot.

## Caesar Salad

1 head lettuce, torn into pieces
1 head romaine or escarole
6 strips bacon, cooked crisp
2 small tins anchovy filets, chopped
1 tablespoon parsley, minced
1 tablespoon lemon juice
1 egg, boiled 1 minute
2 teaspoons onion juice
1 clove garlic, crushed
pinch Accent
1/2 teaspoon salt
1/4 teaspoon black pepper, freshly ground
2 cups small bread cubes, toasted and buttered
2/3 cup Parmesan cheese
French dressing

Crush the garlic and add with the onion juice to the French dressing. Let it stand in the refrigerator for several hours and strain. Add the Accent. Tear the salad greens into a good size bowl. Crumble the bacon and add. Mix in the chopped anchovies. Boil the egg for one minute or less (it should be almost liquid and very soft). When it cools, beat it in a bowl and pour over the salad. Beat the French dressing until thickened and cloudy looking, and pour a little over the egg. Sprinkle on a little salt and pepper. Toss gently until the egg disappears from sight and each piece of leaf glistens. Just before serving add the crisp cubes of bread, Parmesan cheese and parsley. Serve while the bread cubes are crisp.

## Sour Cream Dressing

1 cup sour cream
1/2 cup vinegar
1 teaspoon salt
1/4 teaspoon pepper
1/4 cup sugar

Blend ingredients together.

## Thousand Island Dressing

2 cups mayonnaise
2 sweet pickles, chopped
2/3 cup chili sauce
pepper to taste
3 eggs, hard-boiled and chopped
salt to taste
lemon juice

Combine mayonnaise, pickles, chili sauce and eggs. Season to taste with salt, pepper and lemon juice. Serve on head lettuce wedges. Make the dressing richer by adding more hard-boiled eggs.

## Asheville Salad

1 can cream of tomato soup
2 packages cream cheese
3/4 cup green pepper, chopped
1 cup mayonnaise
3/4 cup celery, chopped
1/4 cup onion, chopped
1 envelope plain gelatin

Bring soup to boil. Add cheese and let melt. Soak gelatin in 1/2 cup cold water and add to soup mixture. Cool. Add vegetables and mayonnaise. Mold. Place in refrigerator until congealed.

### Sam's Salad

*Mary Ann Griffin*

1 head romaine lettuce
1 head endive lettuce
2 tablespoons sugar
Swiss cheese strips
salt
pepper
anchovies, if desired
1 head iceberg lettuce
1/2 can Le Seur Garden peas
1/2 cup mayonnaise
1 onion, thinly sliced into rounds
bacon, (if desired), fried and chopped

Break lettuce and stack with peas, onions, cheese, sugar and mayonnaise in casserole style. Repeat until all ingredients are used, then cover and place in refrigerator. Chill at least one hour. Before serving, toss and add bacon and anchovies if desired.

### Dressing for Tossed Salad

olive oil
herbs and spices
vinegar

Mix 3 to 4 parts olive oil to 1 part vinegar. Add herbs and spices as desired. Shake well.

### Tossed Salad

iceberg lettuce
cucumber
avocado
radishes
green onions
blue cheese

Tear lettuce apart. Add radishes, cucumber and onions. Top with avocado and blue cheese. Add dressing; toss.

## Kitty's Salad Dressing

*Julia Dyar*

3 tablespoons vinegar
pepper
12 tablespoons Wesson oil
1 teaspoon salt
1 teaspoon garlic powder or garlic to taste, crushed

Blend ingredients.

## Tomato Soup French Dressing

*Aline Burgess*

1 can tomato soup
3/4 cup vinegar
1/4 cup sugar
1 teaspoon salt
onion or garlic
1 cup Wesson oil
dash of Tabasco
1 tablespoon Worcestershire sauce

Mix all ingredients together.

## Cream of Peanut Soup

1/4 cup butter
1 medium onion, finely chopped
1 cup creamy peanut butter
1 cup celery, thinly sliced
2 tablespoons flour
2 quarts chicken stock
1 cup light cream

Melt butter in large saucepan over low heat and add celery and onion. Cook until tender but not browned. Add flour and stir until mixture is smooth. Gradually add chicken stock and bring to a boil. Blend in peanut butter and simmer about 15 minutes. Stir in cream just before serving. Makes about 8 servings.

## President Eisenhower's Nasturtium – Vegetable Soup

*Kay Savage*
*Detroit Free Press*

1 soup bone
2 pounds stewing beef
water to cover
1 teaspoon salt
dash pepper
1 clove garlic
1/3 cup barley
1 can tomatoes
1/2 cup fresh peas
1/2 cup canned corn
1/2 cup nasturtium stems
1/2 cup shredded cabbage
2 potatoes, diced
3 stalks celery
1 onion, diced
3 carrots, diced
1 turnip, diced
1/2 teaspoon onion salt
1/2 teaspoon garlic salt
1 teaspoon Worcestershire sauce

Place soup bone, meat, water, salt, pepper and garlic in soup pot and simmer very slowly for several hours, adding water to cover meat as needed. Strain, reserving meat. Cool and remove fat; reheat and add barley. Cook about 15 minutes. Add pieces of meat, tomatoes, peas, corn, cabbage, diced potatoes, celery, onion, carrot and turnip with seasonings and cook until all are tender. Add chopped nasturtium stems and cook 5 minutes longer. Serves 6 to 8.

## Nasturtium French Dressing

*Kay Savage*
*Detroit Free Press*

1/2 cup nasturtium stems, chopped
1/3 cup red wine vinegar
1/2 teaspoon coarse black pepper
1 cup salad oil
1/2 cup celery, finely diced
1/4 cup onion, finely chopped
1 1/2 teaspoons salt
1/4 teaspoon thyme
1/4 teaspoon basil

Combine all ingredients in a pint jar, cover and shake well to dissolve salt. Let chill several hours to blend flavors.

## Gazpacho

*Fred Zapico*
*White House Inn*

Soup

1 clove garlic
1 medium onion, sliced
1 cucumber, sliced
1 green pepper, seeded
3 tomatoes, peeled
4 raw eggs
1/8 teaspoon salt
1/8 teaspoon cayenne pepper
1/4 cup vinegar
1/4 cup olive oil
3/4 cup tomato juice

Garnish

1 cup bread cubes
2 tablespoons olive oil
1 clove garlic, minced
1 cucumber, diced
1 onion, chopped
1 green pepper, seeded

*Soup:* Puree garlic, onion, cucumber, tomatoes, green pepper and raw eggs in blender. (Or, put vegetables through a food mill and mix well with beaten eggs.) Season with salt, cayenne, vinegar, olive oil and tomato juice. Chill.

*Garnish:* Brown the bread cubes in oil with garlic. Add croutons, cucumber, onion and green pepper just before serving. Serve ice cold.

## Green Pea Salad

*Aline Burgess*

1 large can tiny peas, drained
1/2 bell pepper, diced
1 1/2 cups sharp cheese, shredded
2 eggs, hard boiled and diced
1 small onion, diced
1/2 cup mayonnaise

Mix all ingredients and chill at least 1 hour before serving.

### Easy Crab Meat Dip

1 can crab meat (6 ounces)
1 package cream cheese (3 ounces)
1 tablespoon onion, minced
1 tablespoon catsup
1/4 cup mayonnaise

Flake crab meat. Beat remaining ingredients until fluffy. Fold in crab meat. Chill.

### She-Crab Soup a la William Deas

*Ben Green Cooper*
*The Jefferson Davis Receipt Book*

1 pound white crab meat
2 quarts plus 1 pint milk
Worcestershire sauce
1/4 pound crab roe, chopped
paprika
1 medium onion, chopped
1 stick cooking butter
1 teaspoon cornstarch
1/2 cup sherry wine

Saute onion over low fire in half of the butter until soft, but not brown. Add the crab meat and heat. Heat the milk in top of double boiler, but do not boil. Add the crab meat mixture and the rest of the butter to the hot milk. Season to taste with Worcestershire sauce and sprinkle with salt. Stir cornstarch in 1/2 cup cold milk. Pour into soup to thicken. Add crab roe (if unavailable, substitute ground cooked yolks of hen eggs) and sherry wine. Stir together well, sprinkle a little paprika on each serving and serve piping hot.

## Japanese Egg Yolk Soup

*Michael Jones-Kelley*

1 quart fish stock
2 tablespoons Kikoman soy sauce
4 fresh eggs
4 leaves fresh spinach

*To make fish stock:* Use the awfuls from any fresh fish you might have around. Use the head, skin, tail, bones, anything that you'd rather not think about. In a large pan, bring the water to a hard boil and dump in the fish awfuls. Add soy sauce and a pinch of salt. Boil rapidly for 20 minutes, covered. Strain through a cheesecloth. (This stock may be used immediately or frozen for future use with any Oriental fish soup recipe.)

*To make egg yolk soup:* This recipe, like most Japanese dishes, depends as much on visual impact as taste for its success. Consequently, it is desirable to use a dark brown or black serving bowl. Bring the fish stock to a hard boil. Cut a strip from each spinach leaf approximately 1/2 inch by 1 inch. Place one spinach strip in the bottom of each serving bowl. Separate the yolk from the egg and discard the white. Carefully place one yolk on top of the spinach strip in each serving bowl. Carefully pour the boiling stock into each bowl. The hot stock will cook the outside of the egg yolk (although the inside will remain raw) by the time the bowls are placed on the table.

## Rumaki

6 chicken livers
18 bacon strips, lean
1/4 teaspoon ginger, ground
18 water chestnuts
1/2 cup soy sauce
1/4 teaspoon curry powder

Cut chicken livers in thirds, fold each third over a water chestnut and wrap with a strip of bacon. Secure with a toothpick. Marinate 2 or more hours in soy sauce and spices. Broil until bacon is cooked. Makes 18 hors d'oeuvres.

## Peasant Soup

*Michael Jones-Kelley*

tail portion of leg of lamb
3 carrots
3 stalks celery
2 cups noodles
1/2 teaspoon oregano
1/2 teaspoon parsley, chopped
pepper
1/2 head of cabbage
2 medium white onions
2 boiling potatoes
3 bay leaves
1/2 teaspoon dried mint
2 cloves garlic
salt
1 quart water

In a large boiler, bring the water to a boil. Drop in the entire tail portion from a leg of lamb. (You may also throw in any fat which you trimmed from the lamb prior to roasting it. The tail portion is that end of the leg which is useless in roasting. Ask the butcher to cut it off for you. But you're paying for it, so use it.) Boil slowly for 45 minutes. Remove lamb and cut usable meat from the bone. Discard the fat and bone, and return remaining meat to the stock. (This will render very little meat, but lots of hearty stock.) Return to hard boil. Chop the vegetables coarsely and add all except the potatoes. When the soup reaches the hard boil again, reduce the heat to low boil and add the potatoes and herbs. Salt and pepper to taste. Boil, covered, over low heat for 30 minutes.

## Water Chestnut Snack

water chestnuts
brown sugar
soy sauce
bacon

Marinate chestnuts in soy sauce a few hours, stirring often. Roll in brown sugar and wrap with bacon. Pin with a toothpick and bake at 350 degrees until rather crisp.

## Egg Drop Soup

*Michael Jones-Kelley*

1 quart chicken stock
2 tablespoons Kikoman soy sauce
3 large eggs
salt

Bring chicken stock to boil, then reduce heat. Add soy sauce. (It is essential to keep the stock just below the boil or the soup won't work. If it's too hot, you'll have boiled eggs; if it's too cold, you'll have egg soup.) Break one egg in a small bowl and stir (do not beat) a few times with a fork. With a large spoon, swirl the soup and pour in the egg. Repeat for the other eggs. Salt to taste and simmer for 5 minutes.

## Jajoukh
(Eastern Cucumber Soup)

*Michael Jones-Kelley*

3 large cucumbers
1/2 pint plain yogurt
1/2 pint sour cream
white pepper
1 pint buttermilk
1/2 cup white vinegar
salt

Peel 2 cucumbers and, removing the seedy inner part, purée in a blender. Add buttermilk, yogurt, vinegar and sour cream and blend until smooth. Add pepper (about one teaspoon) and salt to taste. Soup should be tart and sour. Peel remaining cucumber and slice into paper-thin slices. Place soup in a large bowl and top with cucumber slices. Chill for a minimum of six hours prior to serving. Serve cold.

VEGETABLES

### Onions in Cheese Sauce

1 cup hot milk
2 tablespoons butter
1/4 teaspoon dry mustard
1/4 teaspoon paprika
dash of Tabasco
2 tablespoons flour
1/4 pound American cheese, (Cheddar if prefer stronger cheese)
2 cans onions

Grate a little of the cheese and set aside. Dice the rest. Put all the ingredients except grated cheese and onions in a blender and turn on high speed for 10 seconds. Pour into saucepan and cook over low heat for 3 minutes, stirring constantly. Season to taste with salt and pepper. Place onions in a shallow baking dish and pour sauce over. Top with grated cheese and sprinkle a little more paprika for color. Serves 6 to 8.

### Pecan – Squash Souffle

2 cups squash, cooked, mashed and measured
1 cup dry bread crumbs
1 cup milk
1 tablespoon onion, grated
salt to taste
3 tablespoons bacon drippings or butter
2 eggs
1/2 cup pecans, finely chopped
pepper to taste

Melt butter in hot milk; pour over bread crumbs; mix well and add to squash. Add seasoning. Beat eggs; add to mixture and pour into baking dish. Bake at 325 degrees. Top with additional buttered crumbs.

### Creamed Corn

butter
corn, cut from cob
pepper
flour
water
salt
sugar
heavy cream

Melt a good chunk of butter in a heavy pan. Add corn and stir to coat each grain. Add a little water and cook until tender. Season with salt, pepper and sugar. Thicken with flour blended into heavy cream.

### Scalloped Corn

1 number-2 can golden cream-style corn (2 1/2 cups)
1 cup milk
1 egg, well beaten
3/4 teaspoon salt
1 1/2 cups cracker crumbs
1/4 cup onions, minced
3 tablespoons pimento, chopped
2 tablespoons butter or margarine
1/8 teaspoon pepper

Heat corn and milk. Gradually stir into egg. Add seasonings, 1 cup cracker crumbs, onion and pimento. Mix well. Pour into greased 8 1/2 X 1 3/4-inch round layer cake pan. Melt butter and pour over 1/2 cup crumbs. Sprinkle buttered crumbs over corn. Bake at 350 degrees for 20 minutes. Garnish with pimento strips. Serves 6.

### Brussels Sprouts with Pecan Sauce

*Julia Dyar*

1 pint Brussels sprouts, boiled and drained
2 tablespoons butter
1 cup cream sauce
1/4 cup pecans, coarsely chopped

Add cream sauce to Brussels sprouts and mix well. Pour into serving dish and top with pecans browned in butter.

### Butternut Squash Souffle

2 cups cooked squash, mashed
1 cup milk
1/2 to 1 stick oleo
cracker crumbs
1 cup sugar
3 eggs, whole
flavoring as desired (1 teaspoon ginger is good)

Mix all ingredients and put in baking dish. Cook at 350 degrees for 30 minutes. Stir once during baking. Cover with cracker crumbs and brown in oven very quickly.

### Cheese Pudding

10 slices bread
1/2 pound cheese
2 cups milk
1 teaspoon salt
3 eggs
butter

Take 10 slices of bread, crusts removed, butter well and cut into cubes. Put in baking dish, alternating with grated cheese, then pour over milk, salt and eggs, beaten. Let stand several hours before baking. Bake at 275 degrees for about 45 minutes. Serves 6.

### Marinated Cauliflower

*Jean Russell*

1/2 cup chili sauce or catsup
1/2 cup oil
1/2 cup vinegar
1 clove garlic, crushed
1 tablespoon sugar
salt and pepper to taste
cauliflower

Separate cauliflower into flowerets and place in quart jar. Mix remaining ingredients well and pour over cauliflower. Refrigerate, turning jar from time to time.

### Corn Pudding

*Jere N. Moore*

1 2-cup package frozen corn
1 can pimento, chopped
1 small bell pepper, shredded
1/2 small onion, grated
2 eggs, well beaten
1 teaspoon salt
1/4 teaspoon pepper
1/2 teaspoon paprika
2 tablespoons of flour
1 teaspoon baking powder
1 cup milk
2 tablespoons butter, melted

Mix all ingredients. Pour into well buttered casserole. Bake covered at 325 degrees for 20 minutes. Remove cover and brown at 350 degrees. Makes 6 servings.

### Squash Casserole

*Shirley McCullough*

1 package Pepperidge Farm stuffing mix
1 can condensed chicken soup
1/2 pint sour cream
1 grated carrot
2 cups cooked yellow squash

Cover bottom of buttered 1-quart casserole dish with part of the stuffing mix. Combine remaining ingredients and pour into casserole. Top with additional stuffing mix and bake at 350 degrees for 35 minutes.

### French Fried Toombs County Onions

*Shirley McCullough*

onions
milk
egg
pancake mix

Peel and slice onions 1/4 inch thick. Let soak in milk to cover for at least an hour. Make thin batter of beaten egg, milk and pancake mix. Dip onions into batter and drop into hot oil. They brown quickly and must be turned quickly, but only once. Drain on paper towel.

## Sour Cream Cabbage

1 small head of cabbage, chopped
1 egg, slightly beaten
1/4 cup cider vinegar
1 tablespoon finely chopped green pepper
1 teaspoon sugar
1 teaspoon salt
1/4 teaspoon pepper
1/2 cup sour cream
1 tablespoon melted butter
1/4 teaspoon paprika

Cook the cabbage in boiling salt water until tender but still crisp, about 5 minutes. Drain very well. In the top of a double boiler, over boiling water, blend together the egg, vinegar, butter, sugar, salt and pepper. Cook, stirring until thick. Cool slightly before stirring in the sour cream and green pepper. Pour over the drained cabbage in a bowl and toss to coat well. Sprinkle with paprika. (When chilled, this may be served as a salad.)

## Aunt Doveye's Stuffed Onions

*Glenn McCullough*

8 large onions, peeled
1 cup pork sausage, seasoned generously with sage
1 cup loaf bread crumbs
1 egg, slightly beaten
salt
pepper
sharp cheddar cheese
1 cup beef bouillon

Boil onions in salt water to cover, about 10 minutes. Drain. Push out the centers to make hole for stuffing. Chop up enough of the centers to make a cupful. Combine the chopped onions with sausage, crumbs, egg, salt and pepper, to taste. Stuff the onion shells with the mixture and place the stuffed onions in a baking dish. Pour bouillon around the onions, cover and bake at 400 degrees for 30 minutes. Remove the cover and baste the onions several times while continuing to cook for 15 minutes. Now place a cube of cheddar atop each onion and return to oven until cheese gets bubbly.

### Scalloped Tomatoes

2 cups peeled and cooked fresh or canned tomatoes
2 cups bread crumbs
1 teaspoon salt
2 tablespoons butter or margarine
1 teaspoon minced onion and green pepper (optional)

Season tomatoes with salt and pepper. Fill baking dish or casserole with bread crumbs and tomatoes in alternate layers, with bread crumbs on top. Dot with butter or margarine. Bake at 350 degrees for about 1/2 hour.

### Okra, Rice and Tomatoes

1 quart okra pods
1 cup uncooked rice
1 cup canned tomatoes or 4 medium-sized fresh, peeled and chopped
2 tablespoons butter or margarine
salt and pepper
sprinkle of paprika
1 onion, sliced

Wash rice and cook in boiling, salted water until tender. Drain and add butter, salt, pepper, and paprika. Cut okra in slices and cook in small quantity of salted boiling water 10 minutes. Add tomatoes, onion, and rice and cook about 5 minutes longer.

### Savory Red Cabbage

4 cups shredded red cabbage
1/4 cup vinegar
3/4 cup water
1/4 cup brown sugar
1/4 teaspoon ground cloves
2 tart apples, diced
1 teaspoon salt

Combine all ingredients and cook at low temperature until cabbage and apples are tender, about 20 minutes.

## Spanish Omelet

2 tablespoons onion, chopped
1 tablespoon green pepper, chopped
2 tablespoons butter
1 can cream of tomato soup
1 small can mushrooms
6 eggs
1/2 teaspoon salt
dash of pepper
3 tablespoons milk
2 tablespoons butter

Make a sauce by cooking onion and green pepper in butter until soft. Add soup and mushrooms and heat thoroughly. Beat eggs well and add salt, pepper and milk. Pour eggs into heavy skillet in which 2 tablespoons butter have been melted. Place over low heat. As omelet cooks, lift edges gently to let uncooked egg flow underneath. When bottom is browned, put 3 tablespoons of the Spanish sauce in omelet and fold over. Serve on platter with more of the sauce poured over it. Serves 4.

## Macaroni Pie

1/2 pound macaroni, broken
1 heaping tablespoon butter
1 1/2 cups sharp cheese, grated
1 pint milk
salt to taste
pepper to taste
1/2 teaspoon dry mustard
3 eggs

Cook macaroni in rapidly boiling water for 10 minutes. Drain. Stir butter and cheese (leaving about 1/2 cup cheese to sprinkle over top of pie) into hot macaroni. Add salt, pepper and mustard. Beat eggs into mixture, add milk and mix well. Put in greased baking dish and sprinkle top with cheese and dot with butter. Bake at 350 degrees until brown.

## Stuffed Green Peppers

6 large green peppers
1 1/2 teaspoons salt
1 1/2 cups cooked white rice, (about 1/2 cup raw)
3/4 teaspoon dried thyme
1 cup onions, sliced and peeled
1 cup condensed tomato soup, undiluted
2 sprigs parsley
1 cup boiling water
3 cups cooked ham, coarsely ground
1/4 teaspoon pepper
1/4 cup butter or margarine
4 peppercorns
6 whole cloves
1 number-2 can tomatoes, (2 1/2 cups)

Wash peppers. Cut thin slice from stem end of each; remove all seeds. Place peppers, water and salt in Dutch oven or deep kettle. Cover and boil 5 minutes. Drain; reserve liquid. Meanwhile, in large bowl, combine ham, rice, pepper and thyme. Lightly fill drained peppers with this mixture. Melt butter in Dutch oven, add onions; sauté until golden. Tie peppercorns and cloves in small piece of cheesecloth. When onions are brown, add remaining ingredients including spice bag and reserved liquid. Arrange peppers upright in sauce. (If peppers do not fill bottom of Dutch oven, and tend to topple over, use inverted custard cups to fill up space.) Cover; simmer 30 minutes and remove spice bag. Serve peppers surrounded by sauce. Makes 6 servings.

## Creamed Chestnuts

1 pound chestnuts
1 pint chicken stock
1 cup heavy cream
dash nutmeg

Cut a gash in the rounded sides of the chestnuts and place in the oven for 15 minutes. Remove the shells and scrape or peel off the inner skin. Boil in the chicken stock until tender. Drain well, combine with the cream and let simmer for 10 minutes. Season to taste with a small amount of salt if necessary, and add a dash of nutmeg.

## Eggplant Casserole

2 medium eggplants
1 medium onion, finely chopped
1 green pepper, finely chopped
6 eggs beaten
salt, pepper and poultry seasoning to taste
1/4 pound butter

Peel and boil eggplants until very soft, then mash. Blend with other ingredients and add enough cracker or bread crumbs to give desired consistency. Pour into casserole and top with additional bread crumbs. Bake at 350 degrees until brown.

## Squash Casserole

*Mrs. Ralph (Frances) Owen*

1 1/2 cups cooked yellow squash
3 tablespoons chopped onion
3 tablespoons butter, melted
3 tablespoons chopped pimento
2 eggs, well beaten
1 cup scalded milk
1 cup cracker crumbs
1 cup grated medium sharp cheese
salt and pepper to taste

Combine all ingredients and pour into a well greased casserole. Bake for 1 hour at 350 degrees.

## Woodchuck

*Mary Anna Bryan*

2 cups medium white sauce
6 hard boiled eggs, chopped
1 small jar pimientos
1 small can mushrooms
1 cup grated sharp cheese
1 large can Chinese noodles

Melt cheese in white sauce. Add eggs, pimientos, mushrooms. Serve over Chinese noodles.

## Vegetable Pilaf

*Julia Dyar*

1/4 cup almonds, slivered
2 cups hot cooked rice
1/8 teaspoon pepper
1/2 teaspoon rosemary
1 can English peas
1/2 cup butter or margarine
1 small onion, chopped
1/2 teaspoon seasoned salt
1 can or jar mushrooms, sliced

Saute almonds in melted butter until golden brown. Add hot rice, chopped onion and seasonings; stir to blend. Add drained mushrooms and peas; heat. Makes 6 servings.

## Eggplant Casserole

1 medium eggplant
salt
butter
cream of mushroom soup
cracker crumbs
1 medium onion
pepper
onion
grated cheese

Boil eggplant until soft enough to peel (approximately 10 minutes). Peel and cut into good sized cubes. Chop fine 1 onion. Put into casserole layer of eggplant, sprinkled with salt, pepper, butter and onion. Repeat layers until entire eggplant is used. Cover with cream of mushroom soup. Sprinkle with grated cheese and cracker crumbs. Bake in medium oven for 30 minutes.

## Stuffed Eggplant

1 medium eggplant
1/2 cup mushrooms, sliced
2 tablespoons onion, chopped
1/2 cup stale bread crumbs
dash of basil
1 clove garlic, pressed
2 tablespoons butter
1/2 cup cream
salt, to taste
pepper, to taste
bacon, crisp and crumbled

Cut eggplant lengthwise and remove meat from shells. Cut meat into small cubes and cook in boiling salt water. While eggplant is cooking, brown mushrooms, onion and garlic in butter. When partially browned, add drained eggplant. Salt and pepper to taste and add dash of basil and cream. Simmer until soft, then stir in bread crumbs and fill shells. Top with crumbled crisp bacon. Bake at 350 degrees for 45 minutes.

## Scalloped Onions

3 cups onions, cooked
2 cups oyster crackers
1/2 cup buttered crumbs
3/4 cup sweet milk
2 eggs
3 tablespoons butter
salt to taste
pepper to taste

Slice or quarter onions and boil until done. Into a baking dish put a layer of onions, butter, salt and pepper. Add a layer of broken crackers, more onions and crackers until all are used. Mix milk and eggs together, pour over the mixture, covering top with buttered crumbs, and bake just long enough to set the milk and eggs. Brown top about 20 minutes. Serve in the dish in which it was baked. Have milk heated just tepid.

## Baked Eggplant

*Catherine Burgess*

4 medium-size eggplants
1 1/2 cups milk
pepper to taste
1 1/2 cups saltine crackers, crushed
4 eggs
salt to taste
1 cup American cheese, grated
1/4 pound butter

Peel, slice and boil eggplant until tender. Drain in colander for 10 minutes. Add eggs, milk and seasonings. Mix well. Pour into baking dish. Have mixture about 1 inch thick. Sprinkle top with grated cheese, then top with crumbs and slivers of butter. Bake at 375 degrees for 20 minutes, or until firm. Serves 6 to 8.

## Spanish Rice

3 tablespoons bacon drippings
1 cup rice, uncooked
3/4 cup onion, chopped
1/2 cup green pepper, chopped
1 cup water
1 1/2 teaspoons salt
1 teaspoon chili powder
1/4 teaspoon basil
1 number-2 can tomatoes

Heat 2 tablespoons bacon drippings in large skillet and add rice. Brown lightly, stirring frequently. Add remaining tablespoon bacon drippings, onion, green pepper and celery. Cook until the vegetables are soft. Add remaining ingredients and cover pan tightly. Simmer without lifting the lid for 30 minutes. If rice is not soft enough, add a very small amount of water; cover. Continue to cook until tender. Serves 6.

### Stuffed Eggplant

1 medium-sized eggplant
  or 2 small ones
2 tablespoons fat
2 tablespoons minced onion
1 teaspoon salt
1 cup canned tomatoes or
  4 medium-sized ones,
  fresh, peeled and chopped
1 cup soft bread crumbs

Wash eggplant and cut in half. Scoop out pulp to 1/2-inch of skin. Dice pulp. Brown onion in fat, add eggplant pulp, tomatoes, bread crumbs and salt. Mix well and fill eggplant shells with mixture. Bake until browned, about 30 minutes at 375 degrees. Makes about 4 servings.

### Spanish Rice

1 pound ground beef
1/2 cup chopped onion
1/2 cup chopped green
  pepper
3/4 teaspoon salt
2 cups rice
1 cup shredded cheddar cheese
1 8-ounce can tomato sauce

Cook rice. Brown beef with chopped onion and chopped green pepper; pour off fat. Add salt. Stir in the rice and cheese. Add can of tomato sauce and heat through. Makes 4 to 5 servings.

### Fried Rice and Shrimp

3 tablespoons olive oil
1 teaspoon salt
dash of black pepper
2 eggs, beaten
1/2 cup sliced mushrooms
1 pound raw shrimp, shelled,
  cleaned and cut into three
4 cups cold, cooked rice
2 tablespoons soy sauce
1/2 teaspoon sugar

Place oil, salt and pepper into iron skillet. Add eggs and fry until firm. Cut fried eggs into small strips. Add shrimp, onions and mushrooms and cook over moderate heat for five minutes, stirring constantly but carefully. Add the rice, soy sauce and sugar and cook over moderate heat, stirring constantly until rice is hot. Use more soy sauce as needed. Before serving, sprinkle with slivered almonds, if desired.

## Italian Rice

3/4 cup rice, uncooked
3/4 pound beef, ground
1/2 green pepper, chopped
2 cups tomatoes, cooked
1 1/2 teaspoons salt
2 teaspoons sugar
2 tablespoons bacon drippings
1 medium onion, chopped
1/3 cup celery, chopped
1/2 cup water
dash of pepper

Cook rice according to package directions. Heat drippings in 10-inch heavy skillet; add rice, ground beef and onion and cook with frequent stirring until meat and rice are brown and onion is soft. Add green pepper and celery and cook slowly 5 minutes, stirring frequently. Then add remaining ingredients, cover, and simmer gently for 30 minutes or longer or until rice is perfectly tender. Stir occasionally. Makes about 5 servings.

## Stewed Corn

*Ben Green Cooper*
*The Jefferson Davis Receipt Book*

corn, cut off cob
pepper
flour
1 1/2 tablespoons butter
salt
cream

Shave corn off cob being careful not to cut into cob. Add 1 1/2 tablespoons butter for each 1 1/2 pints corn. Add salt, pepper and just enough water to cover. Put into a skillet, cover and cook rather slowly for 45 minutes. Stir often with a spoon as it must not brown. Add more water if necessary. Thicken with a little flour and cream.

## Macaroni and Cheese Deluxe

3 1/2 cups cooked macaroni
1 4-ounce can mushrooms, chopped and drained
1/4 cup chopped pimento
3/4 cup milk
1 teaspoon Worcestershire sauce
1 1/4 cups sharp cheddar cheese, grated
3 tablespoons minced onion
2 teaspoons dry mustard
1 teaspoon salt
1/4 teaspoon black pepper

Mix macaroni, mushrooms and pimento in greased 1 1/2 quart baking dish. Stir remaining ingredients except macaroni over low heat. Then stir in macaroni, topping with thin strips of cheese. Bake in 350-degree oven for 25 minutes. Serves 6.

## Cheese Souffle

1 cup grated cheese
1 tablespoon butter
2 tablespoons flour
1/2 cup milk
3 eggs
1/2 teaspoon salt

Melt butter, add flour and salt, making smooth paste. Add the milk slowly, stirring while the sauce thickens. Remove from heat and add grated cheese and egg yolks, stirring until cheese is melted. While still hot, pour slowly into stiffly beaten egg whites, folding carefully with spatula. Pour into ungreased baking dish and bake 45 minutes in slow (300 degrees) oven. Serve at once. In a round baking dish, a crown may be created by inserting broad side of silver knife and making a furrow in a circle. This does nothing for the taste, but enhances the appearance.

## Tuna Beans

4 cups white beans, cooked
3 tablespoons lemon juice, fresh
salt
tuna fish, drained
1/2 cup olive oil
1/2 cup onions, finely chopped
black pepper, freshly ground

Drop the cooked beans into a bowl and stir in the olive oil, lemon juice and salt and pepper to taste. Add the chopped onions and toss about with the beans. Then set aside for an hour or more at room temperature.

Mound the beans on individual plates and top each serving with a few chunks of drained imported tuna fish which have been packed in olive oil. Garnish with halved hard-cooked eggs and wedges of lemon. Sprinkle with a little chopped parsley. This is more than adequate as a first course for 6.

## Green Bean Casserole

2 tablespoons butter
1 tablespoon parsley, minced
1 teaspoon salt
1/2 teaspoon lemon peel, grated
1/2 cup yellow cheese, grated
1/2 cup onions, sliced
2 tablespoons flour
1/2 teaspoon pepper
1 cup sour cream
5 cups Blue Lake beans
2 tablespoons butter, melted
1/2 cup cracker crumbs

Cook sliced onions and parsley in butter until tender. Add flour, salt, pepper, grated lemon peel and sour cream. Mix well. Stir in beans, place in greased casserole and top with cheese. Combine remaining 2 tablespoons melted butter and cracker crumbs. Sprinkle over cheese. Bake at 350 degrees for 30 minutes. Makes 6 servings.

## Broccoli Ring

1 package chopped broccoli, thawed
1 cup thick cream sauce
onion juice
1 cup mayonnaise
6 eggs, beaten
salt
red pepper

Mix and season lightly with salt, red pepper and onion juice to taste. Add 6 well beaten eggs. Pour into greased ring mold. Cook in pan of water until firm – about 45 minutes, in slow oven 300 degrees. Fill with creamed chicken.

## Never Fail Cheese Souffle

*Jere N. Moore*

1/4 cup margarine
1/4 cup flour
1 1/2 cups warm milk
1 teaspoon salt
dash paprika or white pepper
1/2 pound processed Cheddar cheese, sliced or grated
6 eggs, separated

Melt margarine in saucepan; blend in flour, milk and seasoning. Cook and stir over low heat until thickened, then add cheese and stir until melted. Remove from heat and add beaten egg yolks. Mix well. Cool mixture slightly and pour slowly over beaten egg whites. Cut and fold together. Pour into ungreased 2 quart casserole or souffle dish. Run the top of a teaspoon around mixture 1 inch from edge of dish, making a light track which will form a "top hat" on souffle as it bakes and puffs. Bake at 300 degrees for 1 1/4 hours. Serve at once. Makes 4 to 6 servings.

### Stuffed Zucchini

6 zucchini, about 6 inches long
1/2 cup chopped onion
2 tablespoons margarine
1 cup chopped tomatoes
1 teaspoon salt
1/2 teaspoon poultry seasoning
1/4 teaspoon pepper
1 cup shredded sharp Cheddar cheese

Wash and trim stem end of zucchini; cut in half length-wise. Cook in boiling, salted water 10 minutes and drain. When cool enough to handle, scoop out center of each. Drain shells upside down; chop scooped-out portion. Saute onion in margarine until tender. Add chopped zucchini and remaining ingredients, mixing well. Spoon mixture into zucchini shells and arrange in baking dish. Bake at 350 degrees for 25 to 30 minutes. Makes 6 servings.

### Lemon-Wild Rice With Shrimp

*Jere N. Moore*

2 tablespoons green pepper, chopped
2 tablespoons onion, chopped
2 tablespoons butter, melted
1 can cream of mushroom soup
2 cups cooked wild rice, packed
3 tablespoons lemon juice
1/2 teaspoon mustard
1 teaspoon Worcestershire sauce
1 cup sharp cheese, cubed
1 pound raw shrimp, cleaned
paprika
parsley
pinch of oregano

Saute pepper and onions in butter until soft. Stir into cooked wild rice. Mix soup, lemon juice, Worcestershire sauce and mustard with rice. Add cheese and shrimp; mix thoroughly. Pour into buttered casserole and bake at 375 degrees for 30 minutes. Garnish with paprika, parsley and oregano. Makes 6 servings.

## Potatoes O'Glenn

(related to Potatoes O'Brien)

*Glenn McCullough*

1/2 cup real butter
1/2 cup sifted flour
1 green onion, finely chopped
dash of Worcestershire sauce
4 cups cooked, diced potatoes
2 cups whole milk
1 cup sour cream
salt
3 cups grated sharp cheddar cheese
1/4 cup chopped pimento
1/2 teaspoon celery seed
1/4 cup green pepper, finely chopped
1 teaspoon chopped green parsley
black pepper

Make a sauce of the butter, flour, Worcestershire and milk. As it thickens add the sour cream and remove from heat, seasoning to taste with salt and pepper. Stir in 2 cups of the cheese, pimento, green pepper, celery seed, parsley and onion. Now place 2 cups of potatoes in electric skillet and sprinkle with salt and pepper. Pour about half the sauce over the potatoes and sprinkle 1/2 cup of cheese over this, add remaining potatoes and top with sauce. Sprinkle remaining cheese over top. Cook at 300 degrees until bubbly, then cut down to 220 degrees and leave for 45 minutes to 1 hour. Serves up to 8. Variation: Substitute whole grain hominy, canned, for potatoes.

## Rice Casserole

1 cup rice (not instant)
1 can onion soup
1 can beef bouillon
1/4 stick oleomargarine
salt to taste

Soak rice in water 45 minutes. Drain and place in casserole, add soup and bouillon, salt and butter. Bake at 350 degrees for 1 hour. Stir occasionally.

### Sweet Potato Souffle

Souffle

2 cups mashed sweet potatoes
1 1/4 cups granulated sugar
2 eggs
1/2 teaspoon cinnamon
3/4 stick butter
1 cup milk
1/2 teaspoon nutmeg

Topping

3/4 cup crushed corn flakes
1/2 cup nuts
1/2 cup brown sugar
3/4 stick butter

*Souffle:* Bake, then mash two large sweet potatoes. Add remaining ingredients and mix well. (If using canned sweet potatoes, use only 1/2 cup milk.) Pour into casserole and bake at 400 degrees for 20 minutes.

*Topping:* Melt butter and combine with crushed corn flakes, nuts and brown sugar. Spread evenly over sweet potatoes and return to oven for additional 10 minutes at 400 degrees.

### Potato Pancakes

*Julia Dyar*

2 cups grated raw potatoes
1 1/4 teaspoons salt
2 teaspoons chopped parsley
2 eggs, lightly beaten
1 1/2 tablespoons grated onion
1/4 cup flour
fat for frying

Combine ingredients and mix thoroughly. Drop batter from tablespoon onto greased, sizzling-hot griddle. Spread thinly to make a 3 1/2-inch cake. Cook until brown, then turn and cook other side. Makes about 12 pancakes.

### Sweet Potato Delight

1 large can potatoes
1 1/4 cups sugar
2 sticks margarine
1 cup pecans, chopped
3 eggs
3/4 cup brown sugar
3 cups corn flakes

Mash potatoes well. Beat eggs, melt 1 stick margarine and mix together. Pour into baking dish. Crush corn flakes and mix with pecans. Sprinkle on potato mixture. Dot with slivered or melted margarine. Bake at 350 degrees for 35 to 40 minutes.

### Turnip Greens

1 piece fatback, medium-size or ham hock
3 pounds turnip greens
3 pounds mustard greens
salt to taste
sugar to taste

Cook meat in a little water. While it cooks, prepare and clean the greens. Add greens to meat; bring to a boil, then cook over medium heat. Season with salt and sugar. Cook approximately 2 1/2 to 3 hours.

### Cheese — Rice Casserole

*Julia Dyar*

2 cups rice, uncooked
1/2 cup vegetable oil
3 medium onions
1 cup parsley, chopped
1 cup cream of mushroom soup
2 teaspoons salt
2 eggs, beaten
2 cups Cheddar cheese, grated
2 green peppers, chopped
garlic to taste

Cook rice and mix with other ingredients. Cook in greased casserole for 45 minutes at 350 degrees.

### Sweet Potato Balls

2 cups fresh or canned sweet potatoes, cooked
1/4 stick of butter, melted
1/8 teaspoon salt
2 tablespoons granulated sugar
1/8 teaspoon cinnamon
1/4 teaspoon vanilla
marshmallows
crushed corn flakes
fat for frying

Mash potatoes and add ingredients as listed, except marshmallows, corn flakes and fat. Mix well and form into balls around marshmallows, roll in corn flake crumbs and fry in deep fat or oil until brown.

### Crab and Mushroom Stuffed Potatoes

4 medium potatoes, baked
1/4 cup heavy cream, heated
1 teaspoon salt
1 can (3 ounces) mushrooms, chopped and broiled
1 can (6 1/2 ounces) crab meat, drained and flaked
1/4 cup butter or margarine, melted
1/8 teaspoon pepper
1 tablespoon onion, grated
1 cup sharp Cheddar cheese, grated

Cut potatoes in half lengthwise. Scoop out all pulp without breaking the skin. Mash or whip pulp and add butter, cream, salt and pepper. Beat until light and fluffy. Drain mushrooms reserving broth for use in soup, sauce or gravy. Add mushrooms, onion, 2/3 cup grated cheese and crab meat. Top with remaining cheese. Bake in preheated oven at 350 degrees for 20 minutes. Makes 8 stuffed potatoes.

## Scalloped Sweet Potatoes

6 sweet potatoes
1/2 lemon, sliced paper thin
1 dozen chestnuts, boiled,
  peeled and thinly sliced
1/2 cup granulated sugar
1/2 cup butter
1 1/2 seedless oranges,
  thinly sliced
1/2 cup light brown sugar
1 jigger brandy

Peel and slice potatoes. In a baking dish, arrange half of the potatoes, and cover with half of the sliced fruit and chestnuts. Mix the brown and white sugar and sprinkle half of it over the potatoes. Pour in the brandy. Repeat the process with remaining ingredients. Bake for 1 hour, basting frequently, at 350 degrees. If it cooks dry, add a little more sugar and water. Serve with game or ham.

## Baked and Stuffed Fluffy White Potatoes

4 baking-size white potatoes
1/2 stick butter
pepper to taste
shredded cheese, if desired
1 teaspoon parsley, chopped
salt to taste
1/2 cup cream
1 egg white

Bake the potatoes in their skins in 350-degree oven for about 1 hour or until done. Cut potatoes in half the long way, and scoop out the contents. Mash and add butter, cream, egg white, parsley, salt and pepper. Beat until very smooth and fluffy. Pack the potato mixture lightly back into the skin to whatever thickness or depth is desired. Dot the tops with butter and 1 teaspoon of shredded cheese. Place back in hot oven and brown. Serve immediately while hot.

## Candied Sweet Potatoes

6 small to medium sweet potatoes
2 tablespoons margarine or butter
4 tablespoons brown sugar
1/3 cup water or orange juice
1 cup dark corn syrup

Wash potatoes and boil until tender but not soft. Drain, peel and cut into lengthwise halves. Pour syrup, sugar, butter and water into heavy skillet. Bring to a boil and add potatoes. Lower heat and allow to simmer until the syrup is thick and the potatoes are well coated. Turn the potatoes gently as they cook. Serves 6.

## Glazed Carrots

2 tablespoons butter
2 tablespoons onion, chopped
2 tablespoons flour
1/2 teaspoon salt
1/2 cup water
10 whole carrots, scraped
1 can consomme

Cook onions in butter until soft. Roll carrots in flour and cook with the onion and butter about 10 minutes. Add consomme, water and salt. Cover tightly and cook until tender. Sprinkle with chopped parsley just before serving. Serves 6.

## Candied Acorn Squash

2 medium acorn squash
1/2 stick butter or margarine
light brown sugar
nutmeg
water

Peel squash and remove seeds. Cut in 1/2-inch widths. Place in shallow pan, sprinkle generously with sugar, dot with butter and pour on water to make syrup. Season to taste with nutmeg. Bake in slow (300 degrees) oven to candy until tender.

## Cabbage au Gratin

1 small cabbage, shredded
1/2 cup cheese, grated
1 cup cream sauce

Boil cabbage and drain. Place in casserole in layers of cabbage, cream sauce and cheese, alternating until all are used. Be sure to have layer of cheese on top. Bake at 400 degrees until bubbly, about 15 minutes. Serves 4.

## Broiled Tomatoes

tomatoes
2 tablespoons butter
flour

Select firm, ripe tomatoes. Peel and cut crosswise in slices 1/2-inch thick. Drain for a minute; dip in flour. Into a heavy fry pan put 2 tablespoons butter. Heat and broil tomatoes on both sides until brown. Turn with batter cake turner. Serve with broiled fish, steak or poached eggs.

## Baked Squash

6 large yellow squash
bread crumbs
2 slices bacon, fried crisp
salt
1 onion
2 tablespoons butter
green pepper, minced
pepper

Cut squash in half lengthwise. (Do not remove skin.) Boil in salted water 10 to 15 minutes, drain, scoop out, leaving 1/4-inch shell. Mash scooped out part and season with chopped onion, minced pepper, salt and pepper. Add crumbled bacon and butter. Fill shells, sprinkle with buttered crumbs. Bake 20 minutes at 375 degrees. Serves 6.

## Carrot Casserole

1 bunch carrots
1 teaspoon Accent
1/2 cup celery, diced
4 eggs, separated
1 tablespoon onion, minced
1/2 cup water
4 tablespoons oleomargarine
1 can cream of chicken soup
1 teaspoon salt
1 teaspoon white pepper
1/2 teaspoon cream of tartar

Scrape carrots and cut into small chunks; cook until you can mash with fork. Add all ingredients except egg whites. Beat egg whites and add cream of tartar. Fold into mixture. Bake at 325 degrees for 1 hour in greased casserole.

## Artichoke and Asparagus Casserole

*Julia Dyar*

2 cans artichoke hearts, sliced
2 large cans asparagus, cut
2 cans (2 1/2 ounces) water chestnuts, sliced
juice from vegetables
2 cups cheese, grated
1/2 cup butter
1 cup flour
almonds
salt to taste
pepper to taste
nutmeg to taste
1/2 cup sherry

Melt butter and brown flour slowly in it. Add juice from vegetables (if too thick add some water). Add grated cheese and sherry. Season with salt, pepper and nutmeg to taste. Combine with other ingredients and pour into casserole. Serve hot.

## Carrots and Cheese

1 cup carrots, shredded
1 cup sharp cheese, shredded
2 eggs
2 tablespoons butter
1 tablespoon milk
salt
pepper

Mix ingredients and fill a buttered baking dish. Dot over the top with butter. Place in a pan containing water and bake at 350 degrees until done, usually about 30 minutes.

## Savannah Red Rice

1/4 pound bacon
2 cups long grain raw rice
1/2 teaspoon salt
1/8 teaspoon Tabasco sauce
1/2 cup onions, chopped
2 cups plum tomatoes, canned
1/4 teaspoon pepper

Slowly fry bacon until crisp. Remove from pan. Cook onions until tender in bacon fat. Add raw rice, tomatoes, seasonings and crumbled bacon. Cook over low heat about 10 minutes. Pour into 1-quart casserole; cover tightly. Bake at 350 degrees for 1 hour, stirring with fork a couple of times. Makes 8 servings.

## Baked Acorn Squash

3 medium acorn squash
1/2 cup honey
salt
3 tablespoons butter
juice of 1/2 lemon

Wash squash and cut in half lengthwise. Scoop out seeds and fibers. In baking dish, place 1/2 inch of water and place squash halves, cut side down. Bake about 30 minutes or until tender. Remove from oven and drain both squash and baking dish. Spread the butter into halves, and salt to taste. Add a few drops of lemon juice and equally divide the honey into the cavities. Return to oven and bake about 15 minutes at 400 degrees.

## Broccoli Souffle

*Julia Dyar*

2 10-ounce packages
  frozen broccoli florets
lemon juice
1 can cream of mushroom
  (or cream of celery) soup
1/2 cup mayonnaise
2 eggs, well beaten
2 tablespoons finely
  chopped onion
1 cup grated sharp
  Cheddar cheese
buttered bread crumbs

Cook broccoli according to package directions; drain well and cool. Dot with lemon juice and stir in remaining ingredients except crumbs. Blend well. Pour into greased 2-quart casserole. Top with crumbs. Bake at 350 degrees for 35 to 40 minutes. Makes 6 to 8 servings.

## Brown Rice

*Carolyn McLeod*

1 stick oleo, whole
1 cup rice
2 cans beef broth
1 cup celery, cut up
1 small onion, cut up
1 small can mushrooms,
  drained

Combine all ingredients and place in 2-quart size baking dish. Cover and bake 1 hour and 15 minutes at 350 degrees.

## Spinach Souffle

*Dot Thomas*

1 package frozen spinach,
  chopped
2 eggs
1 can cream of mushroom
  soup, undiluted
crushed cheese crackers

Thaw and drain spinach well. Mix with eggs and soup and pour into well greased casserole. Top with cheese crackers. Bake at 375 degrees for about 35 minutes.

## Hopping John

*Julia Dyar*

2 cups dried black-eyed peas
1 pound bacon
2 cups long-grain rice
1/2 teaspoon pepper
1 1/2 quarts cold water
5 cups boiling water
1 tablespoon salt

Combine peas and cold water in a large, heavy container with a tight fitting cover. Bring to boil. Cover and cook over medium heat for 1 hour. Remove cover, turn heat to high and cook until peas are almost dry. Cut bacon into 1 1/2 inch lengths. Add bacon, boiling water, rice, salt and pepper. Stir; bring to boil. Cover and simmer for 25 minutes or until moisture is absorbed and rice is tender. Serve topped with bacon pieces. Makes 8 to 10 generous servings.

## Asparagus Casserole

*Julia Dyar*

2 tablespoons butter
2 tablespoons flour
1 cup sweet milk (or 3/4 cup and 1/4 cup asparagus juice from can)
salt to taste
1/2 stick butter
1 cup grated cheese
1 number-2 can asparagus
1 can sliced water chestnuts (drained)
2 pimentos, diced
pepper to taste
2 cups waverly wafer crumbs

Melt 2 tablespoons butter and add flour. Mix well, place over low heat and stir in milk or milk and asparagus juice combination. Cook until sauce begins to thicken. Add salt and pepper to taste. Stir in 1 cup grated cheese. Place asparagus, water chestnuts and pimentos in casserole. Melt remaining butter and stir into wafer crumbs. Spread on casserole and bake at 350 degrees until golden brown. Serve hot.

## Asparagus Pie

1 can green asparagus
1 cup mayonnaise or salad dressing
1 cup cheese, grated
1/2 can cream of mushroom soup
3 eggs

Beat all together and put in casserole. Bake in slow oven at 225 degrees for one hour.

## Fresh Asparagus With Vinagrette Sauce

3 tablespoons melted butter or oil
2 tablespoons cider vinegar
1 tablespoon parsley, chopped
1 tablespoon onion, grated
1 teaspoon salt
1/2 teaspoon paprika
cayenne pepper to taste
1 tablespoon tarragon vinegar

Melt butter; add vinegar and the seasonings. Heat and pour hot over asparagus and serve immediately.

## Pickled Beets

1/2 teaspoon dry mustard
1 tablespoon sugar
1/2 teaspoon salt
1/2 teaspoon cloves, powdered
1/2 clove garlic, peeled
pinch of fennel
6 tablespoons vinegar
1/4 cup water
2 cups cooked or canned beets, sliced and drained

Combine first five ingredients. Stir in vinegar and water slowly. When smooth, pour on beets. Chill; remove garlic. Serve with meat or fish. Makes 6 servings.

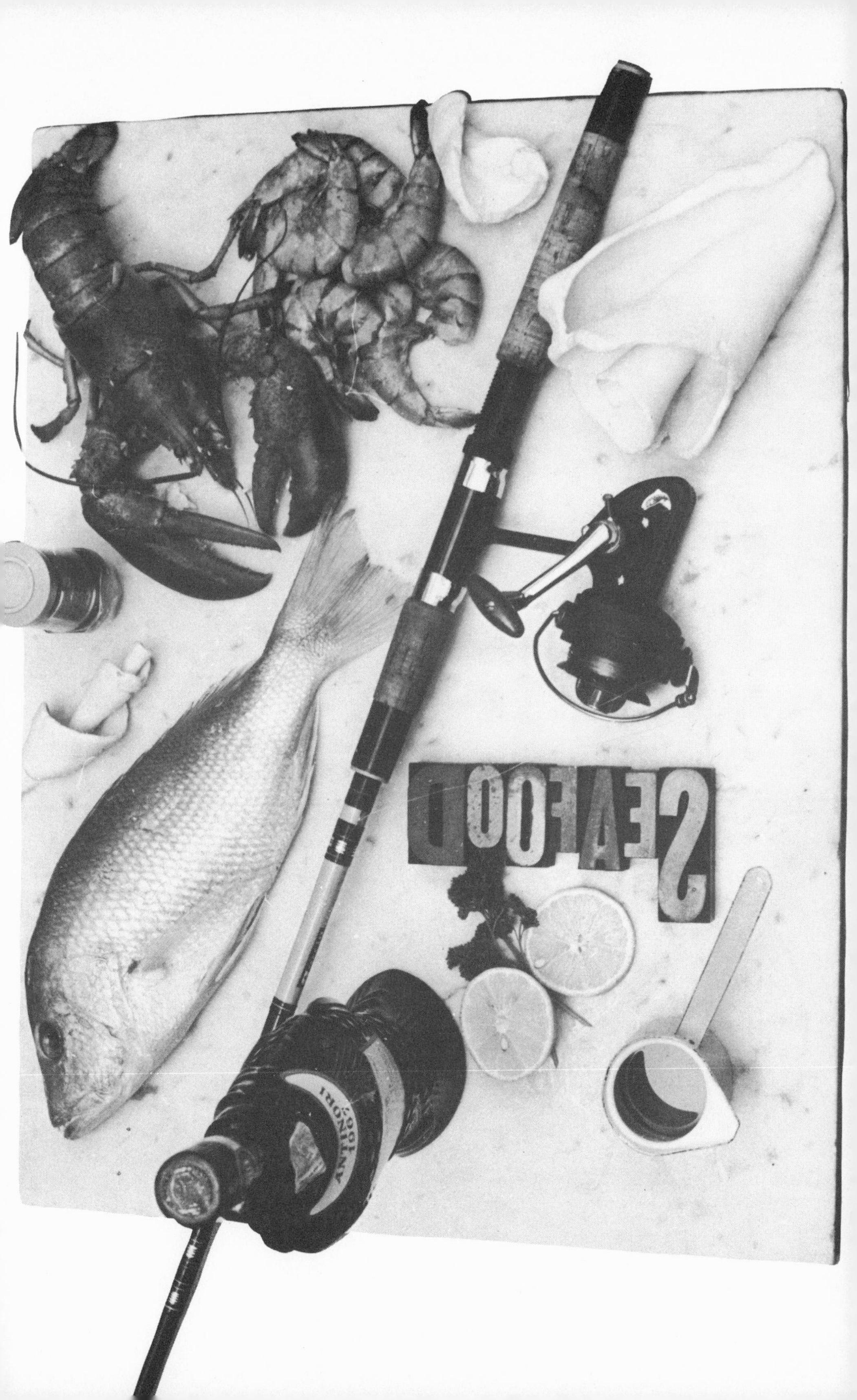

## Oysters Rockefeller

6 oysters in the half shell
3/4 cup sour cream
3 cloves garlic
salt
pepper
3 tablespoons cheese, grated
bread crumbs
1 tablespoon butter
1/2 cup whipped cream
1 cup raw spinach, chopped

Remove the oysters from their shells, mix 1/4 cup sour cream with a little crushed garlic, salt and pepper and put a teaspoon of the mixture in the bottom of each oyster shell. Cover the top with the oyster and cover the oyster with the spinach which has been mixed with the rest of the sour cream, a little garlic, salt and pepper. Sprinkle with a little grated cheese and bread crumbs and dot with butter. Brown under the broiler; remove and put a tablespoon of whipped cream on the top of each oyster and brown under the broiler again.

## Boneless Baked Shad

3 or 4 pound shad
1 quart water
4 or 5 strips bacon
1 tablespoon vinegar
salt to taste
pepper to taste

Boil shad in water and vinegar with seasonings for 20 minutes. Drain off water; put in a heavy, tightly covered roaster and cook in oven slowly (200 degrees) for 5 or 6 hours. Add roe about 30 minutes before fish is done. Put strips of bacon across the shad and place under broiler for bacon to brown. This is delicious. When done, the bones are completely dissolved. Serves 6.

## Scalloped Oysters

*The Jekyll Islander*

1 quart large oysters
2 cups crackers, crumbled
1 egg
1/2 cup sweet milk
salt and pepper to taste
butter

Clean oysters and warm slightly, drain off juices. In baking pan, put a layer of oysters, salt, pepper and butter and crushed crackers. Continue until all are used. Mix beaten egg and milk. Pour over mixture. Cover with buttered cracker crumbs and bake in moderate (350 degrees) oven for 30 minutes. Serve immediately.

## Oyster Stew

*The Jekyll Islander*

1 quart oysters
1 quart sweet milk
3 tablespoons butter

Melt butter, add to milk. Put in oysters but do not allow mixture to boil. Keep it warm until oysters are cooked. Serve with oysterette crackers, and season with salt as needed.

## Chicken With Oysters

*Mrs. Phil Landrum*

6 chicken breasts
1 pint oysters (large or small)
1/2 stick butter
1 cup sweet milk
1 cup cream
1 teaspoon salt
1/4 teaspoon salt

Saute chicken in butter until golden brown. Place chicken breasts in casserole, season and pour milk over them. Cover and cook 1 hour in 350-degree oven. Remove from oven, cover chicken with oysters and add cream. Return to oven for 15 minutes longer. Serves 6.

## Scalloped Oysters

*Julia Dyar*

2 dozen or more oysters, drained
1 box oysterettes crumbs (at least 2 cups)
1/2 cup melted butter or margarine
dash cayenne pepper
2 tablespoons sherry wine
2 tablespoons oyster liquid
1/2 teaspoon salt
1/8 teaspoon pepper
2 tablespoons cream or top milk
1 teaspoon Worcestershire sauce

Drain oysters, reserving 2 tablespoons liquid. Combine crumbs and butter, using 1/2 of them to cover bottom of shallow, greased baking dish. Arrange half of the oysters on top. Combine remaining ingredients and cover with 1/3 more of crumbs. Arrange remaining oysters on top. Pour on remaining sauce; top with crumbs and dot with butter. Bake at 400 degrees until browned. Serves 4.

## Seafood in Tomato Shells

6 medium, ripe tomatoes
1 1/2 cups seafood*
1 cup celery, diced
1/2 cup diced bell pepper
1/4 teaspoon salt
salad greens

Cut a slice from stem end of each tomato, remove pulp and drain. Combine pulp with other ingredients, tossing lightly. Line salad plates with greens, centering the tomato shell. Fill with mixture and top with French dressing.

* Best with flaked crab meat, but chopped shrimp, lobster or canned tuna or salmon may be used.

### Oysters a la Poulette

1 pint shucked oysters
1 pint chicken or turkey, coarsely diced
1 1/2 cups chicken or turkey broth
1/2 cup butter
1/2 cup flour
salt to taste
pepper to taste

Place oysters in casserole dish and place in 400-degree oven until oysters are reduced to approximately 1/2 size. Drain liquid and set them aside. Make roux of butter and flour. Mix broth and oyster liquid and bring to a rolling boil. Add roux to liquid until it becomes a thick sauce. Add chicken or turkey and oysters. Serves 6 to 8. Serve on rissotto.

### Salmon and Mushroom Stuffed Potatoes

4 medium potatoes, baked
1/4 cup heavy cream, heated
1 teaspoon salt
1 can (3 ounces) mushrooms, chopped and broiled
1 can (7 3/4 ounces) salmon, drained and flaked
1/4 cup butter or margarine, melted
1/8 teaspoon pepper
1 tablespoon onion, grated
1 cup sharp Cheddar cheese, grated
1/8 teaspoon dill weed

Cut hot potatoes in half lengthwise and scoop out all pulp without breaking the skin. Mash or whip the pulp and add butter, cream, salt, pepper and crushed dill weed. Beat until light and fluffy. Drain mushrooms, reserving broth for use in soup, sauce or gravy. Add mushrooms, onion and 2/3 cup grated cheese. Bake in oven preheated to 350 degrees for 20 minutes or until cheese melts. Makes 8 stuffed potato halves.

### Baked Oysters

1 quart oysters
3 tablespoons Worcestershire sauce
salt to taste
cracker crumbs
1 stick butter, melted
1 tablespoon catsup
2 eggs, well beaten
pepper to taste

Into a pyrex dish put 1 thin layer of cracker crumbs, 1 layer of oysters and pour egg mixture over oysters. Top with cracker crumbs and bake 40 minutes at 350 degrees.

### Baked Stuffed Pompano

1 pompano, about 3 pounds
1/2 cup heavy cream
2 tablespoons sherry
1/8 teaspoon pepper
2 tablespoons saltine crackers, crushed
6 tablespoons heavy cream
3/4 pound boiled shrimp, finely chopped
1/2 teaspoon salt
3 tablespoons mushrooms, chopped
1 egg

Bone and dress the pompano. Mix the other ingredients, with the exception of 6 tablespoons cream, and stuff the fish. Sew and place in a roasting pan or a heat proof baking dish. Lightly sprinkle with sauce, pour 6 tablespoons of cream over it and bake in a moderate oven at 350 degrees until tender (approximately 30 minutes).

## Crab Imperial

1 pound crab meat
1 small pimento, chopped
1 egg, beaten
1/4 teaspoon pepper
1 teaspoon dry mustard
1/3 green pepper, chopped and boiled
1/3 cup mayonnaise
1/2 teaspoon salt

Combine all ingredients gently and place in casserole. Bake about 15 minutes at 350 degrees until puffy all the way through. Serves 4.

## Scallops au Gratin

1 package scallops, frozen
4 tablespoons butter or margarine
1 1/2 cups bread crumbs, soft
1 medium onion
1 cup light cream
4 stalks celery
1/2 cup Cheddar cheese, grated
1/2 teaspoon salt
1 small green pepper
dash pepper

Butter a 1-quart casserole or baking dish and preheat oven to 350 degrees. Cover scallops with cold water and bring to a boil. Drain immediately.

Melt 2 tablespoons butter or margarine and mix with bread crumbs. Cut green pepper, onion and celery into chunks and cook slowly in remaining butter or margarine for about 5 minutes.

Arrange layers of scallops, vegetables, bread crumbs and cheese in casserole. Season layers with salt and pepper. Pour cream over the top and bake 30 minutes. Makes 4 servings.

### Crabmeat Au Gratin

*John Sutlive*

3 tablespoons butter
1/2 green pepper, minced
1/2 onion, chopped
3 tablespoons flour
2 cups milk
2 cups boned crabmeat
dash nutmeg
1/2 teaspoon salt
1/2 cup grated cheese
buttered bread crumbs

Melt butter; add pepper and onion and cook for 5 minutes. Add flour and milk, then crabmeat, salt and nutmeg. Cook 10 minutes. Pour in shallow buttered baking dish or use crab shells. (Single-serving French pottery casseroles are perfect). Sprinkle with grated cheese and buttered bread crumbs and bake at 350 degrees until cheese is brown.

### Jiffy Creamed Eggs And Seafood

*Jere N. Moore*

2 cans (14 1/2 ounces each) condensed cream of mushroom soup
1/2 pint (1 cup) light cream
1 6-ounce can broiled mushroom crowns, drained
6 hard cooked eggs, halved or quartered
1 tablespoon cornstarch
18 oysters, fresh, frozen or canned
1 cup shrimp, cooked or canned
1 cup Taylor Sauterne or dry sherry
2 tablespoons cold water

Blend soup and cream into saucepan. Combine cornstarch and cold water; add soup mixture with mushrooms, eggs, oysters and shrimp. Stir over low heat until edges of oysters curl. Just before serving, add wine. Reheat; do not boil. Serve on toast or toasted English muffins. Makes 6 servings.

## Fried Catfish

*Mary Alice Quinn, Food Editor*
*The Commercial Appeal, Memphis*

catfish
buttermilk
corn meal
flour

Combine corn meal and flour in ratio of 2 parts corn meal to 1 part flour. Dip each fish into buttermilk, then into corn meal mixture. Fry in deep fat until golden brown.

## Crab Cakes

*Ben Green Cooper*
*SAVANNAH'S COOKIN'*

3 eggs, lightly beaten
1/2 teaspoon salt
1/8 teaspoon black pepper
1 tablespoon white Bordeaux wine
2 cubic inches mild Cheddar cheese, grated
1 teaspoon olive oil
1 tablespoon Italian hard cheese, grated
1/2 cup white flake crab meat
dried French bread crumbs, enough to thicken
4 strips double thick bacon
2 tablespoons butter

Beat eggs and add Italian cheese, salt, pepper, crab meat, wine, French bread crumbs and Cheddar cheese. Mix well.

Fry bacon in large iron skillet and drain on paper. Pour off the fat and wipe out the skillet with paper toweling, gently. Add 2 tablespoons butter and 1 teaspoon olive oil to skillet. Heat to the popping stage when a drop of water hits fat, as the butter starts to brown. Use a large kitchen spoon, dip up spoonsful of the crab meat mixture and drop gently into the skillet. After all the mixture is in the skillet, lower the heat and let the cakes brown on one side, turn up heat slightly, turn the cakes over with a spatula, lower the heat again and let that side brown. Remove with a spatula to paper, drain and serve with the bacon strips.

## Fish Chowder

*Lois W. McCrory*

1 cup Irish potato, blocked
1/2 cup onion
water
1 cup fish
pepper
salt
3 cups milk
saltine crackers (1 dozen)

Cook onion and potatoes in small amount of water. Add fish and season with black pepper and salt. Add approximately 3 cups milk and saltine crackers. Have finished dish soupy.

## Deviled Crab Casserole

1 pound crabmeat
1 1/2 cups breadcrumbs
1/2 cup chopped celery
1/2 cup chopped onion
1/2 cup chopped green pepper
1/2 cup melted butter or margarine
1/4 cup milk
1 teaspoon dry mustard
1/2 teaspoon salt
2 tablespoons A.1. Sauce

Mix together crabmeat, crumbs, celery, onion and green pepper. Add melted butter and milk and mix well. Add mustard, salt and A.1. Sauce. Mix well and pour into casserole. Bake at 350 degrees for 30 minutes. Serves 6.

## Crab Mornay

*Mrs. Charles L. (Paula) Hardy, Jr.*

1 pound white crab meat
1/2 pound grated cheese
1/2 cup butter
3 tablespoons flour
2 teaspoons white pepper
1 teaspoon salt
1 pint milk

Make thick cream sauce of butter, flour, salt, pepper and milk. Into a greased baking dish, place layer of crab meat, layer of cheese. Pour in some cream sauce and continue until dish is filled. Bake at 325 degrees for 25 to 30 minutes.

## Seafood Chowder, Pilau, Gumbo

*Ben Green Cooper*

1 package fish filets, frozen
2 small yellow onions, coarsely chopped
2 branches celery, chopped
1 small can stewing oysters, fresh
black pepper to taste
1 small can claw crab meat
parsley
thyme
Worcestershire sauce
1 small can early June peas
mushrooms, chopped
1/2 pint strong stock
2 small white onions, coarsely chopped
2 cloves garlic, chopped
12 langostinos
1 small can shrimp, drained
celery salt to taste
1 small can clams, minced
basil
oregano
1 pound okra, sliced
1 cup white rice or 2 Irish potatoes, peeled and cubed

*WEBSTER:* GUMBO, also GOMBO, African origin, a soup thickened with the mucilaginous pods of the okra; okra soup.

CHOWDER, French chaudiere, a kettle or pot, a dish made of fresh fish or clams, biscuit, onions, etc., stewed together.

PILAU, PILAW (persian and Turkish, Pilaw), Rice boiled with meat, fowl or fish, spices, etc., Oriental, variations, Pilaf, Pilaff.

Put a package of frozen fish filets (cod, haddock, flounder, sole or snapper) in a pot with water to cover and add a half pint of strong stock made of Virginia ham bone, turkey, beef or chicken; bring to boil. Add chopped yellow and white onions, celery, garlic, oysters, langostinos (tiny deep sea lobsters), shrimp (4 1/2 ounces), black pepper and celery salt to taste. Let come to a boil, cover, and cook on low heat for 2 hours. Remove lid and add claw crab meat, minced clams with the juice, parsley, basil, thyme, oregano, Worcestershire sauce, okra, peas and (for pilau or gumbo) a cup of white rice, or (for chowder) Irish potatoes. Let mixture cook on low heat, uncovered, about 35 or 40 minutes, or until rice or potatoes are done. It can be served as a seafood soup without the rice or potatoes, and the okra may be omitted if using as a fish soup.

### Tuna and Ripe-Olive Loaf

1 cup cracker crumbs
1 1/2 cups milk
3 eggs, slightly beaten
2 6 1/2- or 7-ounce cans tuna, flaked
1/2 cup ripe olives, chopped
dash pepper
1 12-ounce can whole kernel corn, drained (1 cup)

Combine crumbs and milk; heat to boiling. Cook, stirring constantly, for 1 minute. Remove from heat. Add small amount of hot mixture to eggs and mix well. Stir into rest of hot mixture. Add remaining ingredients. Mix well. Put in greased 8 1/2 X 4 1/2 X 2 1/2-inch loaf pan. Place in shallow pan, surrounded by 1 inch of hot water. Bake at 375 degrees for 1 hour, or until loaf is firm. Turn onto hot platter. Garnish with sliced ripe olives. Serves 6.

### Deviled Crab

1 cup crab meat
1/2 teaspoon mustard
1 dessertspoon Worcestershire sauce
2 tablespoons dry bread crumbs, white
cayenne pepper
2 tablespoons cream
salt
pepper
1 tablespoon Parmesan cheese, grated
2 tablespoons fat or olive oil

Put crab meat in a bowl. Add the mustard, Worcestershire sauce, bread crumbs, cream, salt, pepper and cayenne pepper. Mix thoroughly and refill crab shells. Sprinkle top liberally with grated cheese and a little fat or olive oil and bake for 5 to 10 minutes in a hot oven.

## Deviled Crab

1 pound lump crab meat
2 or 3 tablespoons flour
salt to taste
1/4 teaspoon Tabasco
bread crumbs, buttered
1 tablespoon butter
1 cup milk
pepper to taste
1 tablespoon Worcestershire sauce

Make thick white sauce with butter, flour and milk; mix with crab meat after cooling. Mix well but not enough to break lumps. Add salt and pepper to taste, Tabasco sauce and Worcestershire sauce. Fill shells and sprinkle with buttered crumbs. Brown lightly under broiler. Serves 6 to 8.

This can also be cooked in pie pan, making cakes or mounds, in case shells are not available. Sprinkle bottom of pan with crumbs.

## Seafood a la King

6 tablespoons butter
1 cup mushrooms, sliced
6 tablespoons flour
1 teaspoon salt
1/8 teaspoon pepper
2 1/2 cups milk
1 1/2 cups cooked seafood, drained, in large pieces
1/2 cup green pepper, slivered
1/4 cup pimento, slivered
buttered toast points

Melt butter; cook mushrooms in butter for 10 minutes. Remove from stove, blend in flour. Add salt and pepper. Slowly add milk, stirring constantly. Continue to cook, stirring until smooth and thickened. Gently stir in seafood, green pepper and pimento. Serve on buttered toast points. Serves 10 to 12.

### Trout Almondine

6 filets trout
1 cup milk
1/2 cup flour, sifted
pepper to taste
1/3 cup butter
1/2 cup almonds, chopped
salt to taste

Dip filets in milk, roll in seasoned flour. Melt butter in skillet and brown filets evenly on both sides. Remove from skillet. Saute almonds. Pour browned butter and almonds over fish. Garnish with parsley and lemon wedges.

### Stuffed Lobster, Jamaica Style

6 lobsters, split
1/4 pound butter
2 onions, chopped
1/4 pound mushrooms, chopped
1 tablespoon flour
1/2 cup stock
1 teaspoon salt
1/4 teaspoon pepper
dash cayenne pepper
1/2 cup bread crumbs
1/2 cup cheese, grated

Remove the meat from the lobsters and cut in small pieces. Reserve the shells. Set aside. Melt 3 tablespoons of the butter in a saucepan. Add the onions and mushrooms and saute for 15 minutes. Add the flour, stirring constantly. Add the stock, continuing to stir until the mixture boils. Add the lobster meat, salt, pepper and cayenne pepper. Cook for 15 minutes. Check seasoning for desired taste.

Place the lobster mixture in the shells. Sprinkle with the bread crumbs and cheese. Dot with the remaining butter. Place on a baking sheet. Bake at 350 degrees for 15 minutes, or until lightly browned on top. Serve with lime or lemon wedges.

### Lobster A La Newberg

1 1/2 pounds cooked lobster
3 tablespoons butter
1 1/2 cups cream
dash cayenne
paprika
3 egg yolks, beaten
1 1/2 cups Madeira wine or sherry
1/4 teaspoon salt

Cut lobster meat into large pieces and heat slowly in butter about 5 minutes. Add wine and simmer slowly until the wine is almost reduced. Beat cream into egg yolks, add lobster and season. Cook, stirring constantly until thickened. Serve at once on hot toast. Serves 8.

### Fish Mulligan

3 strips bacon, diced
3 medium onions, sliced
1 1/2 pounds fresh or quick-frozen fish fillets, thawed
1 1/2 pounds white potatoes, cut in 3-4-inch cubes
1/2 teaspoon celery seed
3 cups boiling water
3 large carrots, cut in 3-4-inch cubes
1/4 cup diced green pepper
4 teaspoons salt
1/4 teaspoon pepper
1 (number-2 1/2) can tomatoes (3 1/2 cups)
2 tablespoons snipped parsley

Saute bacon in deep kettle or Dutch oven until lightly browned; set aside. In same kettle, saute onions until tender. Add fish, cut into 2 1/2-inch pieces, potatoes, celery seed, carrots, green pepper, salt, pepper and water. Simmer, covered, until vegetables are tender – about 25 minutes. Add tomatoes; heat. Garnish with parsley and bacon bits. Makes 6 servings.

## Frog Legs Provencal

8 frog legs
5 tablespoons butter
2 tablespoons chives, finely chopped
2 or 3 teaspoons garlic, crushed
salt
pepper
2 tablespoons fresh tarragon, finely chopped
2 tablespoons parsley, finely chopped
2 tablespoons lighted dry white wine
1 tablespoon lighted brandy

Wash frog legs very well in lemon juice and water, dry and dust lightly with seasoned flour. Put butter in a pan, heat to foaming and add crushed garlic. Cook for 1 minute, put in frog legs and shake until golden on each side; then add salt, pepper, tarragon, chives and parsley. Cook for another minute; then pour over brandy and wine. Serve at once in very hot dish.

## Lobster Newburg

2 cups lobster (about 5)
2 tablespoons flour
4 egg yolks
1/2 teaspoon salt
dash nutmeg
6 tablespoons butter
1/3 cup sherry
1 cup cream (1/4 milk)
dash cayenne

Boil lobster and pick out. Melt butter; add flour and cream. Add eggs, salt, cayenne and nutmeg. Add lobster and cook about 30 minutes. Just before serving, add sherry. Serve over rice or in pastry shell.

## Artichoke – Lobster Newburg

1 package (9 ounces) artichoke hearts, frozen
2 teaspoons onion, chopped
2 tablespoons sherry
1/2 teaspoon salt
1/8 teaspoon pepper
1/2 cup Cheddar cheese, grated
1 bay leaf (optional)
1 can (10 1/2 ounces) cream of mushroom soup, condensed
1/8 teaspoon garlic salt
1 cup lobster (5-ounce can), cut in bite-sized pieces

Cook artichoke hearts as directed on package; add bay leaf during cooking. Drain. Combine soup, onion, sherry, salt, garlic salt and pepper. Arrange artichoke hearts and lobster in 1-quart casserole. Add soup mixture. Top with cheese. Bake in hot oven (400 degrees) about 15 minutes. Serve with wild rice, rice, noodles or toast points. Makes 4 servings.

## Quick Seafood Bisque

1 cup seafood, cooked
3 tablespoons sherry
1 can condensed tomato soup
1 can condensed pea soup
1 can consommé
1 1/4 cups hot rich milk or cream

Use crab meat, lobster, shrimp, oysters or any desired combination of seafood. Soak it in sherry for 10 to 15 minutes. Combine tomato soup, pea soup and consommé in medium saucepan and place over low heat until hot. Slowly stir in the milk or cream and add the seafood. Simmer until steaming hot but do not boil. Serves 6.

## Lobster Salad Supreme

2 cups flaked lobster, cooked
1/4 cup stuffed olives, chopped
1 teaspoon capers
1/3 cup French dressing
2 hard-cooked eggs

Combine all ingredients and chill for 1 hour before serving. Serve on lettuce and garnish with lobster claws. Serves 6.

## Tuna Bake with Cheese Swirls

*Julia Dyar*

1 medium onion, chopped
3 tablespoons butter
3 cups milk
dash lemon juice
dash salt
dash pepper
biscuit dough
2 pimentoes, diced
1/2 green pepper, chopped
6 tablespoons flour
1 can tuna fish, drained and scalded in strainer with hot water
1 can mushrooms, chopped
1 cup cheese, grated

Saute onion and pepper in butter; add flour and then milk to make sauce. After all grease is removed from tuna, dry between paper towels and add tuna to sauce. Add lemon juice and mushrooms and set aside.

Roll out biscuit dough in rectangular shape. Over this put grated cheese and diced pimentoes. Roll dough like jelly roll and place in refrigerator to chill. Slice 1/4-inch thick and put on top of tuna mix in greased casserole. Bake at 400 degrees for 20 to 25 minutes.

### Easy Shrimp Curry

1/2 cup chopped onion
2 tablespoons butter or margarine
1 (5-ounce) can shrimp
1/2 teaspoon curry powder
1 cup sour cream
1 (10-ounce) can frozen, condensed cream of shrimp soup
1 teaspoon Worcestershire sauce
salt and pepper to taste

Saute onion in butter until yellow but not browned. Add shrimp soup. Stir to break up. Add shrimp and heat to boiling. Simmer gently for about 5 minutes. Add seasonings and sour cream. Serve over hot rice. Serves 4.

### Shrimp de Jonghe

*Albert Crews*

1/2 cup butter
2 cloves garlic, minced
1/3 cup parsley, snipped fine
1/2 teaspoon paprika
dash cayenne
monosodium glutamate
salt
pepper
1/2 cup sherry
2 cups soft bread crumbs
4 cups cleaned, cooked shrimp

Melt butter; add garlic, parsley, paprika, cayenne and wine. Mix well and stir in bread crumbs. Place shrimp in 12 X 1 1/2 X 2-inch baking dish and spread butter mixture on top. Bake in 350-degree oven for 25 minutes, or until crumbs are brown. Sprinkle with more parsley and paprika, if desired. Serves 6.

## Shrimp & Rice

*Julia Dyar*

2 pounds shelled, deveined shrimp, or 2 7-ounce packages shelled and deveined frozen shrimp
1 cup raw long-grain rice
1 small bayleaf
3 tablespoons parsley
1/2 teaspoon dried marjoram
1 teaspoon chili powder
2 tablespoons butter
1/3 cup chopped onion
1 minced clove garlic
2 cups chicken broth
1 1-pound, 12-ounce can tomatoes
2 teaspoons salt
1/8 teaspoon pepper
dash of cayenne

Preheat oven to 350 degrees. If using frozen shrimp, defrost them. Melt butter in small skillet. Add onion and garlic and brown lightly. Blend all ingredients in 2-quart casserole. Cover and bake for 1 hour or until rice is dry and fluffy and liquid is absorbed. Makes 6 servings.

## Shrimp Rice – Jambalaya

*Edda R. Agee*

1 1/2 cans (1 pound) stewed tomatoes
1/2 cup water
1 teaspoon salt
1 teaspoon garlic salt, rounded
dill weed
1/8 teaspoon pepper
1/2 cup finely chopped celery
1/2 cup finely chopped green olives
1 1/3 cups Minute Rice
1 pound fresh shrimp, cleaned and cooked

Combine stewed tomatoes, water and seasoning in skillet. Cover and bring to a boil. Add Minute Rice directly from the box. Add shrimp, cover and simmer for 7 minutes. Garnish with dill weed. Serves 6.

### Stuffed Avocados

avocados
chili sauce
dash lemon juice
shrimp or crab meat
mayonnaise

Cut avocados lengthwise, leaving skin on. Remove seed. Fill with small shrimp or crab meat mixed with sauce made of 1/3 chili sauce, 2/3 mayonnaise and a dash of lemon juice.

### Beer-Batter Shrimp

1 can light domestic beer (12 ounces)
1 tablespoon salt
16 medium shrimp, raw
2 cups flour, sifted
1 tablespoon paprika
juice of 2 lemons
cooking oil

Pour beer into mixing bowl. Sift 1 cup all-purpose flour, salt and paprika into the beer, stirring with a wire whisk until the batter is light and frothy. Beer batter may be used at once or after standing several hours. When using the batter, whisk it from time to time to keep it thoroughly mixed.

Have shrimp at room temperature. Carefully peel off the shells, leaving the tail intact. Make an incision from the base of the tail down the center. Wash each shrimp under running water and remove the dark vein. Dry them and sprinkle with lemon juice.

Heat several cups of oil or fat in a fryer. Dredge the shrimp in flour, coating them entirely, then grasp by the tail and dip into the beer batter, coating well. When the temperature of the oil or fat has reached 375 degrees, drop the shrimp in one by one and cook until they are golden brown and crisp. Drain on paper toweling. Serves 4 to 6.

### Shrimp Remoulade

3 pounds shrimp, boiled
1 teaspoon salt
1 teaspoon pepper
1 tablespoon creole mustard
3 hard boiled eggs, finely chopped
1/2 pint olive oil
1/4 pint vinegar

Mix salt, pepper, mustard, olive oil and vinegar in bowl and add chopped eggs. Add shrimp, mix well and serve on lettuce with sliced tomatoes.

### Shad Roe Spread

1 can shad roe
1/2 teaspoon prepared mustard
2 tablespoons celery, chopped very fine
1/4 teaspoon garlic salt or juice
1 tablespoon onion, chopped
1 teaspoon horse-radish
1/4 teaspoon salt
1/4 teaspoon onion salt
4 tablespoons mayonnaise
1/2 teaspoon Worcestershire

Break up the shad roe and mix with all of the ingredients except the mayonnaise. Add the mayonnaise to make the desired spreading consistency. Spread on crackers.

### Deviled Salmon

canned salmon, flaked
2 tablespoons onion juice
1/2 teaspoon mustard
2 tablespoons butter
2 teaspoons Worcestershire sauce

Flake canned salmon. Mix with butter, onion juice, Worcestershire sauce and mustard. Serve on crackers.

## Baked Fish

*Pat C. Barron*

2 pounds boned fish
  (halibut is best)
1/4 teaspoon celery salt
1/4 teaspoon black pepper
1 teaspoon minced parsley
1 sliced onion
2 tablespoons flour, sifted
2 tablespoons butter
1 cup whole milk

Season fish with celery salt and pepper. Arrange in a well buttered baking dish. Cover with onion rings and sprinkle with flour. Melt butter in warm milk. Do not boil. Pour over fish and sprinkle with parsley. Bake at 350 degrees until the milk is nearly absorbed, usually about 30 minutes. Serves 4 to 6.

## Creole Shrimp

4 tablespoons bacon
  drippings
2 onions, medium
1 green pepper
1 1/2 cups celery
1 teaspoon sugar
1 quart tomatoes, canned
3 tablespoons tomato paste
salt to taste
pepper to taste
3 cups cooked shrimp

Cut up onions, green pepper and celery and fry in bacon drippings for 15 or 20 minutes. Add quart can of tomatoes, sugar and paste. Let this mixture simmer slowly to thick consistency for 30 to 45 minutes. Add pepper and salt. Fifteen minutes before serving, add cooked shrimp. This should be served with rice. Serves 6 to 8.

### Shrimp Stuffed in Bell Peppers

6 bell peppers, medium
2 cups shrimp, cooked and picked
1 cup bread crumbs
2 eggs, beaten
1/2 cup milk
3 tablespoons butter
3 tablespoons celery, chopped
1 tablespoon onion, chopped
1 tablespoon bell pepper, chopped
1 teaspoon salt
1/8 teaspoon black pepper
1 tablespoon Worcestershire

Cut off tops and remove seeds from peppers. Cook pepper shells in boiling water for five minutes and then put at once into cold water. Cut shrimp slightly. Combine with eggs, crumbs and milk. Saute chopped ingredients in butter for three minutes, and add to shrimp mixture. Add seasonings and stuff into pepper shells, putting a few bread crumbs and a dot of butter on top of each. Bake 30 to 40 minutes at 375 degrees. Serves 6.

### Shrimp and Crabmeat Casserole

1 green pepper, chopped
1 onion, chopped
1 cup celery, chopped
1 12-ounce can white crabmeat
1 12-ounce can cooked shrimp
1/2 teaspoon salt
1 tablespoon Worcestershire sauce
1 cup mayonnaise
1 cup bread crumbs, buttered
slivered almonds, toasted
1/2 teaspoon pepper

Combine all ingredients except almonds and bake at 350 degrees for 30 minutes or until done. Sprinkle almonds on top if desired.

## Shrimp Sea Island

8 ounces frozen shrimp, peeled and deveined
1/8 cup catsup
1/8 cup chili sauce
salt
1/4 cup mayonnaise
1/4 cup tartar sauce
1 onion, shredded
cayenne pepper

Boil shrimp according to package directions. Combine with remaining ingredients, seasoning with salt and pepper. Chill in refrigerator for 2 to 3 hours before serving.

## Crab Louis

*Mary Cullen, Food Editor*
*Oregon Journal*

1 pound fresh crab
Western iceberg lettuce
lemon wedges
ripe olives
tomato wedges
2 hard-cooked eggs, quartered

Dressing

1 cup mayonnaise
1/2 cup chili sauce
2 teaspoons horse-radish
1/4 cup sweet pickle relish
2 tablespoons lemon juice
2 tablespoons chopped green onion
1 teaspoon salt
1/4 teaspoon pepper

Shred crab, reserving leg pieces for garnish. For each salad, pile shredded lettuce into a lettuce cup. Top with approximately 1/2 cup crab. Cover with 3 to 4 tablespoons dressing. Garnish with reserved crab legs, tomato wedges, eggs, lemon and olives. Serve additional dressing on side. Makes 4 salads.

To make dressing, blend all ingredients and chill. Makes approximately 2 cups dressing.

### Scalloped Shad Roe

*Ben Green Cooper*
*The Jefferson Davis Receipt Book*

shad roe
1/2 tablespoon vinegar
parsley
thin white sauce
salt
egg yolk, hard-boiled
lemon juice
Tabasco

Wash the roe and cook for ten minutes in boiling water, salt and 1/2 tablespoon vinegar. Then plunge in cold water. Draw and break lightly with a fork, sprinkle a layer of roe in a shallow dish, then rub the yolk of a hard-boiled egg through a strainer. Add a sprinkling of parsley if wished and a little lemon juice. Moisten with a thin white sauce, with a drop or two of Tabasco in it. Then add another layer of roe, egg and seasoning and white sauce. Cover with buttered crumbs and bake until golden brown.

### Deviled Shrimp

2 teaspoons onion, minced
1 teaspoon paprika
1/2 teaspoon salt
1/3 cup flour
1 tablespoon lemon juice
1/4 cup margarine
1 teaspoon prepared mustard
dash cayenne
2 cups milk
2 cups shrimp, cooked

Sauté onion in margarine. Add paprika, mustard, salt and cayenne. Gradually stir in flour; add milk. Stir constantly until sauce thickens, then add lemon juice and cooked shrimp. Serve over rice or chow mein noodles or in baking dish.

## Savannah Shrimp

- 2 cups shrimp, seasoned and cooked
- 3 onions, sliced
- 1 cup water
- 1 tablespoon flour
- 2 teaspoons salt
- 1 tablespoon vinegar
- 1/2 cup sherry wine
- 2 cups canned tomatoes
- 1 small can LeSeur peas
- 2/3 cup celery, chopped
- 2 tablespoons bacon drippings
- 1 teaspoon sugar
- 2 tablespoons chili powder

Sauté onions and celery in bacon drippings. Add flour and tomatoes and other ingredients except wine. Cook 15 minutes, add wine and serve on rice as soon as mixture is very hot.

## Boiled Trout

- 2 good-sized trout
- 3 teaspoons salt, or more if desired
- 4 strips bacon
- 2 hard-cooked eggs, sliced

Cut the fish in half and remove the backbone. Sprinkle each piece with salt. Add the salt to approximately 1 1/2 quarts of water or enough to cover the fish well. Put fish pieces in the water and allow to boil for 15 to 20 minutes, or until the fish is tender but will still hold together. Remove carefully from the water and place on platter, meat side up. While fish is cooking, cut the bacon strips in pieces and fry slowly. The hot grease should be poured over the fish as soon as it has been put on the platter. Decorate with the bacon curls and slices of egg. If trout is not available, rock fish, flounder, or fresh mackerel can be used.

## Sole in Wine Sauce

1 1/2 pounds broccoli
juice of 1 lemon
1 cup mushrooms, fresh
2 tablespoons flour
1/2 teaspoon salt
1 cup sharp Cheddar cheese
1 1/2 pounds filet of sole
1 cup white table wine
2 tablespoons butter
1/2 cup table cream (or homogenized milk)

Cook broccoli until just tender. Sprinkle sole with lemon juice and let stand a few minutes. Drain, and poach in heated wine. Place broccoli at either end of shallow rectangular baking dish. Place fish in center of dish. Slice mushrooms and sauté lightly in butter. Blend in flour. Stir in cream and 1/2 cup wine in which fish was poached. Cook and stir until mixture boils and is thickened. Blend in salt and grated cheese, and stir over very low heat until cheese is melted. Pour over fish. Bake in moderate oven at 350 degrees for 20 to 30 minutes. Serves 4.

## Brook Trout Almondine

4 whole brook trout, cleaned
salt
pepper
4 tablespoons almonds, sliced
4 tablespoons butter
2 tablespoons lemon juice
flour

Wipe season and lightly flour trout. Brown in foamy hot butter in chafing dish pan over direct flame on both sides. Remove to hot platter and sprinkle with lemon juice. Add sliced almonds to butter in pan and toast. Pour butter and almonds over trout and serve at once.

### Fried Bass Filets

10 filets (from 2 to 3 pound bass)
3 cups yellow corn meal
1 cup flour, unsifted
salt
pepper
skim milk
vegetable oil

Soak filets in skim milk for 1/2 hour. Shake filets in meal, flour and seasoning. Preheat oil in frying pan until water jumps 6 inches or more when dropped in oil. Place bass in hot oil. Cut stove down to medium and cook until brown and crispy. Serve with ample lemon wedges and tartar sauce if desired. Serves 6 to 8.

### Creole Shrimp

4 tablespoons butter
1 medium onion, chopped
1/2 green pepper, chopped
1 cup celery, chopped
1/4 to 1/2 teaspoon sage, crushed
1 teaspoon salt
1 cup tomato juice
2 cups shrimp, cleaned and cooked
2 cups rice, steamed

Melt butter in heavy skillet. Add onion, pepper and celery and brown lightly. Add sage, salt and tomato juice and bring to boil. Add shrimp and simmer for 30 minutes. Serve on steamed rice. Serves 4. If sauce is too thin thicken with cornstarch.

### Baked Flounder with Sauce

1 flounder, baked
1 can frozen shrimp soup
1/4 cup cheese, grated
2 teaspoons A.1. sauce
2 tablespoons onion, grated
bread crumbs

Cook fish first for a few minutes. Place onion on fish, then pour sauce of shrimp soup, A.1. sauce and cheese over it. Sprinkle bread crumbs on top and brown.

## Bayou Pie

4 slices bread
4 tablespoons catsup
1 1/2 pounds shrimp, cleaned and cooked
1 teaspoon Worcestershire sauce
3/4 cup milk, canned
1 medium onion, grated
3/4 cup water
1 egg, slightly beaten
2 tablespoons sherry wine
dash Tabasco

Soak bread in milk and water until thoroughly moistened. Add remaining ingredients and pour into buttered casserole. Dot with several hunks of butter and bake at 350 degrees for 30 to 45 minutes.

## Clam Chowder

20 clams
1 slice fat salt pork
1 onion, sliced
1 tablespoon Worcestershire sauce
4 pilot biscuits*
1 teaspoon salt
2 tablespoons butter
4 potatoes, diced
1 cup fish stock
2 cups scalded milk

Wash clams and scald them in their own liquor. Then, remove clams and strain juice through cheesecloth. Cut pork into cubes and fry out. Cook onions in pork fat 5 minutes, then strain fat into soup kettle. Parboil potatoes in 1 cup water and add water and potatoes to fat. Cover and simmer 10 minutes. Add fish stock and clams. Add hot milk, salt, butter and Worcestershire sauce. Split pilot biscuits, soak in a little cold milk and add to chowder. Serves 4.

* Four hard, unleavened crackers or bagels may be substitued for pilot biscuits.

6
FOWL

## Turkey Carving

### Traditional Method

1. *Remove drumstick and thigh* – To remove drumstick and thigh, press leg away from body. Joint connecting leg to backbone will oftentimes snap free or may be severed easily with knife point. Cut dark meat completely from body by following body contour carefully with knife.

2. *Slicing dark meat* – Place drumstick and thigh on separate plate and cut through connecting joint. Both pieces may be individually sliced. Tilt drumstick to convenient angle, slicing towards plate.

3. *Slicing thigh* – To slice thigh meat, hold firmly on plate with fork. Cut even slices parallel to the bone.

4. *Preparing breast* – In preparing breast for easy slicing, place knife parallel and as close to wing as possible. Make deep cut into breast, cutting right to bone. This is the base cut. All breast slices will stop at this vertical cut.

5. *Carving breasts* – After base cut, begin to slice breast. Carve downward, ending at base cut. Start each new slice slightly higher up on breast. Keep slices thin and even.

## New Side Method

1. *Carving position* – Place turkey on its side, breast away from carver. Remove wing tip and first joint. Hold tip firmly, lift up, and sever at joint. Set this aside for other dishes and leave second joint of wing attached to turkey.

2. *Remove drumstick* – Slice dark meat off drumstick and thigh until thigh bone is exposed. Lift drumstick and cut off at thigh joint. Slice meat from drumstick.

3. *Cut away thigh bone* – Steady turkey with fork. Run knife point completely around thigh bone, loosening it. Pry one end up, grasp and pull free. With thigh bone gone, generous portions of dark meat can be sliced from turkey.

4. *Slicing dark meat* – Slice dark meat away from turkey just above removed thigh bone. As you work deeper into the meat, you will discover the "oyster." This choice piece may be lifted whole from spoon-shaped section of backbone.

5. *Slicing white meat* – Breast meat, like dark meat, is much easier to carve if turkey stands 20 to 30 minutes after roasting. Make deep vertical cut in breast just in front of wing joint to serve as base for all breast meat slices.

6. *Breast slices* – Start from center of breast and cut toward you, making large, even slices. When more slices are needed, turn turkey and repeat process. Remove stuffing from a hole cut under thigh.

## Low Country Fowl Bog

*S. Marvin Griffin*

1 6-pound hen or
  6 pounds chicken meat
black pepper
salt
2 pounds smoked sausage
4 medium onions
1 50-cent sack long
  grain rice

This is a dish with many variations. Ducks may be used to advantage, but chicken, which is plentiful, makes a tasty-toothy dish.

For a recipe to serve 10 hungry folks, get about a 6-pound hen or about 6 pounds of chicken meat. Disjoint the fowl and put into a cauldron or pot with a lid. Cover the meat with water, and add a copious amount of black pepper and two hands of salt.

Put the pot on top of the stove and set the heat on high until the water begins to boil, then cut down to medium on the heat. It will take about 3 hours for the meat to cook so it will fall off the bones. Remove the bones and put the meat back into the pot. If there is too much stock, pour some of it off. Too much stock will make the final dish too gummy.

Cut up about 2 pounds of smoked sausage into 1-inch lengths, and quarter about 4 medium-sized onions. Put these into the pot after the meat and stock come back to a slow boil.

Dump in a 50-cent sack of long grain rice (no instant rice, please). Stir the rice good one time, and then put the lid back on. Don't be peeping into the pot, or the rice wont't stand out and will be soggy.

Some French bread with garlic butter toasted in the oven will make this a good meal.

### Chicken in Wine

*Glenn McCullough*

chicken breasts
pepper
dash of oregano
1 cup wine vinegar
fat
salt
2 or 3 bay leaves
1 clove of garlic
1 cup Dago Red Wine or
  cooking sherry

Salt and pepper chicken breasts (whole or cut in half) and brown thoroughly in deep fat. Pour off fat and place in covered pan or Dutch oven. Add bay leaves, oregano, garlic, wine vinegar and sherry. Simmer, covered, for 1 hour.

### Chicken Roll with Mushroom Sauce

4 chicken breasts, cut in
  half lengthwise and boned
salt
pepper
8 tablespoons green onion,
  chopped
2 tablespoons ginger
1/4 pound butter, cut in
  8 pieces
1/2 cup flour
1 can cream of mushroom soup
8 tablespoons parsley,
  chopped

Remove skin from chicken. Place each piece between two pieces of plastic wrap. Working from center, pound with wooden mallet to form cutlets not quite 1/4-inch thick. Peel off plastic wrap; sprinkle chicken with salt and pepper. Measure 1 tablespoon each of onion and parsley and sprinkle over each cutlet. Roll as jelly roll, tucking in sides of meat. Press to seal well. Roll in flour which has been blended with ginger. Place in baking dish and put 1 pat of butter on each piece of chicken. Bake at 350 degrees for 1 hour. Spoon the undiluted mushroom soup over each piece and cook 10 minutes more.

## Party Chicken

*Laura Conway*

8 large chicken breasts (skinned and boned)
8 slices bacon
1/2 pint sour cream
1 package (4 ounces) chipped beef
1 can undiluted mushroom soup

Wrap each chicken breast with piece of bacon. Cover greased pan with chipped beef and arrange chicken over it. Mix soup and sour cream and pour over chicken. Bake at 275 degrees, uncovered, for 3 hours. Serves 8.

## Chicken Salad Casserole

*Glenn McCullough*

3 cups diced, boiled chicken
1 can condensed chicken soup
1 can cream of mushroom soup
2 cups diced celery
1 medium sized onion, chopped
1 cup pecans, chopped
1 teaspoon salt
1/2 teaspoon black pepper
juice of half a lemon
1 cup mayonnaise
5 hard boiled eggs
2 handfuls crushed potato chips

Cross slice the eggs and place in casserole with all ingredients except potato chips. Sprinkle potato chips over top and bake at 350 degrees for about 20 minutes. Garnish with fresh green parsley or butter lettuce and serve with cranberry sauce. Serves about 8.

## Grace's Sourdough Chicken Pie

*Dorothee Polson*

1 pound butter
2 recipes plain biscuit dough
2 chickens (3 pounds each) cooked, boned, cut in bite-sized pieces
2 cups milk
1 recipe sourdough*
pepper
10 eggs
2 1/2 to 3 cups chicken stock
2 tablespoons flour

*Sourdough here refers to a recipe of biscuit dough made with 2 cups of flour, covered and left in the refrigerator for 3 days. See recipe in bread section.

Line bottom and sides of large baking pan with half of the plain biscuit dough, rolled thin. Place about 1/3 of the cooked and boned chicken over the pastry and dot with butter.

Roll sourdough very thin and cut into dumplings; place layer over chicken and sprinkle with pepper. Over this, break 6 whole raw eggs to make a layer; dot with butter. Cover with another layer of sourdough dumplings. Repeat layer of chicken, butter and dumplings. Add remaining 4 eggs and remainder of chicken. Dot with butter and cover with chicken stock seasoned to taste. Sprinkle with flour; add milk.

Roll out remainder of biscuit dough; cut into 4 equal pieces. Place on top of pie, trim off excess, press edges of dough together to seal. Dot with butter. Bake at 300 degrees for 2 hours. Serves 15.

## Delicious Patio Chicken

5 2-pound fryers, halved
1 1/2 large bottles Durkees dressing
1/2 cup vinegar
juice of 6 lemons
1 tablespoon prepared mustard
2 tablespoons sugar
salt and pepper to taste
1 pound butter

Prepare and dry chicken halves. Combine remaining ingredients and blend into sauce. Dip chicken into sauce mixture and place on grill over coals which have burned to gray ash. Keep turned to prevent scorching; dip chicken into sauce 3 or 4 times during cooking. Cook approximately 2 1/2 to 3 hours.

## Steamed Chicken Mold

*Mrs. Phil Landrum*

2 cups cooked chicken
2 tablespoons butter
1 cup bread crumbs
1 cup milk
1 cup stock
1 tablespoon parsley
1 tablespoon grated lemon rind
2 eggs
1 cup cooked celery
1/2 cup blanched almonds
salt and pepper to taste

Melt butter in saucepan. Add crumbs, milk and stock. Cook 5 minutes, stirring constantly. Add chicken, cut in small pieces, slightly beaten eggs and seasoning. Mix well and turn into well greased ring mold. Place in shallow pan of hot water and bake at 375 degrees for about 30 minutes. Take out of mold and fill center with peas and garnish with carrots cut with fancy cutter. Serves four to six.

### Chicken Champignon

1 pound chicken breasts
2 tablespoons flour
1/2 teaspoon salt
1/8 teaspoon pepper
1 small garlic clove, minced
1/2 cup green pepper strips
2 tablespoons butter or margarine
1 medium onion, sliced
1 can (10 1/2 ounces) mushroom gravy

If desired, remove skin from chicken breasts. Dust chicken with flour, salt and pepper. In skillet, brown chicken with garlic in butter. Add onion and mushroom gravy. Cover; cook over low heat or at 375 degrees for about 30 minutes, basting occasionally with gravy. Add green pepper. Cover; continue cooking about 15 minutes longer or until chicken and green pepper are tender. Makes 3 servings.

### Charcoal Broiled Chicken

*Phil Landrum*

2 chickens (2 to 2 1/2 pounds) split
garlic salt
butter

Season chicken with garlic salt and brush with butter. Let stand until they are room temperature – about 30 minutes. Start cooking in oven broiler very slowly, skin down, until inside is lightly brown. Then transfer to wire holder and finish over the outdoor charcoal fire until the skin is brown and crisp, and the inside is quite brown, giving the longest cooking time to the skin side which was not cooked indoors. Baste with sauce made from 1 stick of melted butter, juice of 3 lemons and 3 tablespoons of Worcestershire sauce.

## Pressed Chicken

*Julia Dyar*

Chicken

1 large cooked hen (diced)
6 hard cooked eggs (chopped)
2 cups celery (chopped)
1 cup almonds, blanched, slivered and toasted
1 pint mayonnaise (homemade)
2 envelopes plain gelatin
1/2 cup cool water
1 cup hot chicken stock
1 tablespoon chow-chow (or relish)
1 tablespoon capers

Boiled Dressing

1 teaspoon salt
1 teaspoon mustard (dry)
1 tablespoon sugar
red pepper to taste
1 tablespoon butter (size of egg)
1 cup vinegar
4 eggs, separated

*Chicken:* Soak gelatin in 1/2 cup of cold water for 5 minutes. Dissolve in 1 cup of hot chicken stock. (Skim off fat.) When cool, add mayonnaise. Mix all other ingredients after chopping well. Put in molds or flat pan. Slice when firm and ready to use. Note: Lemon juice may be added for tartness.

*Dressing:* Boil salt, mustard, sugar, butter and pepper in vinegar. Beat egg yolks and whites separately, then together. Pour hot vinegar mixture over eggs. Cook until slightly thickened. Cool.

## Chicken — Sausage Casserole

*Mrs. Ruth Bridges*

1 chicken (hen)
1 can cream of mushroom soup
1 pound of sausage
1 cup yellow rice
1 medium onion
1 medium bell pepper
1 tablespoon butter

Boil chicken until done and remove from pot. Cook yellow rice in chicken broth. Let chicken cool, then cut up in small pieces. Cook sausage. Saute onion and pepper in butter. Place in casserole, alternating layers. Cook at 350 degrees until bubbly hot.

## Chicken Curry

*Mrs. Belmont Dennis*

1/4 cup butter
1 cup minced onion
1 cup celery, diced finely
1/2 teaspoon curry powder
1/4 teaspoon salt
1/4 teaspoon pepper
1 can tomato soup
2 cans chicken soup with rice
2 cups sweet milk

Melt butter in deep kettle and add onion and celery. Cook until tender. Combine with remaining ingredients, cover and simmer 15 to 20 minutes, stirring often.

## Gourmet Broiled Chicken

1 large fryer, cut into pieces
3 tablespoons lemon juice
3 tablespoons Worcestershire sauce

Dry, salt and pepper chicken. Arrange in baker or similar vessel, skin side down. Make sauce of Worcestershire and lemon juice. Dredge chicken thoroughly. Cover baker with chef foil, or close fitting lid. Place in 275-degree oven. Cook about 2 1/2 hours, turning last 30 minutes to brown top side of chicken.

## Chicken Bourguinone

6 - 8 chicken breasts, boned
1 can small white onions, drained
salt
pepper
1 can large button mushrooms
1 1/2 cups chicken bouillon
1 1/2 cups burgundy
flour

Salt, pepper and flour chicken. Brown in little oil in skillet. Add onions and mushrooms. Add chicken bouillon and burgundy. Simmer covered over low flame until tender. More bouillon and burgundy may be added to keep sauce from becoming too thick. Serve over wild and white rice.

## Chicken Ravioli

1 4 or 5-pound hen
1 pound ground beef
2 large onions
1 large can tomatoes
1 large can mushrooms
3 boxes spaghetti
1 pound grated sharp cheese
red pepper
1 teaspoon celery salt
1 tablespoon chili powder (or more if desired)
3 pods garlic
1 large green pepper
2 cups chopped celery
salt
black pepper

Salt and pepper hen to taste. Boil until tender, saving all broth. When cool, remove all bones and chop chicken as for salad. Fry chopped onion and green pepper in fat, then add ground beef and celery. Cook until it changes color. Add other ingredients (hen, tomatoes and chili powder) and cook 2 hours. Add broth to prevent mixture from drying out. Cook spaghetti in boiling salt water, drain and add to the cooked meat. Mix thoroughly. When cool, refrigerate overnight. Reheat in large casseroles in oven, mixing in grated cheese and thin with stock. Serves 12 to 15. Serve with green salad and French bread.

## Country Captain Chicken

3 pounds chicken breasts
flour
salt
pepper
lard, or other shortening
2 medium onions, minced
2 bell peppers, minced
1 garlic clove, pressed
1 1/2 teaspoons salt
1/2 teaspoon white pepper
3 teaspoons curry powder
2 number-2 cans tomatoes
1/2 teaspoon chopped parsley
1/2 teaspoon powdered thyme
1/4 pound blanched, toasted almonds
1/2 cup currants
3 cups cooked rice
water cress

Remove skin from chicken breasts and roll in flour, salt and pepper. Brown in lard. Remove from pan, but keep hot. Put onions, peppers and garlic into the lard and cook very slowly, stirring constantly. Season with salt, pepper and curry powder. Add tomatoes, parsley and thyme. Put chicken in roaster and pour mixture over it. Add sufficient water to cover. Cover the roaster and bake for 45 minutes in 375-degree oven. Put chicken in center of large platter and put rice around it. Place currants into sauce mixture and pour over the rice. Scatter almonds on top and garnish with water cress.

## Parsley Dumplings

1 1/2 cups sifted flour
1 1/2 teaspoons baking powder
1 teaspoon salt
2 eggs, beaten
1 tablespoon finely chopped fresh parsley
2 tablespoons melted butter
1/3 cup milk

Sift flour, baking powder and salt into bowl. Stir in parsley. Combine eggs, butter and milk. Add to flour mixture and mix lightly to make soft dough. Drop by tablespoons into boiling chicken soup, beef stew or into beef bouillon and simmer 10 minutes uncovered and 10 minutes covered. Serve at once. Serves about 4.

## Chicken Casserole

chicken breasts, medium
potatoes
1 can cream of mushroom soup
1 package dry onion soup mix

Place as many medium-sized chicken breasts as desired in casserole dish. Slice potatoes over them and cover with one can cream of mushroom soup. Sprinkle with one package dry onion soup mix. Cover and bake at 375 degrees for 50 minutes.

## Greek Chicken and Rice

*Nancy Cucich*

1 fryer, cut up
juice of 1 lemon
oregano
garlic powder
salt
pepper
butter
rice

Place fryer in low baking dish and sprinkle each piece with salt, pepper, garlic powder and oregano. Top each piece with pat of butter. Fill baking dish about 1/2-inch deep with water and place in oven preheated to 300 degrees. Bake 15 minutes then remove from oven, turn chicken pieces, season again and add butter. Squeeze lemon juice over each piece and return to oven. Bake for 1 hour, basting every 15 minutes.

Boil about 2 cups of water on stove. After chicken is baked, remove from pan and add enough water to double liquid in pan. Add about 1 1/2 cups of rice – or as much as needed to absorb sauce in pan. Place in oven to cook rice. Keep water boiling on top of stove to add to rice if needed (add in small amounts to be safe).

When rice is cooked, place in serving dish and mix in chicken to increase flavor.

## Chicken-in-a-Beerpot

*Aline Burgess*

1 5 to 6 pound chicken
2 teaspoons salt
2 cups beer
1 cup celery, sliced
1/4 cup parsley, chopped
16 small new potatoes, peeled
16 small mushrooms, whole
1 10-ounce package frozen peas
lemon juice
pepper
2 large onions, chopped
1 garlic clove, chopped
8 carrots, scraped and cut into 2-inch pieces
16 small white onions, peeled
paprika

Rub chicken inside and out with lemon juice, then sprinkle inside and out with salt and pepper. Tie legs together and put chicken in a large kettle or Dutch oven. Add beer, onions, salt, celery, garlic and parsley. Cover tightly and simmer for 1 1/2 to 2 hours or until chicken is tender, adding more beer as necessary to keep desired level of liquid.

When chicken is tender, add whole potatoes, onions and carrot pieces. Cover and simmer until vegetables are tender, then add mushrooms and peas. Cover and cook 5 additional minutes. Sprinkle chicken with paprika. Serves 6 to 8.

## Chicken Breasts with Rice

4 chicken breasts, cut in 1/2
1 stick butter
1 can cream of mushroom soup
1 can cream of celery soup
1 can cream of chicken soup
1 1/2 cups rice, uncooked
salt to taste
pepper to taste

Melt butter in baking dish. Stir in undiluted soup and rice. Mix well. Pat chicken dry; salt and pepper. Rub butter over chicken to coat. Place chicken on top of rice and soup mixture. Bake, uncovered, for 2 hours at 250 degrees. If desired, add onion juice, cheese or pimento.

## Plantation Fried Chicken 'n Gravy

*Mrs. Sanders (Betty) Camp*

frying-sized chicken
salt
sifted flour
whole milk
2 tablespoons black pepper
iron skillet
cup of corn oil

Place cleaned and cut-up frying-sized chicken in salt water and leave overnight in refrigerator. (A gallon mayonnaise jar serves well for the container.) Use about 2 or 3 tablespoons of salt per gallon of water and stir until dissolved.

When ready to fry, drain chicken and blot dry with paper towels. Place chicken pieces in large paper bag containing about 2 cups of sifted flour and 2 tablespoons of black pepper. Shake well until chicken is coated. Heat corn oil in iron skillet at medium low heat. Place chicken in skillet and cook until downside is golden then turn, cooking until other side is golden. Do not cover. It is important that the chicken be turned but once. When done, remove from skillet and let drain on several thicknesses of paper towels.

To make gravy, drain off excess oil from skillet, leaving about 3 tablespoonsful. Add about 3 tablespoonsful of the leftover flour, being sure to sift again. Stir thoroughly. Slowly add a mixture of half water and whole milk, stirring constantly until desired thickness is reached.

### Char-broiled Chicken Halves

*Glenn McCullough*

chicken halves
olive oil
fresh pressed garlic cloves

Make a charcoal fire in grill and wait until a white ash forms on the coals before placing cut side of chicken halves down on the grill. Turn at intervals during the first hour of cooking. Now brush with a simple solution of olive oil and garlic cloves – no salt, no pepper, no nothing else. Keep turning until golden brown. It may be necessary to chunk the coals and if so, add but a few new briquettes at a time to avoid flame-up. Most of the garlic flavor is kept out of the chicken by juices oozing out, so do not fear overdoing it.

### Chicken Kiev

2 small chickens
lump butter
garlic, chopped
fresh parsley, finely chopped
salt
flour
1 egg, beaten
few bread crumbs
fat
water cress
pepper

Remove breast of chickens from bone and carefully take off skin. Carefully cut in half and place between 2 pieces of waxed paper. Beat with a wooden mallet until very thin. Remove paper. In the center of each place a small finger of firm butter and the garlic. Sprinkle with parsley and season with salt and pepper. Roll up and tuck in each end. Roll in flour, brush with beaten egg, roll in bread crumbs, and fry in hot fat until golden brown (approximately 3 minutes). Remove and drain well on paper. Stick with a cocktail stick and arrange on a hot serving dish. Garnish with watercress and serve at once.

## Liver Stuffed Chicken Breasts With Sauce

Chicken

4 whole broiler-fryer chicken breasts, boned
1/4 teaspoon thyme, powdered
1/2 pound chicken livers
4 ounces (1 cup) Swiss cheese, grated
1 cup fine dry bread crumbs
1/2 teaspoon salt
1/4 teaspoon pepper
1/2 cup margarine
2 teaspoons instant minced onions
1 egg, beaten

Sauce

1/4 cup margarine, melted
2 cups chicken broth, canned
1/2 cup evaporated milk
2 tablespoons cornstarch
1 tablespoon lemon juice

*Chicken:* Pound chicken breasts between sheets of waxed paper until thin. Sprinkle with 1/4 teaspoon salt, pepper and thyme. Melt 1/4 cup margarine in a small skillet. Add chicken livers, minced onion and remaining 1/4 teaspoon salt. Cook about 5 minutes or until livers are tender. Stir in Swiss cheese; divide into 4 parts and place on chicken breasts. Fold chicken breasts so that stuffing of liver is completely concealed; fasten with toothpicks. Dip each into egg then roll in crumbs. Line large shallow baking dish (about 13 X 9 X 2 inches) with foil. Bake in 350-degree oven about 1 hour; remove foil and continue baking 15 minutes or until chicken is tender and brown. Serve with sauce. Makes 4 servings.

*Sauce:* Melt margarine in medium saucepan, add cornstarch and blend. Add chicken broth; boil 5 minutes stirring constantly. Add lemon juice and undiluted evaporated milk. Heat but do not boil.

## Chinese Style Chicken Livers

1 package pineapple chunks, frozen
1 package spinach, frozen
2 packages (1 pound) chicken livers, frozen
1/4 cup salad oil
1 tablespoon soy sauce
1/2 cup almonds, blanched and halved
1/4 cup vinegar
1/4 cup sugar
1/4 teaspoon salt
2 tablespoons cornstarch

Thaw pineapple chunks, spinach and chicken livers according to package directions. Then drain pineapple and add enough water to juice to make 1 1/4 cups.

Heat salad oil in large saucepan. Cut chicken livers in half and dip each half in soy sauce. Brown in salad oil for 10 to 15 minutes. Add pineapple and almonds and cook 1 minute longer.

Mix diluted pineapple juice, vinegar, sugar, salt and cornstarch in a bowl until smooth. Add to liver mixture, dump in spinach, cover and cook 5 minutes. Stir occasionally. Serve with hot steamed rice. Serves 4.

## Sautéed Chicken Livers

1 pound chicken livers
1/4 cup olive oil
1/4 cup sherry
1/4 cup soy sauce
garlic, grated
dry mustard

Marinate chicken livers in oil, sherry and soy sauce, seasoned with grated garlic and dry mustard (a touch of curry powder can be added for variation). Let them marinate at least 3 or 4 hours. Pour everything into a large saucepan and cook until livers are done. Serve over rice for dinner, or with eggs for breakfast.

## Smothered Marsh Hens

8 marsh hens, skinned
2 cups chicken stock or 1 can chicken soup
6 tablespoons bacon drippings
salt water
6 tablespoons flour, browned
salt to taste
pepper to taste

Parboil skinned birds in salt water just long enough to take out the blood and keep the shape. Drain and put in deep frying pan on top of stove. Add gravy made of chicken stock or soup, flour, bacon drippings and salt and pepper to taste. Cover birds with gravy and cook about 1 hour, then uncover and slip under the broiler flame for 15 minutes.

## Chicken Newburg

2 cups cooked chicken, diced large
2 tablespoons flour
1 cup cream
pepper to taste
1/4 teaspoon paprika
2 tablespoons butter
2 cups chicken stock
2 egg yolks
salt to taste
1/2 cup sherry or white wine
2 teaspoons lemon juice

Melt the butter, blend with flour, add cream and chicken stock and simmer 30 minutes. Pour over beaten egg yolks and beat constantly with a wire whip. The sauce must not boil again. Add the sherry, lemon juice, paprika and season to taste. Combine with the chicken, which has been kept hot in a little chicken stock. Serve in patty shells or timbales.

## Wild Duck

duck
vinegar
onions
salt
1 cup sherry wine
flour
salt water
celery
bacon
pepper
2 tablespoons onion, grated
cream

Soak duck in salt water and a little vinegar for an hour or two after cleaning. Dry and fill with celery and onions for flavor. Rub breast with fat and place in roaster. Lay strips of bacon on each breast. Salt and pepper. Brown at 400 degrees about 1/2 hour. Reduce heat to 300 degrees and cook for 2 hours until tender. Add cup of sherry wine for flavor. Brown grated onion in gravy, then add flour and hot water to thicken. Just before taking up, add a little cream.

## Quail Continental

*Mrs. Carl T. (Ann) Martin*

6 quail
flour
salt
1 medium onion, sliced in rings
6 tablespoons Wesson oil, butter flavored
pepper
1 1/2 sticks butter
juice of 2 to 3 lemons

Squeeze lemons on birds, then salt and let stand about 1 hour. Heat Wesson oil in pan, flour birds and brown in the oil. Meanwhile, saute onion rings in melted butter. When clear take off stove. After birds are browned in skillet place in roaster pan. Pour butter and onions over them and squeeze lemon juice over all. Add enough water to cover the birds partially. Put lid on roaster and bake at 350 degrees for 2 1/2 to 3 hours. This recipe makes its own gravy, but it may need salting.

## Hawaiian Duck

2 tablespoons butter
1 onion, minced
1 tablespoon flour
2 tablespoons curry powder
1 teaspoon salt
3 cups chicken stock
1 cup pineapple juice
3 cups duck, cooked
1 can pineapple chunks

Cook onion with butter in chafing dish pan over direct flame until soft. Add flour mixed with curry powder. Add stock and juice and cook until thickened. Add duck and pineapple. Heat well. Serve with rice, chutney and shredded coconut.

## Roast Duck

*Glenn McCullough*

Duck

duck, dressed out to
 about 5 pounds
salt
pepper
sherry or vinegar soaked
 cloth

Apricot Sauce

12 canned apricot halves
1 medium apple, peeled
 and cored
1/2 cup orange juice
 concentrate
1/2 cup brown sugar

*Duck:* Using sherry or vinegar soaked cloth, wipe duck thoroughly inside and out. Sprinkle with a mixture, half and half, of salt and pepper, without rubbing in. Place a quartered apple in the cavity and roast at 325 degrees for half an hour per pound. (If duck is to be stuffed, omit the apple.) In the last half hour of baking, drizzle apricot sauce over the bird and return to oven, basting several times.

*Apricot sauce:* Place all ingredients into blender, cover and mix until smooth.

## Duck Stuffing

*Glenn McCullough*

3 cups stale bread, crumbled
1 cup corn bread, crumbled
2 tablespoons fat or butter
duck liver and heart, boiled and chopped
1 teaspoon salt
2 tablespoons concentrated orange juice
1 egg, beaten
1/4 teaspoon pepper
big pinch powdered ginger
big pinch pulverized sage
little pinch oregano
some green parsley, minced
grated rind of an orange
apple, chopped, peeled and cored

Soak bread in water, then squeeze dry. Place shortening in skillet and bring to moderate heat. Stir in bread until all the shortening is soaked up and remove from heat. Add all other ingredients except egg and mix thoroughly. Add beaten egg and stir thoroughly again. Stuff mixture into cavity of the duck and roast.

## Potted Doves

6 doves
1 cup catsup
3 tablespoon Worcestershire sauce
salt
pepper
6 slices bacon
1 small onion, sliced
1 tablespoon butter
red pepper or hot sauce (small amount)

Steam birds for 20 minutes on top of stove with a little water. Then add seasoning and catsup, and lay bacon on top of the birds. Cook covered for about 1 1/2 hours or until very tender. Remove cover and brown in oven.

### Southern Smothered Pheasant

- pheasant
- 2 tablespoons bacon drippings
- 3/4 cup hot water
- 1 tablespoon lemon juice
- flour
- 2 tablespoons shortening
- 1/4 cup sherry wine
- 1/4 teaspoon basil
- 1 small can mushrooms

Thaw pheasant and split in half, allowing 1/2 bird per serving. Flour heavily. In heavy skillet mix bacon drippings and shortening. When grease is hot, brown bird on both sides until outer skin is crisp. If cooking more than one bird, add more fat as needed. Drain half excess fat. Replace browned birds in skillet and cover with the sherry wine mixed with 3/4 cup hot water per bird, basil and lemon juice. Cover tightly with skillet lid and bake at 375 degrees for 1 1/2 hours. When cooked, remove birds to serving platter.

Thicken skillet drippings with flour and water. Add one small can of mushrooms and a dash of sherry. Bring to boil and pour over birds. Garnish with parsley just before serving.

If cooking several birds, place browned birds in large roaster to bake.

### Soy Squabs

- 4 squabs
- 1 teaspoon ginger, ground
- salt
- 3 tablespoons soy sauce
- 4 tablespoons peanut oil
- pepper

Split squabs. Clean and dry, then rub with ginger, salt and pepper. Marinate in soy sauce for 10 minutes. Heat oil in chafing dish pan over direct flame and brown squabs until tender and brown. Serve hot.

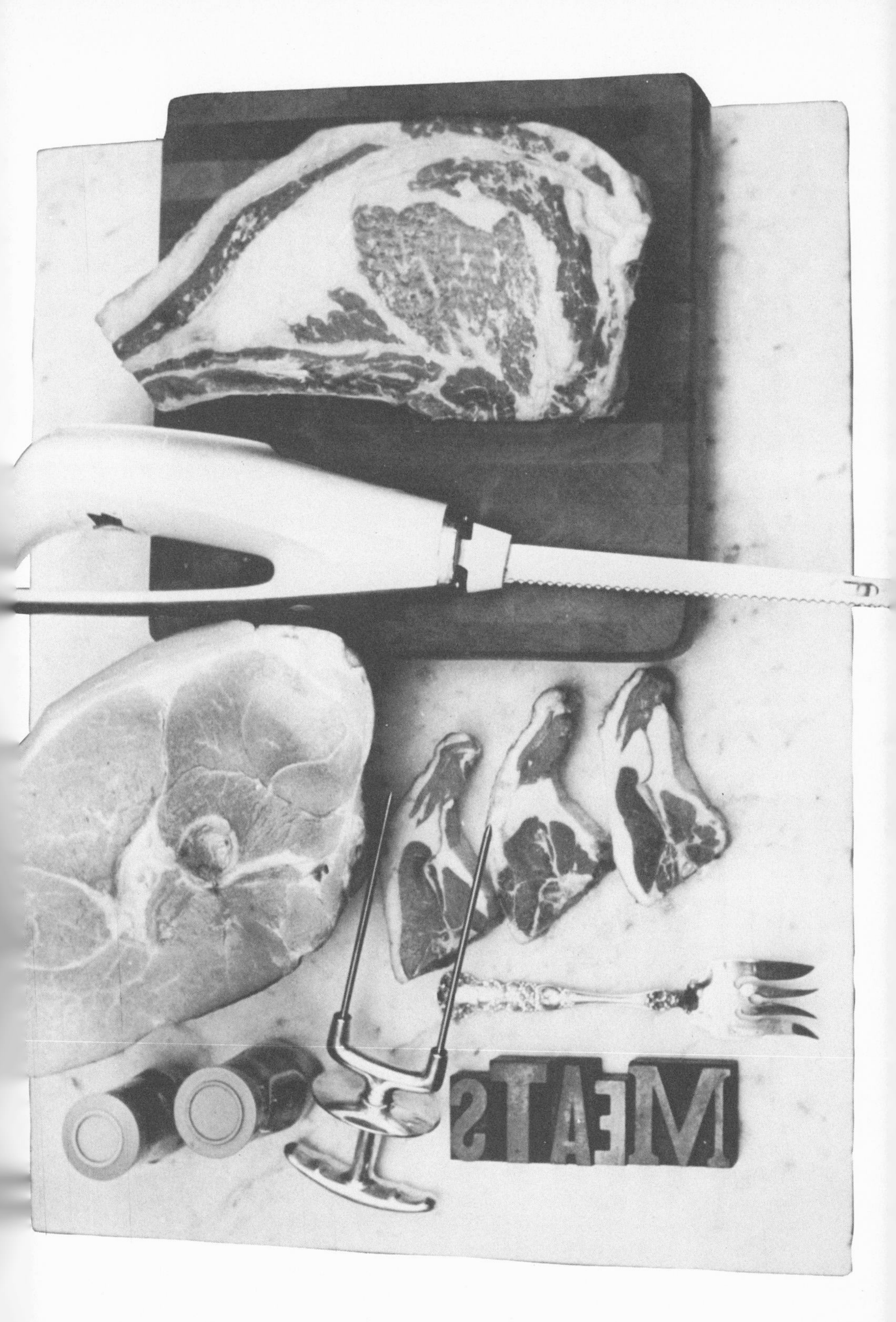
MEATS

## Beef Ribs A La Griff

*S. Marvin Griffin*

| | |
|---|---|
| heavy beef ribs | pepper |
| choy sauce | salt |
| Worcestershire sauce | 1 lemon (for each 6 ribs) |
| barbecue sauce | cooking sherry |

Buy the desired number of good heavy beef ribs from your favorite butcher. Have him remove excess fat.

Place the ribs in a shallow pan. Sprinkle a liberal portion of choy sauce, Worcestershire sauce, and barbecue sauce on one side of the ribs and repeat the process on the other side, adding pepper as desired, but no salt at this stage. Squeeze about 1 lemon over about 6 ribs.

Place the ribs in an oven set on bake (not broil) at a temperature of 350 degrees and bake for 1-1/2 hours. Take the ribs out of the oven and salt them to taste. Sprinkle them with more barbecue sauce and then douse or drench them with some good cooking sherry.

The ribs are then ready to be placed on top of a charcoal grill. Grill the ribs about 15 minutes on each side, and a few wet hickory chips to set up a good smoke will add even a little more to the taste. Take off the grill and serve.

These ribs eat mighty well with paella rice and French bread with garlic butter. (Cook's note: If the beef ribs appear to be a little tough, sprinkle on a little tenderizer before putting them in the oven. Beef ribs cost about 69 cents a pound, and a portion that costs about $1.25 is more than the average fellow can eat at a sitting.)

## Steak Casserole

*Mrs. Wassie K. Vickery*

1 1/2 pounds round steak or minute steak
1 large onion
1 package dry onion soup
flour

Cut steak in about 2-inch squares, salt and pepper and roll in flour. Quick brown in skillet of 1 stick margarine. Place pieces in large casserole so that meat does not have to be stacked.

Slice onions in rings, separating rings and place over steak. Make large bowl of gravy where steak has been cooked. Add onion soup. After well blended, pour over steak.

Cover entire pan with foil so that it does not harden on bottom, and cook at 325 degrees for about 1 hour.

## Sausage Casserole

*Mrs. Jeanette Ensley*

1 pound hot or mild sausage
1 medium onion, chopped
1 medium bell pepper, chopped
1/2 cup chopped celery
1/2 cup chopped pimento
1 can cream of chicken soup
1 can cream of mushroom soup
1 can water
1 cup rice
1 cup grated Cheddar cheese, sharp or mild

Brown sausage and drain. Saute onions, celery and pepper. Add to sausage, then mix in pimento, soups, water, rice and 3/4 of the cheese. Add remaining cheese to top of mixture. Bake, covered, in large casserole for 1 to 1 1/2 hours at 325 degrees.

## Tournedos

*Dorothy Sinz, Food Editor*
*Dallas Times Herald*

Steaks

4 tournedos, fillets of beef, about 6 ounces each
pepper, freshly ground
4 tablespoons butter
2 tablespoons olive oil
4 rounds of bread, about 3 inches in diameter
additional butter
lemon juice

Sauce

1/2 cup Madeira
1/2 cup beef stock
2 tablespoons butter
2 tablespoons finely chopped truffles (or mushrooms)

*Steaks:* Sprinkle pepper on beef. Put butter and olive oil in skillet and cook fillets over high heat for about 5 minutes each side so that meat will be brown on outside and rare inside. Transfer to warm serving dish. Pour off all fat in pan. Saute bread in about 2 tablespoons butter until golden and then drain on absorbent paper. Place a fillet on a bread round and spoon a sauce, such as Madeira over it.

*Sauce:* Add Madeira to pan and cook until reduced to about one half. Add beef stock and truffles or mushrooms. Add butter and mix well. Serve hot over steaks.

### Steak With Rice

*Clara Rountree*

cubed round steak
cooking oil
green peppers, sliced
white onions, sliced
uncooked rice
salt
pepper
boiling water

In heavy frying pan, pour enough cooking oil to lightly cover bottom. Brown desired number of cubed round steaks on both sides. Top each steak with a circle slice of green pepper, onion, salt, pepper and 1 tablespoon of uncooked rice. Pour enough boiling water over all to cover rice. When water begins to bubble steadily, cover and reduce heat. Cook 45 minutes or longer.

### Me Jane Steak

*Jane Fleetwood*

8 Delmonico steaks
1 large eggplant
1 box cherry tomatoes
10 large fresh mushrooms, or 1 big can
2 1/2 sticks butter
1 teaspoon garlic salt
boiling water
salt
flour

Skin tomatoes in boiling water. Melt 1 stick of butter, stir in garlic salt and simmer with tomatoes for 2 minutes.

Heat 1 inch of cooking oil. Peel and cut eggplant in 1/4-inch thick slices. Salt and flour eggplant slices and fry 5 minutes or until brown. Place on paper towels in warm oven.

Slice mushrooms and simmer in 1/2 stick butter.

Melt 1 stick butter in frying pan and cook steaks about 10 minutes. (Rare.) Place steaks on plate and cover with eggplant, tomatoes and mushrooms.

## Beef Stew

2 pounds bottom round,
  2 inches thick
2 tablespoons fat
water
3 medium potatoes
4 scraped carrots
1 cup diced celery
1 cup thinly sliced onion
1 tablespoon salt
2 cans bouillon
1/2 teaspoon black pepper
1 teaspoon Worcestershire
  sauce
3 tablespoons flour

Cut the steak into 2-inch squares and roll it in flour, seasoned with pepper and salt. Brown in fat, turning to all sides. Remove beef from skillet and add remaining seasoned flour, stirring well. Put the beef and skillet contents into stewing pot and cover with bouillon. Simmer for one hour, adding water when necessary. Add all other ingredients and cook for another hour. This gets better each time it is reheated. Serves about 12.

## Green Peppersteak

1 1/2 pounds boneless chuck
2 tablespoons salad oil
1/2 teaspoon salt
water
2 cloves garlic, minced
2 cups thinly sliced celery
4 green bell peppers, cut
  in strips
10 green onions, bulbs thinly
  sliced, leaves cut in 1-inch
  pieces
1 tablespoon soy sauce
2 beef bouillon cubes
1 1/2 cups water
arrowroot
2 cans Chinese noodles

Cut meat into strips, 1/2 X 2 inches; sprinkle with tenderizer if necessary. Brown the beef in oil. Add salt and a cup of water. Cover and simmer about 15 minutes or until tender. Add remaining ingredients except arrowroot and noodles. Cook about 10 minutes until tender but still crisp. Thicken with arrowroot mixed with bit of water. Serve topped with noodles. Serves 4 to 6. It may be served over hot cooked rice or egg noodles.

### Marinated Steak

2 1-inch thick rib steaks
2 tablespoons lemon juice
black pepper, freshly ground
1/2 cup olive oil
salt

In shallow dish large enough to hold the two steaks in one layer, mix together the olive oil and lemon juice. Lay the steaks in the marinade, then turn them over to moisten each side; cover the dish with plastic wrap. Marinate the steaks at room temperature for 4 to 6 hours, turning every hour or so.

Set broiling grid 2 inches from the source of heat, drain the steaks, and broil them as desired. Steaks may be brushed lightly with olive oil. Sprinkle with salt and pepper and surround the steaks with lemon quarters. Serves 2 to 4.

### Chili con Carne

2 cans kidney beans
1 can tomato paste
1 1/2 to 2 pounds beef, ground
4 tablespoons shortening or oil
1/4 teaspoon salt
1 teaspoon sugar
1 can tomatoes
1 can tomato sauce
1 to 2 cloves garlic
1 large onion, chopped
2 teaspoons chili powder
1/2 teaspoon black pepper
6 ounces water

Brown ground beef, onion and garlic in hot shortening (or oil) in skillet. In large saucepan combine tomatoes, kidney beans, tomato paste and sauce and seasonings with water. Bring to boil, add meat, garlic and onion that has been browned. Lower heat and cook slowly until liquid begins to thicken (about 45 minutes).

### Scotch Steak and Kidney Pie

1 pound beef round steak
1/4 cup flour
1/8 teaspoon pepper
3 tablespoons lard or drippings
1/4 teaspoon thyme
1 1/2 cups water
1 beef kidney
1 teaspoon salt
1 medium onion, chopped
1/4 cup pimento, chopped
2 tablespoons Worcestershire sauce
pastry for one-crust pie

Cut round steak in 3/4 to 1-inch cubes. Remove tubes and fat from kidney and cut in 3/4 to 1-inch cubes. Combine flour, salt and pepper. Dredge steak and kidney cubes in seasoned flour (reserving any extra flour) and brown in lard or drippings. Remove meat from frying pan. Add onion to drippings and cook over low heat until transparent. Pour off drippings, add pimento, Worcestershire sauce, thyme and water to onion in frying pan and bring to boil. Stir in browned meat cubes and any remaining seasoned flour. Invert 9-inch pie plate over pastry rolled to about 1/8-inch thickness. Cut a circle about an inch from rim of plate for top crust. Cut a design in crust to allow steam to escape. Cut a second circle about 3/4 to 1 inch from edge of top crust to provide pastry to circle edge of pie plate. Moisten edge of plate and top with outer circle of pastry, adjusting to fit. Turn meat mixture into pie plate and cover with top crust. Seal top pastry to edge and flute. Bake in 325-degree oven for 1 1/2 hours. Makes 6 servings.

### Batter Fried Chitterlings

chitterlings
salt
black pepper
buckwheat flour
soda
1 egg

Prepare the chitterlings for cooking. Cover with water and parboil until tender. Cool. Make a batter of remaining ingredients, dip chitterlings into the batter and fry until golden brown in 1 inch or more of hot fat in a heavy skillet.

## Swiss Steak

2 pounds beef, round, rump or chuck
1/3 cup seasoned flour
3 celery stalks, chopped
1 onion, sliced
1 bell pepper, sliced
1 1/2 cups tomatoes, stewed or canned

Have beef cut 1 to 1 1/2 inches thick. Wipe with cloth and rub seasoned flour into steak or pound it in with a wooden mallet (or the edge of a heavy plate). Brown the meat on all sides in a little fat in a heavy skillet or Dutch oven. Add onion, pepper, celery and tomatoes; cover and simmer about 1 1/2 hours or until meat is tender.

## Pepper Steak

1 pound round steak
1/4 cup salad oil
1 teaspoon salt
1/8 teaspoon pepper
1/4 cup onion, diced
1 clove garlic, minced
4 green peppers, diced
1 cup celery, sliced
1 cup beef bouillon
2 tablespoons cornstarch
1/4 cup water
1 teaspoon soy sauce

Cut steak in 1/4-inch diagonal slivers. In a heavy skillet, place oil, salt and pepper. Add meat and brown. Add onion, garlic, green peppers, celery and bouillon. Cover with tight fitting lid and cook 10 minutes over low heat. Mix cornstarch, water and soy sauce and add to mixture and cook until juice thickens. Serve with hot rice. Serves 4.

## Round Steak Supreme

1 pound round steak
1/2 teaspoon salt
1/8 teaspoon pepper
2 onions, thinly sliced
1 green pepper, chopped
1/2 box macaroni, cooked
1 can tomatoes
butter for searing

Sear steak quickly in butter on both sides. Salt and pepper and place in casserole. Over this, put the sliced onions then the green pepper. Season with salt and pepper. Next add a layer of macaroni and top with canned tomatoes. Bake at 400 degrees for 1 hour. During last half hour of baking, remove lid to allow the top to brown.

## Beef Stew a – Eloise

*Aline Burgess*

2 pounds stew meat
1 clove garlic
1 teaspoon salt
1 teaspoon sugar
1 teaspoon Worcestershire sauce
6 potatoes
1 cup peas
1 onion, sliced
1 bay leaf
1/4 teaspoon pepper
1/2 teaspoon paprika
3 cups water
6 carrots
6 onions
1/4 cup flour

Brown stew meat slowly in skillet. Add 1 sliced onion, garlic clove, bay leaf, salt, pepper, sugar, paprika, Worcestershire sauce and 3 cups water. Simmer for 1 1/2 hours. Add carrots, potatoes and onions; cook 30 minutes. Remove vegetables and thicken with 1/2 cup water and 1/4 cup flour. Add peas and cook 10 minutes.

### Easy Pot Roast

1 envelope dried onion soup
1 pot roast
salt
1 can mushroom soup, undiluted
pepper

Sprinkle dried soup over roast with salt and pepper. Then pour undiluted mushroom soup over all. Cook covered at 350 degrees for 1/2 hour per pound. Turn roast over when half done.

### Liver and Onions

1 pound beef liver, sliced
8 slices bacon
1/4 cup flour
1/4 teaspoon pepper
2 medium onions, sliced and cut into rings
3/4 teaspoon salt
1/3 cup wine vinegar

Cook bacon in large skillet until crisp. Remove, crumble and set aside. Add onions to bacon drippings, cooking slowly until tender. Remove and set aside. Combine flour, salt and pepper. Coat liver with seasoned flour and sauté quickly in the same skillet over high heat, taking care not to overcook. When liver is still pink in center, add wine vinegar and remove any browned bits. Remove to serving platter and top with crumbled bacon and onion rings. Spoon wine vinegar glaze over each serving of liver. Makes 4 servings.

### Roast Venison

1 haunch venison
1 bottle port wine
1 large jar crabapple jelly
black pepper, coarsely ground
salt to taste

Hang haunch for 6 to 7 days or refrigerate 10 days. Cook venison as for rare roast beef. Season with salt and pepper. Baste venison while cooking with sauce made of wine and melted jelly. Serve with wine sauce over venison.

### Country Fried Steak

| | |
|---|---|
| round steak | flour |
| salt | pepper |
| fat | |

Pound flour which has been seasoned with salt and pepper into the meat. Brown on both sides in a small amount of fat over moderate heat. To make rich gravy, add water gradually and allow to simmer until the meat is fork tender. For an even richer gravy, add a beef bouillon cube dissolved in hot water. Thicken gravy with paste made of flour and cold water if needed.

### Venison Steaks

| | |
|---|---|
| venison | salt |
| onion | 1 cup hot water |
| 1 medium onion | 1 celery stalk |
| 1/2 cup chili sauce | juice of 1/2 lemon |

Wash steaks and sprinkle lightly with salt. Wrap closely with a cut onion in oiled paper. Chill overnight. Heat pan and sear meat, add hot water and cook slowly until well done. Cover with sauce made from onion, celery, chili sauce and lemon juice.

### Baked Country Ham

| | |
|---|---|
| 1 12-pound ham | 3 cups pineapple juice |
| water | 1/2 glass brandy (2 tablespoons) |
| 1 cup sugar | |

Soak the ham in water overnight. Change the water and cook the ham for 4 hours. The water should cover the ham. Let it cook in the water in which it boiled. When cool, trim off excess fat and place ham in roasting pan. Pour pineapple juice and brandy over ham, sprinkle the sugar over the top and let it cook in the oven slowly, about 1 hour at 325 degrees. Baste frequently. Serve hot or cold.

### London Broil

1 clove garlic
1/2 cup cider vinegar
1 teaspoon salt
2 teaspoons Worcestershire sauce
few drops Tabasco sauce
1 cup corn oil
1/4 teaspoon pepper
2 teaspoons dry mustard
dash cayenne
1 2-pound top quality flank steak

Slice garlic into large shallow pan. Add corn oil, vinegar, salt, pepper, dry mustard, Worcestershire sauce, cayenne and Tabasco sauce. Stir to blend. Trim excess fat and membrane off flank steak and score surface on both sides. Place steak in pan and spoon marinade over it. Let stand overnight if possible, but not less than 3 hours, turning steak 2 or 3 times. Remove from marinade. Preheat broiler. Broil steak 2 or 3 inches below heat, allowing 3 to 4 minutes for each side. Remove steak to a heated platter. Carve diagonally across grain into thin slices.

### Calf's Liver in Wine

12 thin slices calf's liver
2 cloves garlic, minced
1 teaspoon salt
1/2 teaspoon pepper
1 bay leaf
1 cup white wine
1/4 cup olive oil

Wash the liver carefully. Combine the garlic, salt, pepper, bay leaf and wine in a bowl. Add the liver and marinate overnight in the refrigerator. Baste occasionally. Heat the olive oil in a frying pan until it smokes. Add the liver slices and wine mixture all at once. Stir gently, but constantly for 5 minutes. Serve immediately.

### Chuckwagon Braised Liver

1 1/2 pounds liver, sliced
  1/2 inch thick
1/8 teaspoon pepper
2 cups carrots, thinly
  sliced
1 medium green pepper, diced
pepper
1/2 cup flour
1/2 teaspoon salt
3 tablespoons lard or
  drippings
1 cup onion, diced
salt
1/4 cup water

Cut liver into serving-sized pieces. Combine flour, 1/2 teaspoon salt and pepper. Dredge liver in seasoned flour and brown in lard or drippings. Arrange vegetables on browned liver. Season vegetables with salt and pepper. Add water, cover tightly and cook slowly until liver is tender and vegetables are done, about 30 to 35 minutes. Makes 6 servings.

### Thursday Pot Roast

3 to 4 pound beef rump pot
  roast
1 1/2 teaspoons salt
1/4 teaspoon marjoram
1 large onion, sliced
6 tablespoons flour
2 tablespoons lard or
  drippings
1/8 teaspoon pepper
1/4 cup water
1 can (4 ounces) mushroom
  stems and pieces

Brown pot roast slowly in lard or drippings. Pour off drippings. Season with salt, pepper and marjoram. Add water and onion. Cover tightly and cook slowly 3 to 3 1/2 hours or until tender. Remove meat to heated serving platter. Measure cooking liquid, add mushrooms including liquid and enough water to make 3 cups. Thicken liquid with flour for gravy. Makes 6 to 10 servings.

### Talmadge Country Fried Ham

*Mrs. Herman (Betty) Talmadge*

warm water or 1 cup
buttermilk and 3
tablespoons brown sugar
ham
1/4 teaspoon brown sugar

Soak ham 15 minutes in warm water or 30 minutes in 1 cup buttermilk and 3 tablespoons brown sugar. (Sweet milk may be substituted.)

Preheat skillet. Brown each side of ham over medium heat. (Do not overheat – this toughens ham.) To make red-eye gravy, add a small amount of water and 1/4 teaspoon brown sugar. Let simmer.

### Rabbit Bourguignonne

*Ted Burgess*

1 rabbit, cut in pieces
onions
celery
Burgundy wine
garlic, crushed
laurel (bay leaf)
mushrooms, cooked
carrots
leeks
parsley
3 tablespoons flour
thyme
bacon, cooked and diced
1 clove, crushed

Cut rabbit in pieces, place in pot and add carrots, onions, leeks, celery and parsley. Cover with Burgundy and pickle overnight.

Remove pieces of rabbit from pot and place into another vessel. Cook in lard until brown, about 20 minutes. Add flour and stir until brown. Add contents of the first pot and more carrots, small onions, celery, parsley, thyme and laurel together with garlic and clove. Place over small flame until cooked. Before serving, add diced, cooked bacon and mushrooms. Serve with red wine or champagne. Serves 4.

## Braised Sirloin

*Julia Dyar*

sirloin steak, cut in bite-sized pieces
salt to taste
8 ounces noodles
1/2 cup hot water
mushrooms, canned or fresh
Crisco
flour for dredging
pepper to taste
1/2 can tomato paste
parsley
1/2 cup Burgundy, for cooking

Brown meat dredged in flour in small amount of Crisco. Add tomato paste, water and Burgundy. Simmer until tender. Add parsley, salt and pepper to taste and mushrooms which have been sauteed in butter. Serve sirloin over noodles (cooked according to package directions).

## Rabbit Pie

1 rabbit, dressed
2 onions, diced
2 carrots, diced
2 or 3 potatoes, diced
pastry dough
water
vinegar
salt
pepper
flour

Cut rabbit into serving pieces. Soak in equal parts of vinegar and water for 12 to 24 hours. Drain and wipe dry. Sprinkle with salt and pepper and dredge with flour. Sear quickly in frying pan. Add water to cover and simmer slowly in covered pot for 1 1/2 hours. Add onions, carrots and potatoes. Cook until vegetables are done. Thicken with flour. Cook in a greased baking dish in a hot oven until bubbling. Cover with pastry dough and return to oven to bake until dough is done and golden brown.

### Venison With Sour Cream

2 pounds venison
1/2 cup fat
1 cup celery, diced
1/2 cup onion, minced
1 bay leaf
4 tablespoons butter
1 clove garlic
1 cup carrots, diced
2 cups water
1 teaspoon salt
4 tablespoons flour
1 cup sour cream

Cut venison in pieces and melt fat in heavy frying pan. Add meat and garlic. Brown all sides and arrange in dish. Put vegetables in remaining fat and cook for 2 minutes. Add salt, pepper and water. Pour over meat. Bake in slow oven until meat is tender. Melt butter in frying pan and stir in flour. Add water that the meat was cooked in and boil until thick. Add sour cream and more salt if necessary. Pour over meat and vegetables. Serve with buttered noodles and currant jelly.

### Roasted Lamb

leg of lamb
2 medium onions
4 to 6 stalks celery
1/2 cup vinegar
salt
pepper

With a sharp knife, cut off most of skin and fat from lamb. Then salt and pepper meat generously. Put it in roast pan with onions, quartered, celery, cut in pieces, and vinegar. Cook, covered, 20 minutes per pound at 325 degrees. Serve sauce (including onions and celery) with meat.

## Lamb In The Ground

along with other things

*Glenn McCullough*

| | |
|---|---|
| leg of lamb | olive oil |
| salt | pineapple spears, drained |
| pepper | 2 teaspoons curry powder |
| fresh mint sprigs | 1/2 cup dark brown sugar |
| wine | 1/2 cup dark rum |
| roasting ears of corn | honey twist |
| fresh coconut | grapefruit sections |
| 1 tablespoon arrowroot | avocado slices |
| 1 teaspoon almond flavoring | butter |

If you're lucky enough to be living yet in an area where open fires are not prohibited and have sufficient space, here's a very good and sort of ritualistic spread which will keep your guests talking about it for months.

The menu consists of avocado-grapefruit salad, fried coconut, curried pineapple, fresh roasting ears, leg of lamb, honey twist bread and coffee. Now, that's enough, unless your wife also wants to do the dessert, which should be something like lime sherbet or lemon chiffon pie.

You start by digging a 2 X 2 X 2-foot pit in the ground and placing therein some hard, big rocks. On the rocks build a fire of soft wood until you've generated some heat, then add a little hardwood and charcoal. Let that go until it glows. In the meantime, you've prepared a leg of lamb by rubbing it with salt and pepper and covering one side with fresh mint sprigs. Cover it with a cheesecloth, wet with wine. Now turn the leg and place more mint on the top side, wrapping completely with the drippy cloth. Put this in heavy foil and seal in completely. Now wrap the leg in heavy brown paper which has been pre-soaked in water. Place directly on the fire, along with roasting ears which have set overnight in water or freshly pulled. The ears are wrapped in foil and sealed in without shucking or seasoning. Quickly cover the fire with the pile of earth you've neatly piled up from the original digging. You can more or less forget it then and look forward to having the dinner some six hours later.

In the meantime, take a fresh coconut and drain the milk, reserving it aside. Crack the hull and remove the meat, slicing it into thin pieces. Add a tablespoon of arrowroot to the milk and simmer, stirring to make smooth, and adding a teaspoon of almond flavoring. Fry the coconut slices in olive oil to avoid burning. After frying, remove them from the pan and dunk them into the milk-almond sauce.

In a baking dish, place drained pineapple spears. Take the juice and put it in a saucepan, adding enough arrowroot to thicken slightly, and add the curry powder and brown sugar. Do not boil. When sauce has thickened slightly, remove from heat and cool before adding rum. Stir the mixture and pour into a baking dish with the pineapple. Cover and place in slow (300 degrees) oven for about an hour.

During all this time, your wife has prepared honey twist (see recipe elsewhere in this book) and you've made a salad of grapefruit sections and avocado slices, covered with French dressing on lettuce. About this time it all comes together and you dig out the lamb and serve in chunks because it is too tender to slice. Then you strip off the foil, shuck the roasting ears and brush with butter. The pineapple and corn and lamb go on one plate, the coconut on a little side dish, the salad in its own thing and the bread wherever you find a place. This is what is commonly called real eating and the goodness of it is worth all the abnormal preparations.

## Broiled Lamb Chops

lamb chops
pepper
salt
melted butter

Prepare lamb chops by removing the outside skin and any extra fat. Have a very hot frying pan or skillet. Place the chops in it and as soon as the side next to the pan is browned, turn. Turn several times, keeping pan hot. Never cover; cook about 8 to 10 minutes. The chops should be about 1 inch thick. When done remove to a hot platter, season with salt, pepper and melted butter. Serve at once.

## Deviled Lamb Chops

6 lamb chops, rib or shoulder
1 tablespoon prepared mustard
1 teaspoon salt
1/2 teaspoon celery, garlic or onion salt
1 tablespoon shortening
1 green pepper
2 medium onions
1/4 cup water
1 lemon rind, grated
dash pepper
1/4 cup flour

Spread one side of chops with thin coating of mustard, then dip chops into a mixture of flour, salt, pepper and either celery, garlic or onion salt. Brown in melted shortening in a skillet.

Meanwhile, cut pepper into rings, onions into slices. Arrange these on top of chops. Add water and lemon rind. Cover and cook over low heat for 45 minutes or until chops are tender.

### Spaghetti Meat Dish

*Mrs. Donna Hunt, Food Editor*
*The Denison Herald*

1 medium can mushrooms (4 ounces)
1/2 pound cooked spaghetti
1 medium onion, chopped
1 medium green pepper, chopped
1 clove garlic, chopped
1/2 cup grated cheese
1 1/2 pounds ground beef
1/2 cup stuffed olives, diced
2 tablespoons Worcestershire sauce
1 1/2 teaspoons salt
1 can tomatoes (medium size)
2 tablespoons shortening
1 can tomato soup

Saute onions, pepper and garlic. Add beef and cook 30 minutes or until done. Add tomatoes, olives, salt and cheese. Cook covered over slow fire 30 minutes, then add Worcestershire sauce, mushrooms and soup. Mix well with cooked spaghetti, put in covered dish and leave in refrigerator for 2 days. When ready to serve, heat again.

### Burgundy Beef Tips With Mushrooms

*Shirley McCullough*

3 pounds lean beef, cut into 1-inch strips
1 cup burgundy wine
3 cups water
dash of garlic salt
10 bouillon cubes
1 tablespoon dehydrated onion soup mix
1 6-ounce can mushrooms

Remove all fiber from beef and cut into 1-inch strips. Place beef in preheated skillet and stir until browned on all sides. Add 1/2 cup wine, water, bouillon cubes, soup mix, garlic salt and 1/2 can mushrooms. Simmer until meat is tender, about 45 minutes. Just before serving, add remaining 1/2 cup wine and 1/2 can mushrooms. Serve over rice or in toasted bread cups.

### South Georgia Brunswick Stew

4 pounds beef
3 pounds pork
1 hen
2 cans tomatoes
2 cans cream style corn
2 cans small butterbeans
1 can sliced okra
2 green peppers, chopped
2 red peppers, chopped
1 pound onions, chopped
1 bottle catsup
4 cups diced, cooked Irish potatoes
1/2 bottle Worcestershire sauce
black and red pepper to taste
salt to taste
3 tablespoons sugar
2 teaspoons prepared mustard
1 stick butter (if meat is not fat enough)

Cook and grind beef, pork and hen with cooked green and red peppers and onions. Cook tomatoes, corn, butterbeans and okra together. Add cooked diced potatoes and combine with beef and vegetable mixtures. Add remaining ingredients and cook until mixture thickens. If too much liquid, bread crumbs may be added to take up surplus. Season to taste.

### Skillet Stroganoff

1 1/2 pounds round steak
3 tablespoons minced onion
3 tablespoons oil
1 package egg noodles
1 can cream of chicken soup
1 cup sour cream

Cut steak in strips. Roll in flour after putting on salt and pepper. Brown steak and onion in oil; add small amount of water and simmer about 1 1/2 hours or until tender. Add enough water to make about 2 cups of water. Add noodles and cook according to directions on package. Add soup and sour cream and heat.

### Mexican Eggplant Skillet

1 pound ground lean beef
1/4 cup chopped onion
1 tablespoon flour
1 8-ounce can tomato sauce
1/4 cup chopped green pepper
1 teaspoon oregano
1 teaspoon chili powder
1/2 teaspoon salt
1 small eggplant, pared, cut in 1/2-inch slices
1 cup shredded sharp Cheddar cheese

In skillet over medium heat, cook meat and onion until meat is browned. Sprinkle flour over meat and stir. Add tomato sauce, green pepper, oregano, chili powder and salt and mix well. Season eggplant with salt and pepper and arrange slices over meat. Cover and cook until eggplant is tender, approximately 10 to 15 minutes. Top with cheese. Just before serving sprinkle with grated Parmesan cheese, if desired. Makes 4 servings.

### Quick Stroganoff

*Mary S. Mallard*

2 pounds ground beef
3 cups chopped onions
4 teaspoons salt
5 tablespoons Worcestershire sauce
3 cups dry noodles
2 tablespoons sugar
herb seasoning, pepper or other seasonings
1 large can (46 ounces) tomato juice
1 1/2 cups buttermilk, or sour cream

Brown onions and beef slightly in minimum fat. Mix all ingredients except noodles; heat to boiling. Sprinkle noodles over top – do not stir in. Cover, let come to boil again. Cut heat and simmer 30 to 40 minutes, or until noodles are tender. Do not stir.

## Beef Stroganoff Casserole

1 1/2 pounds ground beef
3 tablespoons green pepper, chopped
2 tablespoons pimento, chopped
1 can condensed mushroom soup
1/4 cup chopped onion
1/2 pint sour cream
1 can oven-ready biscuits

Heat 2 tablespoons of cooking oil and add beef, onion and pepper. Brown very slightly and salt to taste. Add soup and simmer for 10 minutes. Stir in sour cream and pimento. Place in an attractive baking dish and top with biscuits. Bake at 350 degrees until biscuits are cooked all the way through and brown (20 to 25 minutes). Add sliced mushrooms, if desired.

## Company Casserole

8 ounces cream cheese
1/4 pint thick sour cream
1 8-ounce package egg noodles (not macaroni)
1 can tomato paste
melted butter
pepper
1 cup cottage cheese
1 small bunch green onions, finely chopped
1 can tomato sauce
3/4 to 1 pound ground beef
salt

Soften cream cheese. Mix cream cheese, cottage cheese, sour cream and onions in bowl. Cook egg noodles as directed on package. Put 1/2 egg noodles in 2-quart casserole, then all of cheese mixture, then rest of egg noodles. Pour 1 to 2 tablespoons melted butter over this. Brown meat in butter in frying pan, add salt and pepper lightly. Add tomato sauce and paste. Put this meat on top of mixture in casserole. Bake at 350 degrees for 30 to 40 minutes. Serves 6. This is fine made a day ahead and cooked the next day.

### Huberto's Own Spaghetti

*Hubert Dyar*

1 large onion, chopped
4 or 5 celery stalks, chopped
3 pounds ground chuck beef
2 cans pears tomatoes
tomato paste
1 large package spaghetti
salt
Parmesan cheese
1 large can mushroom bits
1 large bell pepper, chopped
oregano
rosemary
thyme
bay leaf
marjoram
pinch of tarragon
garlic salt
olive oil

In large Dutch oven or heavy pan, place onions, bell pepper and celery; cover with olive oil and saute until brown. Stirring constantly, add beef and saute until beef is light in color and separates. Add tomatoes and tomato paste; sprinkle with Italian spices, using plenty of garlic salt or 1 or 2 finely chopped garlic cloves. Cook, the longer the better, over low heat. Stir occasionally. During last 30 minutes, add drained mushrooms. Cook spaghetti according to directions on box, then drain, cover with sauce and top with Parmesan cheese.

To serve, use shakers of Parmesan and Mozzarella cheese for additional topping. Serve with garlic French bread and tossed salad with Italian dressing.

## Brunswick Stew

*Julia Dyar*

3 pounds pork, ground
3 pounds beef, ground
2 cans corn
2 cans tomatoes
large lump of butter
3 hens
salt to taste
pepper to taste
red pepper to taste
bottle of catsup
3 large onions

Grind corn, tomatoes and onions. Cut up boned and chopped hens and add to ground meats. Add seasonings and cook slowly for several hours until desired taste is reached.

## Lasagna

1 pound ground beef
2 cloves garlic, crushed
1 8-ounce can tomato sauce
1 number-2 can tomatoes, whole
1/2 cup grated Parmesan cheese
8 ounces wide noodles
1/2 pound Mozzarella cheese, sliced
3/4 pound cottage cheese
1 1/2 teaspoons salt
1/4 teaspoon pepper
1/2 teaspoon oregano

Brown meat with garlic; add tomato sauce, canned tomatoes, salt, pepper and oregano. Cover and simmer 20 minutes. Cook noodles until tender. Rinse in cold water and drain. Arrange in alternate layers in baking dish with noodles on bottom, followed by Mozzarella cheese, cottage cheese, meat sauce and Parmesan cheese. Continue until dish is filled, ending with Parmesan cheese. Bake at 375 degrees for 45 minutes.

## Sauerbraten

4 pounds beef, rump, chuck or sirloin, cut in serving-size pieces
2 quarts vinegar
1 quart water
1 large onion, sliced
gingersnaps
3 bay leaves
3 whole cloves
1 teaspoon salt
2 1/2 tablespoons fat
2 tablespoons flour
1/2 cup red wine
noodles or rice

Place meat in large crock or mixing bowl and pour a marinade of the liquids and spices over meat, allowing to stand for 4 days. Turn meat each day and save vinegar-water mixture. On fourth day, flour meat and brown on all sides, adding vinegar-water mixture. Remove to covered pan and bake meat, covered, in 350-degree oven for 2 1/2 hours, basting frequently. About half an hour before meat is done add the wine to the juices. Thicken gravy with 2 or 3 crumbled gingersnaps. Remove excess grease. Serve with noodles or rice.

## French Chop Suey

2 pounds round beef, ground
1 large can tomatoes
4 tablespoons butter
salt to taste
1 package macaroni (1 pound)
2 onions, medium
1/2 pound cheese, sharp
pepper to taste

Fry onions in butter, add meat and brown well. Add tomatoes and seasonings. Let simmer 30 minutes. Boil macaroni until tender. Add to other mixture. Bake in casserole with grated cheese on top in moderate oven (375 degrees) until brown. Serves 10.

### Corned Beef

2 1/2 pounds corned beef
4 cloves, whole
2 bay leaves
3 onion slices
6 black peppers, whole
1/2 teaspoon rosemary

Cover beef with water and add remaining ingredients except cloves. Bring to boil and simmer for 4 hours. Remove from oven; make diagonal cuts 1/8-inch deep and 3/4-inches apart. Stud with cloves and brown sugar. Broil in shallow pan until glazed.

### Island Ham Rolls

6 pineapple spears
6 slices ham, boiled
banana, strawberries, or other fruit
salad greens
avocado cream
fresh mint sprigs

Roll pineapple in boiled ham slices, tucking a sprig of mint into one end. Arrange as spokes on bed of greens, garnishing with banana slices, berries or other fruit. Pour avocado cream over this when ready to serve.

### Creole Spareribs

6 pounds spareribs
1 teaspoon salt
1/2 cup molasses
6 cloves
6 peppercorns
3 tablespoons soy sauce
1/2 cup water
2 medium onions, chopped
3 tablespoons prepared mustard
3/4 cup chili sauce

Place spareribs on rack over fire and cook 3/4 to 1 hour, basting with molasses barbecue sauce. To make sauce, combine remaining ingredients and heat for 30 minutes.

## Meat Loaf

1/2 pound ground pork
1 pound ground beef
2 eggs
1 1/4 cups bread crumbs
1 1/2 cups tomatoes (canned)
1 teaspoon Worcestershire sauce
1 small onion, finely chopped
1/2 green pepper, finely chopped
1 teaspoon salt
1/4 teaspoon pepper
2 tablespoons catsup
1 1/2 teaspoons parsley

Combine ingredients and shape into loaf. Bake 15 minutes at 450 degrees and 30 minutes at 325 degrees.

## Tortilla Flats

*Kay Jarvis, Food Editor*
*San Diego Evening Tribune*

1 1/2 pounds stew meat
1 1/2 cups water
salt and pepper to taste
1 clove garlic, minced
1 teaspoon Kitchen Bouquet
1 teaspoon oregano
1 tablespoon chili powder
1 can (7 ounces) green Mexican chiles
1 can (1 pound) tomatoes
flour tortillas

Cut meat into bite-sized chunks and cook with water and seasonings until tender, adding liquid if needed. Add chiles and tomatoes and simmer, uncovered, until cooked down and fairly thick.

Meanwhile, brown the tortillas quickly in a little oil in a skillet and then keep warm in oven. With oven at low temperature, these can be left for hours – the crisper the better.

To serve, place a tortilla on a plate, top with meat mixture, another tortilla, more meat, and so on to the size of the appetite. Serves 2 to 3 hearty eaters.

## Moist Meat Loaf

*John Sutlive*

1 1/2 pounds ground beef
1/2 pound pork sausage
bell pepper, diced
onion, diced
1 egg
Lea and Perrins
  Worcestershire sauce
tomato sauce
garlic salt (slight and
  optional)
slice of bread, soaked
  in milk and torn apart
salt
pepper
Accent (MSG)

Combine all ingredients except tomato sauce, and place in pan. Cover with tomato sauce and foil, and bake at 350 degrees for 1 hour. Remove foil for the last 15 minutes so top will get slightly crisp or brown.

Be generous with onions and bell peppers – a little bit doesn't add enough taste.

## Blue Cheese Steaks

*Mrs. Joseph B. Parham*

1 1/2 pounds ground chuck
  or round steak
1 tablespoon instant
  minced onion
1 teaspoon salt
2 ounces blue cheese,
  crumbled

Combine ingredients gently but thoroughly. Shape into 4 steaks. Heat heavy skillet until fairly hot and sprinkle lightly with salt. Brown steaks over medium heat, turning carefully. (Blue cheese tends to make them break easily.) Brown on both sides, cover, and turn heat very low. Cook for 20 minutes. Pour liquid over meat when serving.

### Fabulous Hawaiian Marinated Steak

*Julia Dyar*

steak (at least 1 inch thick)
2 jiggers soy sauce
1 jigger peanut oil
1 jigger wine vinegar
juice of 1 fresh lime
1 pinch ginger
pinch black pepper
1 tablespoon garlic puree

Combine ingredients and use to soak steak for at least 3 hours per side. Charcoal broil steak and use remaining sauce for basting while it broils.

### Summer Meat Loaf

*Jere Moore*

1 pound ground sirloin
1/2 pound ground lean pork
1/2 pound ground veal or venison
1 cup wheat germ
2 eggs
1 medium onion
1 clove garlic
1 teaspoon salt
1/2 teaspoon ground pepper
2 tablespoons catsup
1 teaspoon Worcestershire sauce
1 bayleaf or 1 teaspoon ground bay leaf
1/4 teaspoon thyme
1 teaspoon ground oregano
6 strips bacon (use thick-sliced bacon)
dash hot pepper sauce

Combine ground meats in large mixing bowl. Stir in wheat germ. Place all other ingredients, except bacon, in blender and liquefy.* Pour liquid over meat; knead with fingers until well blended. Place 3 strips of bacon in bottom of lightly greased loaf pan, and place meat loaf mixture into pan, patting down and shaping into loaf. Place 3 strips of bacon across top. Bake at 350 degrees for 1 1/2 to 1 3/4 hours or until meat is cooked through.

* If electric blender is not available, use a mortar and pestle after chopping onion and crushing garlic.

### Diet Meat Loaf

1 1/2 pounds ground beef
1 slice green pepper, finely chopped
2 beaten eggs
1 1/2 teaspoons salt
celery seed to taste
Worcestershire sauce
1 medium onion, finely chopped
1 stalk celery, finely chopped
pepper to taste
2 tablespoons milk
2 slices bacon

Combine ground beef, onion, green pepper and celery. Add beaten eggs, salt, pepper, celery seed and milk. Place in baking dish and rub top of loaf with Worcestershire sauce. Top with bacon. Bake 1 hour at 350 degrees.

### Barbecue Hamburgers

*Julia Dyar*

1 cup bread crumbs
1/2 cup milk
1 pound ground beef
2 tablespoons vinegar
1/4 cup sugar
1 cup catsup
pepper to taste
1/2 cup Worcestershire sauce
1 medium onion
1/2 teaspoon salt

Combine bread crumbs, milk, meat, onion, salt and pepper. Form into flat round balls and brown on both sides in fat. Combine Worcestershire sauce, vinegar, sugar and catsup. Place meat balls in baking dish and pour sauce over them. Bake in slow oven (350 degrees) about 30 to 40 minutes.

## Swedish Meat Balls

3/4 pound lean ground beef
1/4 pound ground pork
1 cup light cream
1 tablespoon butter or margarine
1 1/2 teaspoons salt
1/4 teaspoon ginger
dash nutmeg
1/2 pound ground veal
1 1/2 cups soft bread crumbs
1/2 cup onion, chopped
1 egg
1/4 cup parsley, finely snipped
dash pepper
1 recipe gravy

Soak bread in cream 5 minutes. Cook onion in 1 tablespoon butter until tender, but not brown. Combine meats, crumb mixture, onion, egg, parsley and seasonings. Beat until fluffy (about 5 minutes at medium speed on electric mixer) plus 8 minutes by hand. Form in 1-inch balls (for easier shaping, wet hands when necessary). Brown only a few at a time, in 2 tablespoons butter, shaking skillet to keep balls round. Remove meat balls and make gravy.

## Swedish Meat Ball Gravy

2 tablespoons flour
1/4 cup cold water
1/2 teaspoon instant coffee
3/4 cup condensed beef broth, canned
meat balls

Stir flour into fat in skillet. Add beef broth, cold water and instant coffee. Heat and stir until gravy thickens. Add meat balls to gravy. Cover and cook slowly about 30 minutes, basting occasionally. Makes enough to cover about 5 dozen.

## Baked Picnic Ham

*Mary S. Mallard*

1 6- to 8-pound picnic ham
1 cup dark brown sugar
3/4 cup flour
1 tablespoon ground cinnamon
1 tablespoon cloves
1 tablespoon dry mustard
vinegar

Mix sugar, flour, cinnamon, cloves and dry mustard. Moisten with enough vinegar to make a medium thick paste. Skin ham, removing most of fat. Coat ham with paste. Place long-size aluminum foil in baking pan (enough to cover ham). Completely seal ham, using "drug store seal". Cook at 325 degrees for 20 to 25 minutes per pound.

## Pineapple Ham Loaf

*Mary Tannor*

1/2 cup brown sugar
2 tablespoons pineapple syrup
1 1/2 cups pineapple chunks, drained
1 1/2 pounds ground smoked ham
1 pound ground chuck or veal
3/4 cup saltine crumbs
1/3 cup chopped onions
1 teaspoon dry mustard
1 cup milk
2 beaten eggs
whole cloves

Make a syrup of the brown sugar and pineapple syrup and pour it into a greased loaf pan. Into each pineapple chunk stick a clove and place the chunks, clove-side down, in a design in the syrup. Combine the other ingredients and press carefully and firmly over the chunks. Bake at 350 degrees for an hour and a quarter. Unmold onto platter and arrange some pineapple chunks and parsley about it. Serves about 8.

## Baked Country Cured Ham

*Mrs. Herman (Betty) Talmadge*

1 country cured ham
water
glaze recipe

Wash country cured ham thoroughly and put in covered roaster, fat side up. Pour two inches of water into pan. (Wine, ginger ale, apple cider, orange juice, pineapple juice or peach pickle juice, Coca-Cola or champagne may be substituted for the water.) Roast in moderate oven at 350 degrees for approximately 20 minutes per pound or until done. Baste often. When nearly cooked, remove the rind and trim off some of the fat. Score the surface of the fat in diamond shapes, and use one of the following glazes:

1. Cover the fat with a paste made of 1 generous teaspoon of dry mustard and 1 tablespoon of prepared mustard. Pour over ham 1 cup of orange juice, pineapple juice or peach pickle juice, and return to 450-degree oven. Uncover. Finish baking, basting frequently.

2. Stud the diamond shapes with cloves and cover with brown sugar and honey. Add apple cider. Glaze in 450-degree oven, basting frequently.

3. Pour 8 ounces of sweet wine over ham, and spread with dark molasses. Glaze in 450-degree oven for 8 or 10 minutes. Baste gently and frequently.

(Many fine old Southern cooks serve their baked hams with the following Brandy Sauce: 1 pound of brown sugar, 6 cloves, juice of 2 oranges. Remove from stove and add 2 ounces of brandy.)

*Note:* If you like your ham mild, soak it in cool water for 12 hours, depending on age of ham. If ham is very old, 24 hours would be better.

### Ham Mousse

2 cups ground ham, cooked (1 pound)
1 envelope unflavored gelatin
2 tablespoons cold water
1/2 cup boiling water
1 teaspoon dry mustard
1 teaspoon salt
1 tablespoon prepared horse-radish
1/2 teaspoon brown sugar
1/4 teaspoon paprika
few grains cayenne
1 cup heavy cream

Grind the ham very fine with food chopper. Soften gelatin in cold water, add boiling water and stir until dissolved. When liquid is clear, add ham and all seasonings; mix thoroughly.

Beat cream until it stands in peaks, then mix or fold the seasoned ham in gently. Mix only long enough to distribute ham evenly. Rinse a 1-quart mold in cold water (this helps to release mousse from mold easily) and pour in ham mixture. Store in refrigerator until chilled and firm.

Unmold and garnish with greens, olives, radishes or pickles. Can be prepared a day ahead. Serves 4.

### Ham and Asparagus Casserole

1 can green asparagus
6 slices ham, baked
2 cups sharp cheese, grated
medium white sauce

Drain asparagus and reserve liquid (using liquid in preparing white sauce). Wrap 3 spears of asparagus in each ham slice and pin with toothpick. Add grated cheese to white sauce. Place ham and asparagus rolls in greased baking dish and cover with sauce. Heat at 375 degrees for 20 minutes.

### Crown Pork Roast with Corn Bread Stuffing

Stuffing

1/4 cup celery, finely chopped
1 tablespoon melted butter
1 1/2 cups corn bread crumbs
1 1/2 cups biscuits or soft bread crumbs
1 egg, beaten
1/4 cup onions, finely chopped
1/4 teaspoon pepper
1/4 teaspoon sage
1 cup warm water with chicken bouillon cube

Roast

pork loin, 10 to 14 ribs
pepper
3 cups water
salt
3 chicken bouillon cubes

*Stuffing:* Cook celery and onions in butter until tender. Combine crumbled corn bread, bread crumbs, sage, pepper and onion mixture. Add bouillon and egg. Mix well. Makes 2 cups of stuffing.

*Roast:* Have crown made at market from strip of pork loin (backbone removed) containing 10 to 14 ribs. Season with salt and pepper. Place in shallow baker, bone ends up; wrap tips in foil to prevent excess browning. Roast uncovered with chicken bouillon cubes dissolved in water in 325-degree oven until meat thermometer reads 185 degrees (well done, not pink) about 35 to 40 minutes per pound. Approximately one hour before done, fill center with corn bread stuffing. To serve, replace foil wraps with spiced crab apples, garnish platter with parsley and frosted grapes.

Makes 10 to 14 servings.

## Pork Chops in Wine Sauce

*Nancy Cucich*

flour
salt
pepper
1 egg
8 lean pork chops, 1-inch thick
1 onion, diced
1 green pepper, diced
1 package frozen mushrooms (or fresh or canned)
butter (about 1 1/2 sticks)
sherry

Saute onions in butter and pour into casserole dish. Cover and place in 350-degree oven. Repeat process with green peppers and mushrooms.

Dip pork chops in egg, then in flour seasoned with salt and pepper. Brown in frying pan in butter, then place in casserole. Be sure to add sherry after each item is added to casserole. After all ingredients are in casserole, sprinkle again liberally with sherry, cover and return to oven for 45 minutes. Keep covered at all times. Serve with wild rice. Serves 4.

## Meat Loaf O'Brien

1 pound ground chuck
1/4 pound pork sausage
3/4 cup canned milk
1/2 cup toasted bread crumbs
4 cups thinly sliced, peeled raw potatoes
1/4 cup chili sauce
snipped parsley
1/4 cup chopped onion
1 teaspoon salt
1/4 teaspoon black pepper
1 thinly sliced medium onion

Arrange evenly in greased 2-quart baking dish the potatoes and onion. Sprinkle with salt and pepper to taste and add parsley.

Mix beef, pork, milk, crumbs, chili sauce, chopped onion, salt and pepper. Spread evenly over potato mixture. Score the top with chevrons, or other design, and fill with chili sauce or catsup. Bake at 350 degrees for 1 hour. Serves 4.

## Barbecued Spareribs

3 to 4 pounds pork ribs, cut in pieces
1 lemon
1 onion, large
1 cup chili sauce
1/3 cup Worcestershire
1 teaspoon salt
1 teaspoon chili powder, (optional)
2 dashes Tabasco sauce
2 cups water

Place ribs in shallow roasting pan, meaty side up. On each piece place a slice of unpeeled lemon and a thin slice of onion. Anchor with a toothpick. Roast in 450-degree oven for 30 minutes. Combine remaining ingredients; bring to boiling point and pour over ribs. Lower heat and continue baking at 350 degrees until tender, about 1 hour. Baste ribs with sauce every 15 minutes. If sauce gets too thick, add more water. Serves 4.

## Backbone

backbone
pepper
flour
salt
2 cups boiling water

Wash backbone and have chopped or cut into pieces convenient to serve. Sprinkle with salt and pepper, place in a baking pan and add 2 cups boiling water. Have oven hot for 10 minutes then cook with medium heat. Baste and turn, cook about 2 hours. If a crusty outside is liked, dredge with flour when 1/2 done and cook uncovered. When ready to serve, remove from pan, pour off all grease from top of gravy and add sufficient browned flour to thicken. Serve with baked sweet potatoes.

## Dixie Pork Chops

4 pork chops
1 8-ounce can tomato sauce
2 cans water (measured in sauce can)
4 slices green pepper
4 slices onion
1/2 cup uncooked rice
salt
pepper

Brown pork chops in skillet and then add rice. Place slices of green pepper and onion over pork chops. Pour tomato sauce and water into skillet. Cover and bake at 375 degrees for 1 hour. May be cooked on top of stove over low heat.

## Lamb Chops with Mint Jelly

lamb chops
pepper
Kitchen Bouquet or Worcestershire sauce
salt
butter
1/2 cup thin brown sauce
1/2 glass mint jelly

Broil chops – salt, pepper and butter over each chop. Have brown sauce ready, add to this mint jelly and blend together well. Add a little Kitchen Bouquet or Worcestershire sauce. Season well with salt and pepper, and pour around the chop. Serve at once.

## Pork Tenderloin

pork tenderloin
pepper
salt
butter

Slice tenderloin about 1/2-inch thick; broil on broiler exactly as steak, giving a little longer time and keep turning. Place on hot platter, season with salt, pepper and butter. Serve with tiny thin hoecakes.

## Shepherd's Pie

roast
mashed potatoes
gravy

Put any kind of roast meat through food chopper; add gravy. Put into a casserole, cover the top with mashed potatoes, and bake for 20 minutes at 325 degrees. Serve with hot bran muffins and pear salad.

## Sherry Roast Pork

1 5-pound loin of pork
1/2 cup brown sugar, packed
1/3 cup orange juice
1 teaspoon bottled horse-radish
1/2 cup cooking sherry
1 tablespoon orange rind, grated
1 teaspoon prepared mustard

Have pork backbone sawed into chops, part way through. This makes it easier to carve meat into chop-size serving pieces.

Place pork loin, ribs down, in shallow roasting pan. In saucepan, combine remaining ingredients and bring to boil. Pour sauce over pork and roast at 325 degrees for 35 minutes per pound, or about 3 hours for a 5-pound loin. Baste often during first 2 hours of cooking.

By the time pork is done, it has a slightly charcoal look and taste. If charcoal appearance is not desired, roast pork 1 hour before adding sauce. Makes 8 to 10 servings.

BREADS

## Glazed Pineapple Fingers

(a delightful breakfast perker-upper)

*Mrs. Sanders (Betty) Camp*

2 cups sifted flour
3 teaspoons baking powder
1 teaspoon salt
1/4 cup sugar
1/4 cup shortening
1 egg
1/4 cup pineapple syrup
1 cup drained, crushed pineapple
lemon frosting

Sift flour, baking powder, salt and sugar together into a bowl and cut in shortening until mixture is crumbly. Add pineapple syrup and beaten egg. Add pineapple. Mix only until flour is well moistened. Using 2 forks drop batter onto greased baking sheet, shaping into long narrow bars. Press the sides smooth to improve appearance of finished product. Bake for 15 minutes at 425 degrees. Frost immediately with lemon frosting.

## Lemon Frosting

1/2 cup fine powdered sugar
1 tablespoon hot milk
dash of lemon extract
grated lemon rind

Mix sugar, hot (but not boiled) milk, a hefty dash of lemon extract and a little grated lemon rind. Spread on the pineapple fingers.

### Blueberry Streusel Muffins

*Dorothy Rhoden*

Muffins

2 cups sifted flour
2 teaspoons baking powder
1/2 teaspoon baking soda
1/2 teaspoon salt
3 tablespoons sugar
1 egg
1 cup sour cream
1/3 cup milk
1/4 cup salad oil
1 1/2 cups blueberries, drained

Streusel

1/2 cup firmly packed light brown sugar
1/4 cup regular unsifted flour
1 teaspoon cinnamon
3 tablespoons butter or margarine

*Muffins:* Into mixing bowl, sift together the flour, baking powder, soda, salt and sugar. Beat egg until thickened and ivory colored. Add sour cream and milk; beat to combine with egg, and stir in oil. Add mixture to sifted flour mixture and stir only until blended. Fold in blueberries. Turn into buttered muffin pans (1/3 cup size wells), filling each 3/4 full. Have streusel ready and sprinkle over batter. Bake at 425 degrees for 15 to 20 minutes or until topping is deep brown. Loosen sides with small spatula and serve at once. Makes 18 muffins.

*Streusel:* In small mixing bowl, stir together brown sugar, flour and cinnamon. With pastry blender, cut in the butter until particles are fine and mixture is crumbly.

## Almond Bread

*Mrs. Sanders (Betty) Camp*

3 eggs
1/2 cup sugar
1 1/2 cups sifted flour
2 teaspoons baking powder
1/2 cup finely chopped almonds

Beat eggs. Add sugar a little at a time and beat until creamy. Sift the flour and the baking powder together, add the almonds and mix well. Add the flour mixture to the eggs and mix until smooth. Pour into well greased loaf pan and bake for an hour at 350 degrees.

## Orange Muffins

*Julia Dyar*

Muffins

1/2 cup Crisco
1 cup sugar
2 eggs, beaten
2/3 cup buttermilk
2 cups flour
1 teaspoon soda
1/4 teaspoon salt
grated rind of 1 orange

Topping

1 cup sugar
juice of 2 large oranges
grated rind of 1 orange

*Muffins:* Blend Crisco and sugar and add eggs, one at a time, beating well after each addition. Sift flour, soda and salt and add to mixture alternately with buttermilk, starting and ending with flour. Blend in orange rind and bake at 375 degrees for 12 minutes. (If using small muffin pans; if using large pans, baking time will be longer.)

*Topping:* While muffins are baking, mix sugar, orange juice and rind. After muffins are baked, place one spoonful of mixture on top of each hot muffin and let cool in pan. Makes about 5 dozen.

## Hot Cross Buns

*Glenn McCullough*

(Traditionally baked and served to our guests by my mother at home following Easter Sunrise Services)

Buns

| | |
|---|---|
| 1/2 cup lukewarm water | 2 eggs |
| 2 packages active dry yeast | 1 cup plumped raisins |
| 1/2 cup lukewarm milk | 1 teaspoon cinnamon |
| 3/4 cup mashed potatoes (unseasoned) | 1/4 teaspoon nutmeg |
| 1/2 cup sugar | 4 1/2 cups sifted flour |
| 1/2 cup butter | 1 1/4 teaspoons salt |

Egg Yolk Glaze

| | |
|---|---|
| egg yolk | 2 tablespoons cold water |

White Icing

| | |
|---|---|
| confectioners sugar | cream |
| lemon or vanilla extract | |

*Buns:* Dissolve the yeast in lukewarm water and stir in until smooth the remaining ingredients, reserving about half the flour for later use. When smooth, add enough of the reserved flour to handle easily, mixing by hand. Turn onto lightly floured board and knead until smooth. Let rise until double (about 1 1/2 hours). Punch down and divide in two. Hand shape each part into 16 buns and place in 2 greased 9-inch round pans or 2 inches apart on greased baking sheet. Let rise until double (30 minutes). Now take a pair of scissors which have been held in boiling water for a minute and make a cross-shaped incision on each bun. Brush with egg yolk glaze. Bake in 375-degree oven for 25 minutes. Allow to cool slightly. Just before serving, make a cross on top of each bun with white icing.

*Glaze:* Mix egg yolk and water with fork. Brush over buns just before baking for glistening golden finish.

*Icing:* Sift sugar and moisten with cream to spreading consistency. Add lemon or vanilla extract and mix.

## Honey Twist Bread

*Shirley McCullough*

Sweet Yeast Dough

1 cup milk, scalded
1/4 cup butter
1/2 cup sugar
1 teaspoon salt
2 packages dried yeast
1/4 cup lukewarm water
4 eggs
4 3/4 cups flour

Honey Topping

1/4 cup butter
2/3 cup confectioners sugar
1 egg white
2 tablespoons honey, warmed

*Dough:* Pour scalded milk over butter, sugar and salt. Dissolve yeast in lukewarm water and when milk mixture has cooled, combine the two. Separate 1 egg and reserve the white; beat the yolk with 3 whole eggs and add to mixture. Add sifted flour to make soft dough. Turn onto floured board and kneed until smooth. Place into greased bowl, cover with damp cloth and allow to double in bulk.

*Bread:* Take sweet yeast dough which has been allowed to rise until double in bulk and work it down. Form into a roll about 1 inch in diameter. Twist the roll as it is coiled into a greased round pan, beginning on the outside edge and covering the pan to the center. Brush with honey topping and allow to rise until double. Bake at 375 degrees for 25 to 30 minutes. Serve hot. Especially good with broiled chicken or barbecue.

*Honey Topping:* Cream ingredients together and brush over prepared twist. Makes enough topping for about 1 10-inch pan of twist.

## Orange Nut Bread

3 cups flour
2 teaspoons baking powder
1/2 teaspoon salt
1/4 cup sugar
1 egg
1/2 cup walnut meats
1 tablespoon orange rind, grated
1/2 cup orange marmalade
1 cup milk

Sift dry ingredients. Add chopped walnuts, grated orange rind and marmalade. Add milk to well beaten egg and stir in all ingredients together. Turn into well greased pan and let rise 15 to 20 minutes. Then bake for 1 hour in 350-degree oven.

## Foolproof Waffles

2 cups flour, sifted
1/4 teaspoon salt
2 eggs
4 teaspoons baking powder
2 tablespoons sugar
1 1/4 cups milk
6 tablespoons fat or cooking oil

Sift all dry ingredients together. Beat eggs and add milk to eggs. Add egg-milk mixture to dry ingredients. Add fat, beat well and cook in hot waffle iron.

## Sweet Potato Biscuits

*Julia Dyar*

2 cups sifted flour
2 teaspoons baking powder
1/2 teaspoon soda (scant)
2 tablespoons sugar
1/2 teaspoon salt
2 tablespoons lard
1 cup mashed sweet potatoes
1 cup buttermilk

Sift dry ingredients. Cut in lard. Add sweet potatoes and sufficient buttermilk to make soft dough. Knead gently on lightly floured board. Roll out and cut. Bake at 450 degrees until golden.

## Coconut Bread

1/4 cup butter or other shortening
1 cup hot water
1 package dry yeast
6 tablespoons sugar
4 to 5 cups flour, sifted
1 teaspoon salt
2 cups coconut, shredded, finely cut
3/4 cup raisins
4 egg yolks

Melt butter in hot water; cool to lukewarm. Add yeast and stir until dissolved; add sugar, salt, coconut and raisins; mix well. Stir in egg yolks; add flour to make a dough which can be easily handled.

Turn out on floured board and knead until smooth. Place dough in greased bowl and brush surface with melted shortening; cover with cloth and let rise in warm place until doubled in bulk. Turn out on floured board and knead again. Shape into 2 loaves and place in two greased 8 X 4 X 3-inch pans.

Brush with melted shortening, cover, and let rise in warm place until doubled in bulk. Bake in moderate oven (350 degrees) for 50 minutes, or until done. (Loaves should be removed from pans at once, and placed on cake racks to cool.)

*Note:* About 5 hours are required to make this bread. This is delightful at any time, but especially so buttered and toasted.

### Popovers

1 1/2 cups flour
1 1/2 cups milk
3 eggs
1/2 teaspoon salt
1 tablespoon sugar

Put all ingredients in mixing bowl and mix well with rotary beater. Grease popover irons or custard cups and heat in hot oven at 450 degrees for 20 minutes. Reduce heat to 350 degrees and bake 15 to 20 minutes longer. At end of baking time open oven door to let popovers dry a few minutes before serving.

### Griddle Cakes

1 1/2 cups flour
3 1/2 teaspoons baking powder
3 tablespoons sugar
3/4 cup milk
3 tablespoons Wesson oil
3/4 teaspoon salt
1 egg, beaten until light

Add milk and Wesson oil to egg. Add flour, salt and sugar and stir vigorously until dry ingredients are mixed. Before baking add baking powder. Bake on heated griddle iron.

### Yorkshire Muffins

1 cup flour, enriched
2 eggs
1 tablespoon fat, melted
1/2 teaspoon salt
1 cup milk

Sift flour, measure; add salt and sift again. Beat eggs, milk and flour together with beater until smooth. Add melted fat; blend. Grease hot muffin pans with more melted fat and pour in batter, making pans a little less than 1/2 full. Bake at 450 degrees for 20 minutes or until golden brown. Turn off heat; prick each muffin at side with sharp fork. Leave in oven 3 to 5 minutes. Makes 16 muffins.

### Orange French Toast

1 teaspoon orange rind, grated
juice of 1 orange
2 eggs
1 tablespoon sugar
8 slices day-old French bread or rolls
butter

Beat eggs with juice, rind and sugar. Dip bread in mixture. Melt butter in chafing dish pan over flame and fry bread until golden on both sides.

### Banana Bread

1 stick butter
1 cup sugar
2 eggs
1/2 teaspoon salt
3 bananas (ripe)
1/2 cup pecans
2 cups flour
1 teaspoon soda

Mix butter, sugar and beaten eggs. Mash and add bananas. Sift flour and soda; add to shortening mixture. Add nuts. Bake at 350 degrees for 1 hour in loaf pan toward back of oven.

### Doughnuts

4 eggs, beaten together
2 cups milk
2 cups sugar
1 teaspoon butter, melted
5 teaspoons baking powder
1/2 teaspoon salt
1/2 teaspoon vanilla
flour for soft dough

Combine ingredients and boil until brown in deep fat.

## Applesauce – Nut Bread

2 cups all-purpose flour, sifted
1 teaspoon salt
1/2 teaspoon cinnamon
1 egg
2 tablespoons shortening, melted
3/4 cup granulated sugar
3 teaspoons baking powder
1/2 teaspoon baking soda
1 cup walnuts, coarsely chopped
1 cup applesauce, canned

Preheat oven to 350 degrees.

Sift together flour, sugar, baking powder, salt, baking soda and cinnamon; add walnuts. In mixing bowl, beat egg; add applesauce and shortening. Add flour mixture; stir just until blended. Pour into pan. Bake 1 hour, or until done, in greased 9 X 5 X 3-inch loaf pan. Cool on rack.

## Batter Bread

1 egg
3 cups flour
1/2 teaspoon soda
1 tablespoon sugar
1 1/2 cups buttermilk
3 1/2 teaspoons baking powder
1 teaspoon salt
2 tablespoons shortening, melted

Beat egg well, add 1/2 cup buttermilk, 1 cup flour with baking powder, soda, salt and sugar. Beat this well, add 1 cup buttermilk, add melted shortening and 2 cups flour and also beat this well. Grease a 9-inch cake pan and have real hot when you pour in the batter. Bake at 400 degrees until brown.

## Orange Pecan Bread

2 3/4 cups all-purpose flour, sifted
2 1/2 teaspoons baking powder
1/2 teaspoon baking soda
1/2 teaspoon salt
2 cups pecans, broken
2 tablespoons butter or margarine
1 cup honey
1 egg
rind of 1 orange
3/4 cup orange juice (about 2 oranges)

Preheat oven to 325 degrees and grease 9 X 5 X 2 1/2-inch loaf pan.

Sift flour with baking powder, soda and salt. Then work butter or margarine until creamy. Stir in honey, unbeaten egg and orange rind. Add flour and orange juice alternately to the butter-honey mixture, mixing well after each addition. Stir in pecans and pour mixture into pan and bake 35 minutes or until golden.

## Easy Banana Bread

*Aline Burgess*

1/2 cup shortening
1 cup sugar
2 eggs, beaten
3 ripe bananas
3 tablespoons water
2 cups flour
1 teaspoon soda
1 teaspoon vanilla
1/2 to 1 cup nuts, broken

Put all ingredients into blender and blend until well mixed. Bake in 9 X 5 loaf pan for one hour in 325-degree oven.

### Corn Meal Muffins

*Julia Dyar*

2 cups boiling water
2 cups white water ground
  plain corn meal
4 teaspoons baking powder
1 teaspoon salt
2 tablespoons butter
1 cup milk
2 eggs, well beaten

Add baking powder, salt and butter to corn meal; pour boiling water over mixture. Mix well and add milk and well beaten eggs. Pour into well greased and preheated tins. Bake for 20 to 25 minutes at 475 degrees. Serve hot. These muffins are crisp on the outside and almost like spoon bread on the inside. They can be made with cracklings by adding 1/2 cup of cracklings to the mixture after adding the eggs.

### Angel Biscuits

5 cups flour
1/4 cup sugar
1 package dry yeast
2 teaspoons warm water
1 teaspoon baking soda
1 teaspoon baking powder
1 teaspoon salt
2 cups buttermilk
1 cup shortening

Sift dry ingredients. Cut in shortening. Dissolve yeast in warm water and add, with the buttermilk, to the dry ingredients. Mix well. Turn the mixture out on a lightly floured board and roll to 1/4 to 1/2 inch thickness. Cut dough with biscuit cutter and place biscuits on a well greased baking sheet. Bake for 15 minutes at 400 degrees.

## Mama's Favorite Corn Bread

*Glenn McCullough*

2 eggs
1/4 pound soft butter
1 teaspoon salt
2 cups corn meal (more or less)
1 heaping teaspoon baking powder
1 heaping tablespoon sugar
2 cups buttermilk
1 level teaspoon soda

Cream the eggs and butter in a bowl. Add buttermilk and stir. Sift dry ingredients together. Add dry ingredients to reach desired consistency. In iron skillet place a tablespoon of lard or other shortening and set on moderate heat. Sprinkle a little corn meal into the grease when hot and pour the mixture into the skillet. Bake at 425 degrees until browned.

## Spoon Bread

1 1/2 cups boiling water
1 cup corn meal
1 tablespoon butter
3 eggs
1/4 teaspoon soda
1 cup buttermilk
1 teaspoon salt
2 teaspoons sugar
1 teaspoon baking powder

Pour boiling water over corn meal and stir until cool to avoid lumping. Add butter and egg yolks and stir until thoroughly blended. Stir in buttermilk, adding salt, sugar, baking powder and soda. Fold in egg whites which have been beaten only enough to hold a soft peak. Pour into greased 2-quart baking dish and bake for 50 minutes in 375-degree oven. Serve hot with butter. Marvelous with fried green tomatoes or spicy corn relish. May be used instead of potatoes with such things as chicken or roasts. This comes out very light, souffle-like and must be served with a spoon directly from the baking dish.

### Coastal Rice Bread

1 cup hot cooked rice
1 tablespoon butter
1 cup milk
3 eggs, lightly beaten
1/2 cup corn meal
1 teaspoon salt

Combine the rice and butter. Add milk to eggs and stir in meal and salt. Add the mixtures and stir well. Pour into 3-inch muffin cups which have been greased and floured – about 1/3 cup batter per muffin cup. Bake at 425 degrees for 25 minutes. Yields 12 servings. Serve hot.

### Party Cheese Biscuits

1/2 pound butter
1 pound sharp cheese, grated
1 teaspoon salt
1/8 teaspoon red pepper
2 teaspoons sugar
4 or 5 cups sifted flour, plain

Sift dry ingredients together. Cream butter and cheese, add dry ingredients gradually. When it holds together make into round roll, wrap in waxed paper and chill in refrigerator. Slice 1/2 inch thick, place on ungreased cookie sheet, and cook at 300 degrees for 25 minutes.

### Soul Food Corn Bread

*Frances Ledford*

1 can (Toombs County) Swift Creek Hush Puppy Mix
1 egg
2 tablespoons bacon drippings
1/2 cup of water (more or less, as needed)

Heat bacon drippings and combine with other ingredients. Bake at 350 degrees until done.

### Sourdough Bread

*Julia Dyar*

1 tablespoon melted butter
1/2 teaspoon soda
2 cups flour
2 cups starter
1 teaspoon sugar

Add butter to starter. Add remaining ingredients and stir into starter, adding enough flour to make a thick dough. Turn out on a board and work in enough additional flour to keep dough from being sticky. Knead until smooth, put in greased bowl and allow to rise in warm place until almost doubled. Form into a loaf and put in a greased tin. Allow to double in width. Bake at 375 degrees for 30 minutes or until brown.

### Sourdough Starter

*Julia Dyar*

1 envelope yeast
2 cups flour
1 tablespoon sugar
2 1/2 cups warm water
2 teaspoons salt

Sprinkle yeast into 1/2 cup warm water and let stand 5 minutes. Stir in 2 cups warm water, flour, salt and sugar. Put in a large crock or bowl (starter will bubble to about 4 times its volume). Cover loosely with a towel. Let stand in warm place (80 to 90 degrees) stirring down daily. In 3 or 4 days it is ready to use. When starter is withdrawn from container, replace it with equal amounts of water and flour.

## Yeast Sally Lunn

1/2 package cake or package dry granular yeast
2 teaspoons sugar
1/4 cup lukewarm water
1 egg
1/2 teaspoon salt
2 cups sifted flour
1/2 cup sweet milk
2 tablespoons lard or shortening

Stir yeast and sugar into lukewarm water. Let stand a few minutes. Add remaining ingredients and blend well. Cover and let rise in a warm place until about doubled in bulk. It is a soft dough. No additional flour is required.

Beat down with a spoon and turn into greased tube pan. Cover and let rise again. Bake at 400 degrees for 25 minutes or until lightly browned. Serve hot.

## Baking Powder Sally Lunn

2 tablespoons butter or margarine
3 tablespoons sugar
1 egg, separated
1/2 cup milk
1 cup sifted all-purpose flour
1/2 teaspoon baking powder
1/2 teaspoon salt

Cream margarine, add sugar and cream together thoroughly. Add the egg yolk and beat well. Sift flour, baking powder and salt and add to mixture alternately with milk. Beat well. Fold in stiffly beaten egg white and pour into a greased 10 X 6 X 2-inch pan. Bake at 400 degrees for 20 to 25 minutes or until golden brown. Serve hot. Serves 6.

## Refrigerator Rolls

*Julia Dyar*

1 envelope yeast
2 cups lukewarm water
1 teaspoon salt
6 cups flour
1/2 cup sugar
1 egg
3 tablespoons Crisco

Place yeast in bowl and add sugar and water. Add well beaten egg and 3 cups flour. Sift flour once before measuring. Beat well and add melted shortening (not too hot). Add rest of flour and beat. Let rise to double its bulk. Punch down and cover tightly. Place in refrigerator. About an hour before baking, remove desired amount and shape into rolls. Let rise to double their bulk slowly. Place in greased pan and bake in hot oven (425 degrees) for 20 minutes or until brown.

## Fruit Bars

2 cups pecans, chopped
1/2 pound crystallized cherries, chopped
1 teaspoon vanilla
1 stick margarine
1 cup flour, unsifted
1/2 pound crystallized pineapple, chopped
1/2 box light brown sugar
2 eggs, beaten

Grease and flour 8 X 12 X 2-inch pan. Put nuts on bottom of pan. Cream butter and sugar; add eggs, flour and vanilla. With wet hands spread batter evenly over nuts. Add pineapple and cherries. Pat into batter. Bake at 300 degrees for 1 hour. Let cool before cutting.

## Scones

2 cups flour
4 teaspoons baking powder
2 teaspoons sugar
2 eggs, well beaten
1/2 teaspoon salt
4 tablespoons butter
1/3 cup cream

Sift dry ingredients together. Chop in the butter, add cream and eggs (reserving a small amount of unbeaten whites). Toss on a floured board. Roll 3/4-inch thick. Cut into small squares. Brush with the reserved egg, sprinkle with sugar and bake in hot oven (400 degrees) for 15 minutes.

## Crumpets

2 cakes or packages yeast
1/2 cup lukewarm water
2 eggs
1 1/2 cups lukewarm milk
2 tablespoons butter, melted
1/2 teaspoon salt
1 teaspoon sugar
3 cups sifted flour

Dissolve the yeast in water. Allow to soften for 5 minutes. Beat the eggs, add milk, butter, salt and sugar. Add the yeast mixture and the flour, beating until smooth and well blended. Cover and set aside in a warm place for 15 minutes. Preheat oven to 400 degrees. Fill buttered muffin tins about half full. Bake at 400 degrees for 15 minutes. Serve hot with plenty of melted butter and raspberry jam.

### Sara's Cheese Wafers

2 cups sharp cheese, grated
2 cups flour
2 cups rice krispies
1 cup butter (2 sticks)
salt

Roll into little balls and mash flat with fork. Bake at 275 degrees on lower rack for 20 minutes and raise to top rack for 20 minutes.

### Echota Hard Bread

1 package active dry yeast
2 tablespoons melted lard, or other shortening
1 cup warm water
1/4 cup tepid water
1/2 teaspoon salt
4 cups sifted flour
1 tablespoon corn meal

Dissolve yeast in 1/4 cup tepid water in large bowl. Stir in lard (cooled) and salt. Add flour alternately with 1 cup water, sifting in the flour a turn at a time and beating well after each turn. Knead in last cup of flour gently, until dough is quite stiff. Dependent upon altitude, humidity and exactness of measure, there may be some flour left over. If so, do not force it into dough. Shape into a ball and place in greased bowl; cover with dry cloth. Let it double in bulk at about 85 degrees, then punch it down. Divide into two equal parts and shape into round flat circle, about 7 inches in diameter. Place one cookie sheet on top of another to prevent bottom burning. Grease the top sheet and lightly coat it with corn meal. Place the circles of dough on it, then cover with clean cloth. Set in warm place (85 degrees) for half an hour, then bake at 400 degrees for about 50 minutes or until lightly browned. Break into pieces for serving while still slightly warm.

## Corn Fritters

*Grandma Pafford*

1 cup plain flour
1 teaspoon salt
1 teaspoon baking powder
2 eggs
1/4 cup milk
1 tablespoon shortening, melted
1 1/2 cups corn

Combine flour, salt and baking powder. Beat eggs with milk and add shortening and corn. Combine the two mixtures lightly. Drop from tablespoon in deep fat and fry until light brown and well done. Drain on absorbent paper. Good served hot with cane syrup or maple syrup.

## Mexican Corn Bread

1/2 pound beef, ground
2 eggs, well beaten
1/2 teaspoon soda
1 number-303 can yellow corn, cream style
1/2 pound cheese, grated
1 cup yellow corn meal
1 cup sweet milk
3/4 teaspoon salt
1/2 cup bacon drippings
1 large onion, finely chopped
4 jalapeno peppers, canned

Sauté ground meat in 1/4 of bacon drippings and drain. Mix together the corn meal, eggs, milk, soda, salt and corn. Grease a big black skillet, heat until hot, and sprinkle thin layer of corn meal in bottom; let brown. Pour 1/2 corn meal batter in skillet and sprinkle evenly with meat, chopped onion and pepper (it is good without pepper). Sprinkle grated cheese onto mixture and pour remaining batter on top. Bake about 45 minutes at 350 degrees or until brown.

### Muffins with Cranberries

6 2/3 cups flour
1 1/2 cups sugar
1 cup lard or margarine
2 cups whole cranberries, canned
2 teaspoons salt
4 eggs
3 heaping teaspoons baking powder
2 cups milk

Cream butter and sugar until light and fluffy. Add milk and unbeaten eggs, salt and baking powder. Beat slightly and fold in cranberries. Bake at 400 degrees about 40 minutes. Brown slowly. Makes 36 to 40 muffins.

### Hush Puppies

*Mary Alice Quinn, Food Editor*
*The Commercial Appeal, Memphis*

2 cups sifted fine corn meal
2 teaspoons baking powder
1 teaspoon salt
1 1/2 cups milk
1 egg, well beaten
1 cup finely chopped onion

Combine corn meal, baking powder and salt. Add milk and beaten egg. Blend in onion. Stir until well mixed, adding more corn meal if necessary to form a stiff batter. Shape into small round balls, about 1 1/2 inches in diameter. Deep fat fry until browned on all sides. Serve immediately, with lots of butter.

### Cracklin' Corn Bread

1 1/2 cups corn meal
1 teaspoon salt
2 tablespoons flour
3 teaspoons baking powder
1 egg, beaten
1 1/4 cups sweet milk
1 1/2 cups cracklings

Sift corn meal, salt, flour and baking powder together. Mix egg and milk and add to dry ingredients. Mix well and add cracklings. Bake in greased pan in hot oven, (425 degrees), about 20 to 25 minutes.

### Southern Corn Bread for Two

1/2 cup corn meal, plain
1/8 teaspoon soda
1 tablespoon lard
buttermilk
1/4 teaspoon salt
1/4 teaspoon baking powder
1 egg

Mix dry ingredients. Add lard and cut into dry ingredients; add egg and enough buttermilk to consistency of cake batter. Pour into hot greased (1 egg) skillet and cook until golden brown at 450 degrees.

### Cream Biscuits

4 cups flour
1/4 stick butter
3 teaspoons cream of tartar
1 1/2 teaspoons baking soda
2 cups rich sweet cream
1 teaspoon salt

Mix ingredients together. Dough should be very soft. Roll thin, cut with biscuit cutter and bake in hot oven at 400 degrees for about 15 minutes.

### Bran Rolls

1 cup bran cereal
1/2 cup sugar
2 teaspoons salt
1 cup shortening
6 1/2 cups flour
1 cup hot water
2 yeast cakes
1 cup lukewarm water
2 eggs, beaten

Cream shortening, add sugar, salt, bran and hot water. Mix well. Let cool. Dissolve yeast in lukewarm water. Add to beaten eggs. Alternate this with flour to first mixture. Refrigerate for at least 12 hours. Let stand at room temperature for 2 hours after forming rolls. Bake at 425 degrees for 20 minutes.

## Corn Sticks

- 1/3 cup enriched flour, sifted
- 1 tablespoon sugar
- 1 teaspoon baking powder
- 1/2 teaspoon soda
- 1/2 teaspoon salt
- 1 1/3 cups yellow corn meal
- 1 egg, beaten
- 1 cup sour cream
- 2 tablespoons salad oil or melted shortening

Sift flour, sugar, baking powder, soda, and salt; stir in corn meal. Combine egg, sour cream, and salad oil. Add to dry ingredients; stir until just blended. Preheat corn stick pans, then grease generously. Fill pans 2/3 full; bake in hot oven (400 degrees) about 25 minutes. Makes 10 to 12 sticks.

## Angel Biscuits

- 1 cake yeast
- 2 tablespoons lukewarm water
- 5 cups plain flour, sifted
- 1 teaspoon soda
- 3 teaspoons baking powder
- 4 tablespoons sugar
- 1 tablespoon salt
- 1 cup shortening
- 2 cups buttermilk

Dissolve yeast in lukewarm water. Into a bowl sift flour with other dry ingredients. Cut in shortening. Add buttermilk, then yeast mixture. Stir until all flour is dampened. Knead on floured board about 2 minutes, roll out to 1/2 inch thickness and cut with biscuit cutter. Bake at 400 degrees about 12 to 15 minutes.

This dough may be placed in refrigerator immediately after mixing and used as needed.

### Never Fail Dumplings

1 1/2 cups flour
1/2 teaspoon salt
3 tablespoons Crisco
1 egg
5 tablespoons water

Mix ingredients; roll out thin and cut into 2-inch squares. Drop one at a time into boiling chicken broth.

### Corn Meal Bread

1 package active-dry or 1 cake compressed yeast
1 1/4 cups lukewarm water
8 cups all-purpose flour, sifted
1 1/4 cups white corn meal
2 1/4 cups water
1 tablespoon salt
1 cup sugar
1 cup raisins

Sprinkle yeast over lukewarm water to soften. (This takes about 10 minutes.) Sift flour.

Cook corn meal and 2 1/4 cups of water together, stirring constantly, until you have a thick mush. Stir in salt, sugar and raisins. Set aside to cool.

Mix softened yeast into 3 cups flour and beat vigorously. Put mixture in a warm spot, away from drafts and let rise until dough is double in size.

Sift remaining 5 cups of flour on a table, dump corn meal and dough on top; knead in all flour well. Let rise in greased bowl until double in bulk.

Shape dough into 3 round loaves. Put on greased baking sheets, let rise 30 minutes longer, then bake at 375 degrees for 50 minutes.

## Easy Ice Box Rolls

*Mrs. Ralph (Frances) Owen*

1 cup shortening
3/4 cup sugar
3 teaspoons salt
1 cup boiling water
1 cup cold water
1/4 cup lukewarm water
2 packages dry yeast
2 eggs
7 cups flour (unsifted)

Pour boiling water over shortening, sugar and salt. Stir to dissolve and add cold water; mix well.

Dissolve yeast in lukewarm water and add to shortening mixture when it has cooled to lukewarm. Add beaten eggs and unsifted flour a cup at a time. Beat well after each addition of flour. Turn into a greased container, cover and refrigerate over night.

When ready to use, roll out onto floured board, cut and brush with melted butter. Place on greased pan and let rise in warm place. Bake 15 to 20 minutes at 450 degrees. Makes about 6 dozen rolls. (Note: dough will keep in refrigerator several days.)

## Grandma's Buttermilk Rolls

*Julia Dyar*

2 cups plain flour
1 scant teaspoon salt
handful pure lard
1 cup buttermilk
1 teaspoon soda

Sift together flour, soda and salt. Combine with buttermilk and lard. Form biscuits by hand and crowd into pan. Bake at 350 degrees until brown. Make at night or lunch. Let stand several hours before baking.

## Country Breakfast Muffins

*Glenn McCullough*

1 egg
1 cup sour cream
2 tablespoons sugar
1 tablespoon soft butter
1 1/3 cups sifted flour
1 teaspoon baking powder
1/2 teaspoon salt
1/2 teaspoon soda

Heat oven to 400 degrees. Grease bottom of muffin cups, or use paper baking cups. Beat egg until light. Blend in cream, sugar and butter. Sift dry ingredients together and stir in. Fill the greased muffin cups to 2/3 full. Bake 20 to 25 minutes or until golden brown. Serve hot.

## Parmesan Casserole Bread

*Shirley McCullough*

1 package active dry yeast
1/4 cup lukewarm water
1/4 cup scalded milk
1 1/2 cups sifted flour
2 tablespoons chopped parsley
1/2 teaspoon salt
1/3 cup butter
1 beaten egg
1/2 cup grated Parmesan cheese
1 tablespoon sugar

Soften yeast in warm water. Cook milk to lukewarm. Meanwhile, sift flour, sugar and salt into bowl. With pastry blender or folk, cut in butter until mixture resembles coarse meal. Add egg, softened yeast and milk and beat well. Stir in cheese and parsley. Turn into greased 8 X 1 1/2-inch round baking dish and cover with damp cloth. Place in warm place until doubled in size. Dot with additional butter and bake at 375 degrees about 25 minutes. Cut in wedges and serve hot, directly from the dish.

## Potato Bread

1 cup riced potatoes
1/2 cup shortening
3 eggs
1 teaspoon salt
8 cups flour
1 cup lukewarm potato water
1/2 cup sugar
1 cup milk
1 yeast cake

Force potatoes through ricer and cool. Cream shortening and sugar. Beat in eggs one at a time. Add potatoes and yeast cake, dissolved in potato water. Add salt, milk and enough flour to make a stiff dough. Mix well. Cover tightly and set in refrigerator overnight. For bread, shape into loaves, cover and let stand in warm place about 1 hour. Bake at 375 degrees for 50 minutes. Brush top with butter. Makes 2 medium or 3 small loaves.

## Dilly Bread

1 yeast cake (or package dry yeast)
1/4 cup lukewarm water
1/4 teaspoon soda
2 tablespoons sugar
1 teaspoon salt
1 tablespoon onion, minced
2 tablespoons dill seed
1 tablespoon butter
1 egg
2 1/2 cups flour
1 cup cottage cheese

Dissolve yeast cake in lukewarm water. Heat cottage cheese to lukewarm. In it dissolve soda, sugar and salt. Add minced onion, dill seed, butter and yeast. Add well beaten egg, then flour in small amount at a time. Makes a soft dough. Let stand in a buttered dish to rise, about one hour. Knead well and place in greased casserole or loaf pan. Let rise again about one hour. Bake at 350 degrees for 40 minutes. Brush with melted butter and sprinkle with salt and dill seed. Very good with spaghetti or Mexican food. Serves 8.

### Yorkshire Pudding

2 large eggs
1 cup milk
1 cup flour
1/2 cup hot fat drippings
1/2 teaspoon salt
1 tablespoon hot drippings
  from roast beef pan

Beat eggs until fluffy. Add milk and beat until well blended. Stir in flour and salt and 1 tablespoon drippings and beat thoroughly. Put 1/2 cup hot drippings (fat) into hot pan and pour in batter which should be about 1/2 inch high in pan. Bake 30 to 40 minutes in 425 degree preheated oven. Serve at once with roast beef and gravy.

### Olivia Risberg's Pizza

*Bill Todd*

1 package hot roll mix
1/4 cup oil
1 number-2 1/2 can Italian-
  style tomatoes, drained
pepper
1/2 pound Mozzarella cheese,
  thinly sliced or garlic
  smoked cheese
oregano
3/4 cup lukewarm water
1 or 2 cloves garlic, minced,
  or garlic salt
salt
cayenne
1 2-ounce can anchovy filets
1/3 cup Parmesan cheese,
  grated

Mix yeast from package with water; stir until dissolved. Add oil and remaining contents of package and mix until smooth dough is formed. Lightly grease top of dough, cover and let rise until double in bulk. Turn onto floured board; knead, and divide into 2 portions. Roll out into 2 very thin, 12-inch rounds. Put on greased cookie sheets and let rise until double in bulk. Brush with oil drained from anchovies, with garlic added. Cover dough with drained tomatoes; season with salt, pepper and cayenne. Arrange sliced cheese and anchovies on top. Sprinkle with Parmesan cheese and oregano. Bake at 400 degrees for 12 to 20 minutes, or until crust is brown. Serve hot, cut in wedges.

DESSERTS
BEVERAGES
FREEZOMINT
CREME DE MENTHE

## The Cracker Crumble

In keeping with the character of The Cracker Crumble, which makes fun and games of nearly everything, presented here for your amusement is the original recipe for Crumble Pie. This fantastically delicious dessert was created for the Cracker Crumble by Henk Versteeg, Convention & Catering Manager of Atlanta's Regency Hyatt House, home of the annual dinner show.

On the other hand, if you're in the mood for a rather large dinner party, you'll find the bulk recipe as submitted by Mr. Versteeg to be usable as well as amusing. The 12-serving version works well and although it hasn't been tested, it is assumed that even that may be halved for six.

The Crumble originated in 1963 as a means of raising funds for the Georgia Press Educational Foundation's scholarship program. It is a political spoof which plays to standing-room-only audiences each fall. The cast is composed of a wide range of personalities from all walks – political, civic, business and professional and none of the players gets paid for their performances.

The Foundation has aided a score of deserving students with grants, loans and scholarships. It has also sponsored workshops for high school publication advisors, provided various services for college journalism teachers and sponsored other community projects aimed at improving newspaper journalism.

### Crumble Pie

Cake

| | |
|---|---|
| 600 eggs | 25 pounds cake flour |
| 37 1/2 pounds sugar | 12 1/2 pounds cocoa |
| 12 1/2 pounds cornstarch | 12 1/2 pounds melted butter |

Filling

| | |
|---|---|
| 100 cups cherries | 12 1/2 gallons cream |
| 100 ounces kirsch | |

*Cake:* Beat egg whites and sugar until stiff peaks form. Sift together cornstarch, cake flour and cocoa. Fold into egg white mixture and add melted butter. Bake at 350 degrees in spring form pans for 25 to 30 minutes. Let cool, then slice into layers of about 1 inch.

*Filling:* Soak cherries in kirsch. Finish cake by alternating layers of cake, whipped cream and cherries. Serves 1200.

To serve 12 (with a 4-layer cake):

Cake

| | |
|---|---|
| 6 egg whites | 1/2 cup cake flour |
| 3/4 cup sugar | 1/4 cup cocoa |
| 1/4 cup cornstarch | 1/4 cup melted butter |

Filling

| | |
|---|---|
| 1 cup red cherries | 1 pint whipping cream (sweetened) |
| 2 tablespoons kirsch | |

## Apple Cake

*Julia Dyar*

Cake

3 eggs
2 cups sugar
1 teaspoon soda
1 teaspoon salt
3 cups flour
1 1/2 cups Wesson oil
3 cups chopped apples
1 cup chopped nuts

Filling

1 1/2 cups light brown sugar
1 stick oleo
1/2 cup pure cream

*Cake:* Place sugar and oil in large bowl. Beat in eggs, one at a time and add other ingredients. Cook in layers with filling.

*Filling:* Boil ingredients and beat well until cool and thick. (Add some nuts to icing.) Bake at 325 degrees for about 50 minutes.

## Apple Crisp

*Laura Conway*

4 large apples, sliced
3/4 cup brown sugar
1/2 cup flour
1/8 teaspoon salt
3/4 cup quick oats
cinnamon
cloves
1/2 – 1 stick butter or oleo

Place apples on bottom of pan. Combine brown sugar, flour, salt and oats with cinnamon and cloves to taste. Put on top of apples. Slice butter over mixture and bake at 350 degrees for about 40 to 45 minutes or until brown on top.

## Grandma's Applesauce Cake

*Julia Dyar*

1 cup sugar
1/2 cup shortening
1 cup raisins
1 cup nuts
2 cups flour
2 cups applesauce with 2 teaspoons soda
1 teaspoon cinnamon
1 teaspoon clove
pinch nutmeg

Cream sugar and shortening. Add remaining ingredients, stirring after each is added. Bake at 350 degrees until done and sides begin to leave pan.

## Oatmeal Cake

*Julia Dyar*

Cake

1 1/2 cups water
1 cup quick oatmeal
1/2 cup Crisco
1 cup light brown sugar
1 cup white sugar
2 eggs, well beaten
1 1/2 cups plain flour
1 teaspoon soda
1 teaspoon salt
1 teaspoon cinnamon
1 teaspoon nutmeg
1 teaspoon vanilla

Topping

1 stick margarine, melted
2 egg yolks
1 cup light brown sugar
1 cup chopped nuts
1 cup angel flake coconut
1 tablespoon milk

*Cake:* Pour boiling water over oatmeal and set aside. Cream the Crisco, brown sugar, white sugar and well beaten eggs. Stir in sifted flour, soda, salt, cinnamon, nutmeg and vanilla. Bake in oblong pan at 350 degrees for 25 minutes.

*Topping:* Combine ingredients and spread over cake. Bake 12 minutes longer at 350 degrees. Cool and cut into squares.

### Old Fashioned Pound Cake

1 pound butter
3 cups sugar
4 cups plain flour
1 teaspoon baking powder
pinch of salt
2 teaspoons vanilla
6 eggs
1/2 cup milk

Let butter and eggs sit at room temperature 1 hour. Sift flour and measure 4 cups. Sift flour, baking powder and salt 3 times. Beat eggs well. Cream butter and sugar. Add eggs and beat well. Add dry ingredients alternately with milk. Add vanilla. Cook in preheated 300-degree oven on middle rack. Cook 2 hours in greased and floured large tube pan. Do not open door while cooking. Turn out on plate as soon as done.

### Pecan Cake

*Lena Sturges*

1 stick butter or margarine
2 cups sugar
4 eggs
2 cups all-purpose flour
2 squares unsweetened chocolate, melted and cooled
6 cups shelled pecans (1 1/2 pounds)

Cream butter or margarine and sugar until light and fluffy. Add eggs, one at a time, and beat well after each addition. Stir in cooled, melted chocolate. Mix flour with pecans, and stir to coat. Add to creamed mixture and stir well (this may have to be done by hand). Grease a 9-inch tube pan and line with greased very heavy paper (this is a very important step). Spoon batter into pan and cover with heavy paper, well greased. Bake at 250 degrees for about 2 hours, or until cake tests done when straw or cake tester is inserted into center of cake. Check carefully after 2 hours to see that cake does not overcook.

## Plum Cake

*Laura Conway*

2 cups self-rising flour
2 jars baby food plums
2 cups sugar
1 cup Wesson oil
1 teaspoon cloves
1 teaspoon cinnamon
3 eggs
1 cup nuts

Mix sugar, oil and eggs. Add plums. Mix spices with flour and combine with plum mixture. Add nuts and bake at 350 degrees for 1 hour.

## Red Velvet Cake

Cake

1/2 cup shortening
2 eggs
1 teaspoon vanilla
1 teaspoon salt
1 teaspoon soda
1 tablespoon vinegar
1 1/2 cups sugar
1 ounce red food coloring
2 tablespoons cocoa
1 cup buttermilk
2 1/2 cups flour

Butter Icing

1/4 cup soft margarine
1 box confectioners sugar (sifted)
3 tablespoons cream
dash salt
1 teaspoon vanilla

*Cake:* Cream shortening, sugar and vanilla. Add eggs one at a time. Make thin paste of cocoa and food coloring and add to creamed mixture. Sift flour and salt together, then alternate buttermilk and flour to creamed mixture one tablespoon at a time beginning and ending with flour. Mix soda and vinegar and add to mixture. Bake in 2 8-1 or 9-inch pans for 30 minutes at 350 degrees.

*Icing:* Beat on low speed until blended, then beat on high speed until thick enough to spread. More cream or confectioners sugar may be added to give desired consistency.

### Brown Sugar Pound Cake

*Mildred Dadisman*

1 pound brown sugar
1 cup white sugar
1 1/2 cups butter
5 large eggs
3 cups flour
1/2 teaspoon baking powder
1 cup milk

Cream butter and sugar. Add eggs one at a time. Add baking powder to flour. Alternate milk and flour to mixture. Bake at 350 degrees for 1 1/2 hours.

### Sunny Coffee Cake

Cake

1 1/2 cups sifted enriched flour
3/4 cup sugar
2 teaspoons baking powder
3/4 teaspoon salt
3/4 cup milk
1 teaspoon grated orange rind
1 egg, beaten
1/3 cup butter or margarine, melted

Icing

1 cup confectioners' sugar
2 tablespoons chopped nuts
2 tablespoons milk

*Cake:* Sift together flour, sugar, baking powder and salt. Stir in orange rind. Combine milk, egg and butter. Add liquid ingredients to dry ingredients, stirring only until well blended. Pour into well greased 5 1/2-cup ring mold. Bake in moderate oven (375 degrees) for 30 to 35 minutes. Cool on rack about 5 minutes. Loosen edges with spatula, invert and remove from pan.

*Icing:* Stir confectioners' sugar and 2 tablespoons milk until smooth. Spread over top of cake and sprinkle with nuts. (For professional touch, allow icing to drip down sides of cake.)

### Franklin Cake

*Julia Dyar*

1 pound butter (or margarine)
2 cups sugar
6 eggs
4 cups flour
1 teaspoon baking powder
1/4 teaspoon salt
1 pound cherries, chopped
1 pound pineapple, chopped
4 cups pecans, chopped
2 teaspoons vanilla

Cream butter and sugar. Add beaten eggs and vanilla. Add 3 cups of flour sifted with baking powder and salt. Dredge fruit and nuts with 1 cup of flour. Pour into tube pan, greased heavily and coated with brown paper. Bake at 250 degrees for 3 hours.

### Carrot Cake

*Mrs. Peter J. Bailey*

Cake

2 cups flour
2 cups sugar
1/4 teaspoon salt
1 teaspoon soda
1 teaspoon baking powder
1 teaspoon cinnamon
1 1/2 cups vegetable oil
4 eggs
2 cups grated carrots

Icing

1 stick butter, (room temperature)
1 box powdered sugar
1 cup chopped nuts
1 8-ounce cream cheese, (room temperature)
2 teaspoons vanilla

*Cake:* Sift dry ingredients together. Beat oil and eggs, then combine with dry ingredients. Fold in carrots. Makes 3 or 4 layers. Bake at 375 degrees for 25 minutes.

*Icing:* Cream butter and cheese. Slowly mix in sugar until creamy. Add nuts and vanilla.

### English Trifle

*Mrs. Joseph B. Parham*

1 one-pound pound cake, cut into thin slices
1 small can sliced peaches (or fresh peaches)
1 Jello Vanilla Pudding made with 2 1/2 cups of milk (not instant Jello)
2 bananas

Arrange one layer of cake in 12 X 8 X 2-inch dish. Place bananas, peaches and a little peach juice on cake, then cover with pudding. Continue in layers, being sure to cover the last layer with pudding. Save a few slices of peaches and bananas for decoration. Cover with wax paper and chill for at least 8 hours before serving.

### Fruited Cheese Cake

*Mrs. Bob Rutherford*

Crust

1 cup graham cracker crumbs
1/8 pound melted butter
2 tablespoons brown sugar

Filling

2 large cream cheese (8 ounces each)
1 can cherry, blueberry or strawberry pie filling
3/4 cup sugar
5 eggs, separated
1 teaspoon vanilla

*Crust:* Work together graham cracker crumbs, butter and sugar and cover bottom of 9-inch spring form pan.

*Filling:* Cream sugar, cream cheese, vanilla and egg yolks. Beat egg whites until stiff. Fold egg whites into mixture and pour into crust. Bake 40 to 45 minutes until nicely browned at 350 degrees. Turn off heat and leave oven door open a few minutes. Chill thoroughly.

Put can of pie filling in cavity a couple of hours before serving.

## "Sweet to Your Heart" Cake
(Low Cholesterol)

*Mrs. Albert S. Jenkins*

1 cup vegetable shortening
1 1/2 cups sugar
4 eggs
2 cups plain flour
1 1/2 teaspoons baking powder
1/2 cup milk or water
2 teaspoons lemon flavoring

Preheat oven to 300 degrees. Line tube cake pan with waxed paper. Grease pan with shortening.

Cream 1 cup vegetable shortening. Add sugar a little at a time. Mix well. Add 1 egg at a time. Mix well.

Measure flour. Sift and measure again. Add 1 1/2 teaspoons baking powder to flour and sift again. (3 times in all). Stir flour, baking powder mixture into first mixture, adding milk (or water) alternately. Add flavoring. Bake at 300 degrees. Brown at 325 degrees. Cook about 1 1/2 hours, or until cake shrinks from edge of pan. Serve warm.

## Lemonade Cake

*Mrs. John Newsome*

Cake

2 cups flour
4 eggs
3/4 cup wesson oil
3/4 cup hot water
1 package lemon jello
1 cup sugar

Icing

1 can concentrated lemonade
1 cup sugar

*Cake:* Blend ingredients and beat until smooth. Bake at 350 degrees for 1 hour.

*Icing:* Blend and pour over cake when baked. Let stand 2 hours.

## Zwieback Cake
(or Torte)

*Julia Dyar*

Cake

1 cup zwieback crumbs
6 eggs, separated
1 cup sugar
1 cup chopped pecans
1 teaspoon cinnamon
1 teaspoon baking powder
pinch of salt

Sauce

2 tablespoons sugar
1/2 pint whipped cream
1/2 cup bourbon
dash of nutmeg

*Cake:* Roll crumbs between sheets of waxed paper. Cream 4 egg yolks with sugar; add crumbs, nuts, spice and baking powder. Then fold in 6 egg whites, stiffly beaten. Put into 2 8-inch layer pans. Bake at 325 degrees for 30 minutes.

*Sauce:* When layers are cool, stack together with whipped cream. Beat in 2 remaining egg yolks, add 2 tablespoons sugar and beat until foamy. Add 1/2 cup bourbon and nutmeg. Fold in whipped cream.

## Grand Ma's Tea Cakes

*Vicki Rogers*

2 1/4 cups (1 pound) sugar
1 cup butter
2 eggs
1 teaspoon cream of tartar
1 teaspoon soda
6 tablespoons warm water
5 cups flour
flavoring

Sift dry ingredients together. Cream butter and sugar. Add dry ingredients and water; knead. Cool, then roll thin. Cut and bake in moderate (350 degrees) oven for 10 minutes. Sprinkle with sugar.

## Fudge Cake

*Mae Chalker*

Cake

2 sticks melted butter
(or oleo)
1 1/2 cups sugar
3 eggs
1/2 cup cocoa
1 cup flour
1/2 teaspoon baking powder
pinch salt
1/2 teaspoon vanilla
1 cup pecans, chopped

Icing

2 cups sugar
1 stick butter
1/3 cup cocoa
1/2 cup milk
1/2 teaspoon vanilla

*Cake:* Add melted butter to sugar and beat. Add 3 eggs, one at a time, beating after each addition. Blend thoroughly with remaining ingredients. Bake at 350 degrees in 9 X 15-inch pan about 25 to 30 minutes.

*Chocolate Icing:* Stir over medium heat until mixture comes to boiling point. Then cook without stirring exactly one minute. Cool and add 1/2 teaspoon vanilla. Beat and spread on cake.

## Papa's Chocolate Icing

*Mrs. Thomas Hubert Frier*

2 squares chocolate, melted
3 cups sugar
3 tablespoons white Karo
syrup
1 cup milk
few grains of salt
1/2 teaspoon vanilla
1/4 cup butter

Combine, then cook over low heat, stirring until sugar is dissolved. Cook to very soft stage (228 to 229 degrees). Remove, add butter and vanilla. Cool. Beat.

## Foolproof Layer Cake

*Mary S. Mallard*

1 package Duncan Hines Yellow Cake Mix
1 package (4 ounces) vanilla jello pudding
4 eggs
3/4 cup Wesson or cooking oil
1 cup water
salt as desired

Mix dry ingredients, add water; beat in eggs one at the time. Add salt and beat in oil slowly. Place in greased, floured cake pans. Bake at 325 degrees for 30 minutes.

## Perfect Chocolate Frosting

*Mary S. Mallard*

2 1/2 squares baking chocolate
2 1/2 cups sugar
2 tablespoons white Karo syrup
2 tablespoons butter
3/4 cup sweet milk
1 teaspoon vanilla
dash of salt

Melt chocolate in milk, strain into sugar. (If cocoa is used, mix 5 tablespoons with sugar, mix thoroughly with hot milk.) Add Karo, mixing well. Boil until mixture forms soft ball in cold water. Remove from heat, add butter and vanilla. Cool about 20 or 30 minutes (according to temperature). Beat until slick and mixture pops when beaten.

## Funny Cake

Pastry

1 recipe regular pie dough
2 8-inch pie tins

Chocolate Syrup

3/4 cup granulated sugar
1/2 cup cocoa
3/4 cup water

Cake Batter

1/2 cup shortening
2 cups granulated sugar
2 eggs
2 cups all-purpose flour
1 teaspoon baking powder
1 cup milk
1 teaspoon vanilla

*Pastry:* Line pie tins with pastry. Set aside.

*Syrup:* Combine sugar, cocoa and water; boil about 10 minutes or until it thickens a little. Cool.

*Cake batter:* Cream shortening, sugar and eggs together. Sift dry ingredients together; add alternately with milk to creamed mixture. Blend in vanilla.

Spread chocolate mixture; dividing evenly, into pastry-lined pie tins. Pour half of the cake batter over each chocolate filled pastry shell. Bake for 35 minutes at 375 degrees. Serve topped with whipped cream or ice cream, if desired.

## Gingerbread

Cake

1 cup molasses
1/2 cup sugar
1/2 cup melted margarine
2 teaspoons ginger
2 teaspoons cloves or allspice
1/2 teaspoon soda
1/2 cup boiling water
1/2 cup apple juice
2 1/2 cups sifted flour
2 well beaten eggs

Sauce

1 cup sugar
1 tablespoon flour
1 cup boiling water
juice and rind of 1 lemon
2 tablespoons butter

*Cake:* Put molasses in bowl, add sugar, melted shortening, ginger and cloves. Dissolve soda in boiling water; add apple juice, and add to first mixture. Then add flour and eggs. Batter will be very thin. Do not fill pan more than 1/2 full. Cook for 30 minutes in 375-degree oven. Store in covered pan.

*Sauce:* Mix first three ingredients and let this come to a boil. Boil several minutes. Add lemon juice and rind. When slightly thick, take off stove and add butter.

## Hot Milk Cake

*Wanda Jared*

3 eggs
2 cups sugar
1 stick margarine or butter
2 cups self-rising flour
1 cup hot sweet milk
1 teaspoon vanilla

Beat eggs, then add sugar and dry ingredients. Melt butter in milk; add it and vanilla to mixture. Bake in 2 9-inch layer pans for 25 minutes at 350 degrees. Frost with chocolate icing.

## Sour Cream Cake

*Linda Cleary*

1/2 pound butter
3 cups sugar
1 cup sour cream
6 eggs, separated
3 cups sifted flour
1/4 teaspoon baking soda
1 teaspoon vanilla

Cream butter and sugar then blend thoroughly with sour cream and egg yolks. Add sifted flour, baking soda and vanilla. Beat egg whites until fluffy and fold into mixture. Bake in greased, floured tube pan at 325 degrees for 1 1/4 hours.

## Cocoa and Cola Cake

*Mrs. Donna Hunt*
*The Denison Herald*
*Denison, Texas*

Cake

1 cup butter, softened
2 cups flour
1 3/4 cups sugar
3 tablespoons cocoa
1 teaspoon soda
1 teaspoon vanilla
2 eggs
1/2 cup buttermilk
1 cup cola
1 1/2 cups miniature marshmallows

Icing

1/2 cup softened butter
3 tablespoons cocoa
1/3 cup cola
3 cups powdered sugar
1 cup toasted chopped nuts

*Cake:* Combine all ingredients except cola and marshmallows. Then add cola and stir in marshmallows by hand. Bake in 11 X 13-inch greased, floured pan at 350 degrees for 40 to 45 minutes.

*Icing:* Combine butter, cocoa, cola and sugar. Stir in toasted nuts.

## Brown Sugar Pound Cake

*Mrs. Belmont Dennis*

3 sticks butter
1 one-pound box brown sugar
3/4 cup white sugar
1 cup sweet milk
5 eggs, separated
3 cups plain flour
1/2 teaspoon Calumet
  baking powder
2 teaspoons vanilla
1 cup finely chopped pecans

Whip egg whites, adding 5 tablespoons white sugar while whipping. Set in refrigerator until rest of cake is mixed.

Cream butter and gradually add rest of white and brown sugar. Beat until light; add egg yolks and beat well. Add flour and milk alternately and beat at low speed. Fold in beaten egg whites and lightly floured nuts. Fold in until lightly mixed. Pour into greased, floured 10-inch tube pan. Bake 1 hour and 40 minutes at 325 degrees.

## Sour Cream Pound Cake

1 carton sour cream
3 cups flour
1 cup butter
6 eggs
3 cups sugar
1/4 teaspoon soda
1/4 teaspoon salt
1 teaspoon vanilla
1 teaspoon almond

Cream butter and 2 cups sugar. Add egg yolks one at a time, beating well after each addition. Sift flour, soda and salt. Sift again. Add flour and sour cream alternately to butter and sugar mixture.

Beat egg whites and last cup of sugar until stiff. Fold into batter. Blend in flavorings. Bake at 325 degrees for 1 1/2 hours.

## Lemon Cheesecake

*Fran Parkman*

Crust

1 cup graham cracker crumbs
3 tablespoons sugar
3 tablespoons butter, melted

Filling

9 tablespoons sugar
1 envelope unflavored gelatin
1 cup milk
2 8-ounce packages cream cheese, cut-up
2 eggs, separated
1/3 cup fresh lemon juice
1 tablespoon grated lemon rind
1 pint whipping cream

*Crust:* Blend cracker crumbs, butter and sugar in bowl. Press 3/4 cup over bottom of 8-inch spring-form pan. (If desired, use all cracker crumbs for crust; top filling with strawberries.)

*Filling:* Mix gelatin and 5 tablespoons sugar in a saucepan; beat in milk and egg yolks. Cook, stirring constantly, until gelatin dissolves. Remove from heat and blend in cream cheese, lemon juice and rind until smooth. Chill, stirring often until mixture mounds lightly.

Beat egg whites until foamy. Beat in remaining 4 tablespoons sugar until meringue stands in firm peaks. Fold meringue, then whipped cream into gelatin mixture. Pour into prepared pan. Sprinkle remaining cracker crumbs on top and chill until firm.

## Famous Orange Chiffon Cake

(Mrs. Nora Lawrence Smith's Favorite)

*Mrs. F. M. Tison*

2 1/2 cups sifted cake flour
1 1/2 cups sugar
3 teaspoons double acting baking powder
1 teaspoon salt
1/2 cup cooking oil (or salad oil)
1/2 teaspoon cream of tartar
5 unbeaten egg yolks
grated rind of two oranges (about two tablespoons)
juice of 2 medium-sized oranges, plus water to make 1/4 cup
1 cup egg whites (7 or 8)

Sift cake flour once. Measure. Add sugar, baking powder and salt, then sift into mixing bowl. Make a "well" in the flour and add cooking oil, unbeaten egg yolks, grated orange rind and orange juice and water. Beat with spoon until really smooth. Place measured egg whites into large separate bowl. Add cream of tartar and whip until whites form very stiff peaks. (Much stiffer than for angel food or meringue.) Do not underbeat. Pour flour and egg yolk batter from first bowl gradually over whipped egg whites, gently folding in with rubber scraper just until blended. Do not stir.

Pour into ungreased 10-inch tube cake pan (4 inches deep), and bake in moderately slow oven (325 degrees) for 65 minutes, or until done. Immediately turn pan upside down, placing tube of pan over neck of funnel or bottle, or rest edges on two other pans. Let stand free of table until cold. Loosen from sides and tube with spatula. Turn pan over and hit edges sharply on table to loosen. Delicious uniced, or served with whipped cream, berries, ice cream or dessert sauce.

## Coffee-Coffee Cake

2 cups sifted all-purpose flour
1 cup sugar
3 teaspoons baking powder
2 teaspoons instant coffee powder
1/2 teaspoon salt
1/2 teaspoon cinnamon
5 tablespoons melted butter or margarine, divided
1 cup milk
1 egg, beaten
1 teaspoon vanilla
1/2 cup crushed corn flakes
2 tablespoons sugar

Mix and sift first 5 ingredients. Combine 3 tablespoons melted butter, milk, beaten egg and vanilla. Stir into dry ingredients. Stir until blended. Turn into greased 8-inch square pan. Combine corn flake crumbs, remaining 2 tablespoons melted butter, 2 tablespoons sugar and cinnamon; mix well. Scatter evenly over batter in pan. Bake at 350 degrees for 45 minutes or until cake tests done. Serve warm, cut into squares.

## Charlotte Russe

3 egg whites
6 marshmallows, chopped
1 bottle Maraschino cherries, chopped
1 pint cream, whipped
1/2 cup sugar
1/2 cup orange juice
1 tablespoon gelatin

Beat cream until stiff. Beat egg whites and add sugar slowly, then fold in cherries, orange juice and marshmallows. Add the gelatin which has been soaked in 1/2 cup cold water for 5 minutes and then dissolved over hot water. When all of this mixture begins to stiffen, put in the cream and turn into a mold.

## Sour Cream Coffee Cake

*Shirley McCullough*

1/3 cup brown sugar, firmly packed
1 cup pecans or walnuts, chopped
2 eggs
2 cups sifted flour
1 teaspoon baking soda
1 cup sour cream
1/4 cup granulated sugar
1 teaspoon cinnamon
1 cup butter
1 cup sugar
1 teaspoon vanilla
1 teaspoon baking powder
1/2 teaspoon salt

Combine brown sugar, granulated sugar, cinnamon and nuts in a bowl; set aside.

Cream butter and sugar until fluffy in bowl. Add eggs, one at a time, beating well after each addition. Add vanilla. Combine sifted flour, baking powder, soda and salt; add to butter and egg mixture alternately with sour cream. Pour half the batter into greased 13 X 9 X 2 pan and sprinkle with half the nut mixture. Top with remaining batter, sprinkling rest of nut mixture on top. Bake at 350 degrees for 35 minutes. Serve hot.

## Cheeseless Cheese Cake

1 package lemon or lime jello
1/2 cup sugar
juice of 1 lemon or lime
1-pound can evaporated milk, chilled
1 cup boiling water
vanilla wafers

Dissolve jello in boiling water; add sugar and lemon juice and chill until slightly congealed. Whip jello, add whipped evaporated milk. Line pie plate with vanilla wafers and pour mixture into it. Sprinkle top with crushed wafers. Chill until firm.

## Mocha Torte

### Torte

4 squares (1 ounce each) unsweetened chocolate
1/2 cup water
2/3 cup milk
1 3/4 cups sugar, divided
2 cups sifted cake flour
1 teaspoon baking soda
1 teaspoon salt
1/2 cup butter or margarine
3 eggs
1 teaspoon vanilla

### Coffee Butter Frosting

1/2 cup sweet butter
cold coffee
3 cups confectioners sugar

### Chocolate Glaze

1 package (6 ounces) semi-sweet chocolate pieces
2 tablespoons milk
1 tablespoon shortening
3 tablespoons light corn syrup

*Torte:* Heat chocolate with water in top of double boiler. Cook and stir over boiling water until chocolate is melted and mixture is thickened. Add 1/2 cup of the sugar. Cook 2 minutes, stirring constantly. Cool to lukewarm. Measure sifted flour. Add baking soda and salt; sift together 3 times. Cream butter or margarine. Add remaining 1 1/4 cups sugar; cream together until very smooth. Add eggs, one at a time, beating thoroughly after each addition. Add flour mixture alternately with milk in small amounts, beating after each addition until smooth. Add chocolate mixture and vanilla. Blend. Bake in 2 greased 9-inch layer cake pans at 350 degrees for about 30 minutes. Cool. Fill and frost top and sides with Coffee Butter Frosting. Pour Chocolate Glaze over top, letting it drip

*Frosting:* Cream butter. Add sugar while continuing to cream, adding enough strong cold coffee to make frosting fluffy and easy to spread on cake.

*Glaze:* Melt package of semi-sweet chocolate pieces and shortening over hot (not boiling) water. Remove from heat. Blend in corn syrup and milk; pour immediately over frosting.

## Lemon Cheese Cake

*Mary (Mrs. Thomas) Burson*

### Cake

- 6 egg whites
- 2 cups sugar
- 1 cup sweet milk
- 1/2 teaspoon salt
- 2 cups flour
- 1 cup butter
- 2 teaspoons baking powder
- 1 teaspoon vanilla

### Filling

- 6 egg yolks
- 2 lemons
- 1 1/2 cups sugar
- butter (egg-sized)

### Seven Minute Frosting

- 2 egg whites, unbeaten
- 5 tablespoons water
- 1 1/2 teaspoons light corn syrup
- dash of salt
- 1/2 cup sugar
- 1 teaspoon vanilla

*Cake:* Sift flour, salt and baking powder together. Cream butter and sugar thoroughly. Add flour mixture alternately with milk, beating well after each addition. Add vanilla and fold in well beaten egg whites. Bake in 3 layers in 9-inch pans at 350 degrees for 20 minutes or until done.

*Filling:* Mix all ingredients together and cook in double boiler until thick enough to spread between layers.

*Frosting:* Combine ingredients except vanilla and place in double boiler. Mix with rotary egg beater. Place over rapidly boiling water, beating constantly, and cook 7 minutes or until frosting will peak. Remove from boiling water, add vanilla, and beat until ready to spread.

## German Chocolate Cake

Cake

1 1/2 sticks butter
1 1/2 cups sugar
1 teaspoon vanilla
3 eggs
3/4 cup milk
2 1/4 cups plain flour
2 1/4 teaspoons baking powder
1 package German chocolate

Filling

4 egg yolks
1 can evaporated milk
  (13-ounce size)
1 1/2 cups sugar
1 teaspoon vanilla
1 cup chopped pecans
1 cup grated coconut
1 stick butter

*Cake:* Cream butter and sugar and add vanilla. Beat eggs and add to milk. Sift flour and baking powder. Add milk and eggs and flour to sugar and butter. Blend in chocolate that has been melted with 1 tablespoon water. Bake in 2 rectangular layer pans, 7 X 11 inches, for 25 minutes at 350 degrees.

*Filling:* Beat egg yolks and mix with milk and sugar, add vanilla, nuts, coconut and butter. Cook over low heat until thick enough to spread on cake.

## Chocolate Ice Cream

5 squares unsweetened
  chocolate, melted
5 cups milk
2 1/2 cups sugar
5 tablespoons flour
3/4 teaspoon salt
4 eggs, slightly beaten
5 cups cream
2 teaspoons vanilla

Scald milk over low heat. Stir in melted chocolate. Combine sugar, flour and salt in a bowl; add eggs and mix well. Pour hot milk over egg mixture carefully, stirring constantly. Cook over low heat until mixture coats a spoon. Chill in refrigerator. Stir in cream and vanilla.

### Chocolate Delight Cake

1 pound sweet chocolate
1 tablespoon flour
2 tablespoons sugar
whipped cream
2/3 cup soft butter
4 eggs, separated
6 teaspoons dark rum

(the above measurements are correct)

Set oven for 425 degrees. Line a round 8-inch cake pan with waxed paper. Melt the chocolate (this must be the sweet variety) in a teaspoon of water in double boiler over hot but not boiling water. Remove from heat and stir in the flour and 1 tablespoon of sugar, which have been sifted together. Stir in soft butter, mixing thoroughly. Stir in vigorously beaten egg yolks, a little at a time, stirring after each addition until smooth. Mix stiffly beaten whites into mixture ever so gently. Transfer to the baking pan and bake for 15 minutes. The cake at this point is still soft, so take care in removing from oven. As it cools it gains a delightful consistency. When cool, remove from pan and cut in wedges.

For topping, combine whipped cream and rum, gradually adding remaining tablespoonful of sugar. Place on top of each wedge of cake. Serves six.

### Chocolate Chip-Mint Ice Cream

4 eggs
2 cups sugar
1/4 teaspoon salt
6 2/3 cups evaporated milk
(4 13-ounce cans)
1 1/2 cups grated milk chocolate
1 1/2 teaspoons mint extract

Add sugar gradually to beaten eggs and continue to beat until stiff. Stir in remaining ingredients.

### Banana Nut Cake

Cake

1 cup shortening
4 eggs (reserve 1 white for frosting)
2 1/2 cups plain flour
1 cup mashed bananas
1 teaspoon soda (dissolved in buttermilk)
1 1/2 cups sugar
1/2 cup buttermilk
1 cup broken pecans

Frosting

1 stick butter
1 egg white
milk to spread
1 box confectioners sugar
1/2 cup broken pecans

*Cake:* Cream together shortening and sugar. Add eggs, one at a time, beating well after each addition. Add flour alternately with buttermilk and soda (beginning and ending with flour). Add bananas and nuts and beat well. Pour into layer pans that have been greased and floured. Bake at 350 degrees for 20 to 25 minutes.

*Frosting:* Cream butter and egg white until smooth. Add sugar and beat until smooth. Add enough milk to spread easily. Add nuts.

### Nut Brittle Ice Cream

vanilla ice cream recipe
2 cups crushed nut brittle

Prepare any vanilla ice cream recipe. Churn for about 15 minutes or until the ice cream has frozen to a mushy consistency. Add crushed nut brittle and continue freezing as directed.

## Walnut Glory Cake

*Mrs. Belmont Dennis*

3/4 cup flour
2 teaspoons cinnamon
2 cups finely chopped
  walnuts
1 teaspoon salt
9 eggs, separated
1 1/2 cups sugar
2 teaspoons vanilla

Combine flour, cinnamon and salt. Beat egg whites in large mixing bowl until soft mounds form. Gradually add 3/4 cup sugar. Continue beating until very stiff straight peaks form. Do not underbeat.

Combine egg yolks, vanilla and remaining sugar in small mixing bowl. Beat until thick and lemon colored. Stir in dry ingredients. Fold batter gently and thoroughly into egg whites, using a wire whip or rubber spatula. Fold in walnuts. Turn into ungreased 10-inch tube pan. Bake at 350 degrees for 55 to 65 minutes. Invert immediately. Cool completely before removing from pan.

Frost with a vanilla glaze. Sprinkle with confectioners sugar or serve with whipped cream.

## Strawberry Sherbet

6 10-ounce packages
  frozen, sweetened
  strawberries, thawed
2 cups milk
1/2 cup orange juice
1/8 teaspoon cinnamon

Puree strawberries and strain through a sieve to remove seeds. Combine them with remainder of ingredients and freeze as directed. Makes about 3 quarts.

## Baked Pears Elegante

4 medium Bartlett pears
1 cup red wine
1 cup sugar
3 inches stick cinnamon
6 whole cloves
1/4 teaspoon salt
6 thin slices lemon

Pare, halve, and core pears; place in 10 X 6 X 1 1/2-inch baking dish. In saucepan, combine remaining ingredients, adding a few drops red food coloring, if desired; bring to boiling point. Pour over pears. Bake, covered, in moderate oven (350 degrees) for 20 minutes. Uncover and bake 10 minutes longer or until pears are tender, basting once or twice to glaze pears. Serve hot in sauce, or chill and top with whipped cream. Makes 4 servings.

## Pound Cake (Variation)

*Julia Dyar*

Cake

1 cup Crisco
2 cups sugar (scant cups)
5 or 6 eggs
1/2 egg shell of water
2 1/3 cups flour
1 teaspoon vanilla

Icing

1/8 teaspoon cloves
1/8 teaspoon nutmeg
1/4 cup butter
1 egg
dash of salt
1 box confectioners sugar
grated rind of 1 lemon
3 tablespoons lemon juice

*Cake:* Cream Crisco and sugar until well blended; add eggs, one at a time, beating well after each addition. Add vanilla and water. Sift flour 4 times and stir into mixture. Bake at 350 degrees for 1/2 hour and at 325 degrees for 1/2 hour.

*Icing:* Place all ingredients in bowl and beat until smooth and fluffy and of spreading consistency.

## Fresh Peach Cobbler

*Grandma Pafford*

2 cups sugar
3/4 cup flour
3/4 stick butter, melted
3 cups peaches
2 teaspoons baking powder
3/4 cup milk
salt

Combine 1 cup sugar, flour, baking powder, milk and salt. Pour into deep dish with melted butter. Do not stir. Add peaches mixed with 1 cup sugar. Bake 1 hour at 350 degrees.

## Praline Cake

1 package cake mix, yellow
1 pound light brown sugar
2 eggs, beaten
1 1/2 cups pecans
1/2 cup butter
2 tablespoons flour
1 teaspoon vanilla

Prepare yellow cake mix according to package directions. Pour batter into 2 greased, floured 13 X 9 X 2-inch pans. Bake in a moderate oven (350 degrees) until done, about 30 minutes. Remove from oven; cool before frosting.

Melt butter in a skillet. Mix brown sugar, flour and beaten eggs. Add to butter in skillet and cook for 3 minutes over low heat. Remove from heat and stir in vanilla and pecans, coarsely chopped. Spread evenly over surfaces of cakes. Return cakes to oven and bake at 400 degrees for 8 minutes in order to set the frosting. Cook, then cut into 1 1/2-inch strips for party service. Makes 60 bite-sized servings.

### Fabulous Vanilla Ice Cream

*Glenn McCullough*

2 quarts milk
12 egg yolks
3 cups sugar
2 quarts whipping cream
2 teaspoons pure vanilla extract

Make custard of beaten eggs, sugar and milk; cooking at low temperature, stirring constantly until thickened. Cool. Whip cream, but not stiff. Add the custard and whip again. Add vanilla, mix and freeze in hand turned or electric freezer.

### Colorful Sherbet Cake

*Mrs. Otis A. (Martha Lee) Brumby, Jr.*

2 quarts sherbet (lime, raspberry, orange or any combination)
1 1/2 to 2 quarts vanilla and pistachio ice cream
1/2 cup shredded German sweet chocolate
1/2 cup toasted almonds
1 pint whipping cream

Fill large angel food cake pan to within 2 1/2 to 3 inches from top with sherbet balls, using approximately 2 quarts sherbet. Place pan in freezer to keep while mixing remaining ingredients.

Soften ice cream in large bowl. Add shredded chocolate and almonds. Pour softened ice cream mixture around sherbet balls and quickly place in freezer. Freeze until firm.

When ready to serve, loosen around edges of pan with warm knife. Turn out on serving platter. Cover top and sides of cake with sweetened whipped cream tinted a pale green. Cake may be garnished with fruits and berries.

### Dark Fruit Cake

*Sara Spano*

5 eggs, separated
1/2 cup molasses
1/4 cup grape juice
1 cup butter
1 cup sugar
1 1/3 cups raisins
1/2 pound candied pineapple, cut up
1/2 pound whole candied cherries
1 1/4 cups chopped dates
1/4 pound chopped citron
1/4 pound chopped orange peel
1/4 pound chopped lemon peel
1 3/4 cups chopped pecans
2 cups sifted flour
1/2 teaspoon nutmeg
1/2 teaspoon ground cloves
1/2 teaspoon mace
1 teaspoon cinnamon
1 teaspoon baking soda

Beat egg yolks; combine with molasses and grape juice. Cream butter and sugar; add egg yolk mixture, blending well. Combine fruits and nuts and mix with 1 cup flour. Place flour-fruit-nut mixture in 200-degree oven and heat for 5 minutes.

Sift remaining flour with spices and soda. Beat egg whites until peaks form. Fold gently into creamed mixture; carefully fold in fruits and nuts and dry ingredients.

Grease 9-inch tube pan, line with brown paper and grease again. Pour in cake mixture and bake at 300 degrees for 2 hours. Place on rack to cool. Wrap securely in foil and store in cold place.

## Japanese Fruit Cake

*Mrs. Belmont Dennis*

Cake

1 cup butter
2 cups sugar
4 eggs
1 cup buttermilk
1 cup raisins
1 cup chopped nuts
3 cups flour
1/2 teaspoon salt
1 teaspoon cinnamon
1 teaspoon allspice
1 teaspoon cloves
1 teaspoon nutmeg
1 teaspoon soda

Filling

2 boxes (6 ounces each) coconut
2 1/2 cups sugar
2 tablespoons flour
2 lemons, grated rinds and juice
1 1/2 cups hot water

*Cake:* Cream butter and sugar; add eggs, one at a time, beating well after each addition with electric mixer. Sift dry ingredients and combine the two mixtures alternately with the buttermilk. Flour raisins and nuts and gently fold into mixture. Pour into 4 layer cake pans that have been greased and lined with greased paper. Bake at 300 degrees for about 50 minutes or until cake leaves sides of pan.

*Filling:* Combine all ingredients and cook until thick. Cool slightly and put between and on top of layers.

## Pumpkin Cake

*Mrs. Belmont Dennis*

Cake

1 1/2 cups corn oil
2 cups sugar
3 cups plain flour
2 teaspoons soda
3 teaspoons cinnamon
1 teaspoon allspice
1 teaspoon salt
2 cups pumpkin
2 teaspoons vanilla
4 eggs
1 cup raisins
1 cup chopped nuts

Icing

1 cup evaporated milk
1 cup sugar
3 egg yolks
1 teaspoon vanilla
1 stick butter or margarine
1 can angel flake coconut
1 cup chopped nuts

*Cake:* Preheat oven to 300 degrees. Grease and flour a 10-inch tube pan.

Combine corn oil, sugar, flour, spices, baking powder, salt, soda and pumpkin. Add eggs, one at a time, beating well after each addition. Toss nuts and raisins in 2 tablespoons flour, then add with vanilla to mixture. Pour into tube pan and bake for 1 1/2 hours.

*Icing:* Combine milk, sugar, egg yolks, margarine and vanilla in saucepan. Cook over medium heat, stirring constantly until mixture thickens. (About 12 minutes.) Remove from heat. Add coconut and pecans. Beat until cool and of spreading consistency.

### Dark Beauty Fruit Cake

*Sara Spano*

2 cups chopped walnuts
1 1/2 cups chopped dates
1 cup chopped mixed candied cherries and peel (orange or lemon)
3 eggs, beaten
1 28-ounce jar ready-to-use mincemeat
1 1/2 cups sifted flour
3/4 cup granulated sugar
1/2 teaspoon baking powder
1/2 teaspoon salt

Combine walnuts, dates, candied fruit and mincemeat. Stir in beaten eggs. Combine remaining ingredients and stir into batter until well blended. Pack into a well greased 9-inch tube pan and bake at 300 degrees for about 2 1/2 hours. Cool completely; remove from pan and wrap in foil for storage.

### Holiday Pound Cake

*Julia Dyar*

6 eggs
4 cups plain flour
1 pound light brown sugar
1 pound butter (do not substitute)
1/2 pound candied cherries
1/2 pound candied pineapple
2 cups pecans
1 1/2 teaspoons vanilla flavoring
1/2 teaspoon salt

Cream butter and sugar slowly. Add eggs, one at a time, beating well after each addition. Add flavoring. Add sifted dry ingredients slowly. Then, add cherries, pineapple and nuts. Bake 1 hour at 300 to 325 degrees, or until well done.

## Rum Cream Pie

*Mrs. James R. Blair*

Crust

16 graham crackers
1/4 cup sugar
1/2 stick softened butter or margarine

Filling

6 egg yolks
1 cup sugar
1 tablespoon plain gelatin
1/2 cup water
1 pint cream
1/2 cup rum
bittersweet chocolate

*Crust:* Roll graham crackers until fine. Work in sugar and butter. Press evenly and firmly into an even layer against sides and bottom of lightly greased pie pan. Bake about 8 minutes at 350 degrees.

*Filling:* Beat together egg yolks and sugar until light. Dissolve gelatin in water and bring to boil. Pour into egg mixture, beating briskly. Let cool. Whip cream until stiff and fold into cooled egg mixture. Add rum. Pour into crust and refrigerate. Grate bittersweet chocolate over top before serving. Serves 6 to 8 people.

## Lemon Pie

*Dana Blair*

1 small can frozen Lemonade concentrate
1 small carton Cool Whip
1 can Borden's condensed milk
1 graham cracker crust

Combine can of lemonade concentrate (mashed with fork) with milk and Cool Whip. Pour into graham cracker crust and chill. May be served after 15 minutes of refrigeration.

## Lemon Chiffon Pie

*Mrs. Belmont Dennis*

4 eggs, separated
1 cup sugar
1 small orange
1 large lemon
pinch of salt
1 teaspoon lemon juice
baked pie crust

With electric mixer, beat egg yolks until fluffy. Add 1/2 cup sugar and grated lemon and orange rinds. Cook in double boiler until thick, stirring constantly. Let cool.

Beat egg whites, remaining sugar and lemon juice until stiff. Fold half into custard mixture, then pour into baked pie shell. Top with remaining half of meringue and cook until brown at 325 degrees for about 15 minutes, or until brown.

## Frozen Lemon Pie

*Mrs. Leo (Ira) Aikman*

2/3 cup vanilla or graham cracker crumbs
juice of 2 lemons
grated rind of 1 lemon
pinch of salt
2 eggs, separated
6 tablespoons sugar
3/4 cup whipping cream

In double boiler, cook for 3 minutes egg yolks, lemon juice, lemon rind, salt and 4 tablespoons sugar. Whip egg whites, gradually adding 2 tablespoons sugar. Whip cream.

Cover oblong pan with half the vanilla (or graham cracker) crumbs.

Blend egg whites into lemon and egg mixture. Fold in whipped cream.

Pour mixture into pan and sprinkle with remaining crumbs. Freeze. Let soften a little before serving.

## Lemon Coconut Pie

*Mrs. Belmont Dennis*

2 tablespoons flour
1 1/3 cups sugar
5 eggs, separated
1 teaspoon lemon extract
1 can flaked coconut
pinch of salt
2 frozen pie crusts
2 cups sweet milk

Thoroughly mix flour and one cup sugar. Beat egg yolks until very light; mix with coconut, salt and milk. Combine with flour and sugar mixture. Add lemon flavor and cook in double boiler until very thick. Spread in baked pie crusts.

Beat egg whites until stiff, gradually adding 5 tablespoons sugar. Spread on top of pies and brown.

## Cherry Cream Pie

*Mrs. Julia N. Haywood*

Crust

1/2 package graham cracker meal
1 stick margarine
2 tablespoons granulated sugar

Filling

1 can cherry pie filling
1 can Eagle Brand milk
2 3-ounce packages cream cheese
3 1/2 ounces Cool Whip
2 lemons
2 tablespoons confectioners sugar

*Crust:* Mix cracker meal, butter and sugar and spread into 2 pie plates. Bake for 15 to 20 minutes at 275 degrees. Cool.

*Filling:* Cream milk, cream cheese and juice of 2 lemons. Fold in Cool Whip. Place in pie shells. Mix confectioners sugar and cherry pie filling. Spread on top of cream filling.

## Butter Pecan Pie Crust

*Mrs. Belmont Dennis*

1/2 cup butter, cold
1/4 cup dark brown sugar
1 cup plain flour
1/2 cup chopped pecans

Preheat oven to 400 degrees.

Using hands, mix all ingredients thoroughly. Spread to a thickness of about 1/2-inch in an ungreased flat biscuit pan. Bake for 15 minutes or until lightly browned. While hot, crush with spoon and press all but 1/4 cup into bottom and sides of ungreased 10-inch pie pan. Cool. Fill with pie filling and decorate top with a circle of the remaining crust. Freeze for 8 to 24 hours before serving. Serves 8.

## Blueberry Pie

*Laura Whorton*

Crust

2 frozen pie crusts
1/4 cup chopped pecans

Filling

1 large creamed cheese
3/4 box confectioners sugar
1/2 teaspoon vanilla flavoring
1 package (2 package, box size) Dream Whip
1 can blueberry pie mix

*Crust:* Slightly thaw crusts. Press chopped pecans into each and bake.

*Filling:* Cream cheese and sugar. Add vanilla. Whip Dream Whip as directed and fold into cream cheese mixture. Pour into baked pie crusts and chill. Pour blueberry mix over and chill.

## Pecan Pie

1 cup sugar
1 cup dark corn syrup
4 eggs
salt
1 teaspoon vanilla
1 1/4 cups pecan halves
  or large pieces

Combine ingredients. Pour into uncooked 9-inch pastry shell. Bake at 400 degrees for 10 minutes, reduce temperature to 350 degrees until knife inserted will come out clean, about 20 to 25 minutes. Do not overcook.

## Mile High Lime Pie

*Connie Harris*

1 package gelatin
1/4 cup water
1 can frozen limeade
green food coloring
5 eggs, separated
1/2 cup sugar
graham cracker crust
lime slices
whipped cream

Combine gelatin, limeade, egg yolks and a little green food coloring. Cook until thick; cool. Beat egg whites and sugar and fold into limeade mixture. Pour into graham cracker crust and chill. Garnish with lime slices and whipped cream.

## Pineapple Chiffon Pie

*Mrs. Emily Thornton*

3/4 cup sugar
2 beaten eggs
1 small can crushed
  pineapple
1 box lemon jello
1/2 teaspoon vanilla
1 large can evaporated milk,
  thoroughly chilled (icy)
2 vanilla cracker crumb
  crusts

Bring sugar, eggs and pineapple to boil and add jello. Mix thoroughly and add vanilla. Whip chilled milk until stiff and fold into cooled mixture. Pour into crusts. May be covered with whipped cream.

## Georgia Lemon Pie

*Dorothee Polson*
*Arizona Republic*

2 large lemons
2 cups sugar
4 eggs, well beaten
pastry for 2-crust, 9-inch pie

Slice lemons as thin as paper, rind and all. Combine with sugar; mix well. Let stand for two hours or longer, blending occasionally. Add beaten eggs to the lemon mixture; mix well. Turn into pastry-lined 9-inch pie pan, arranging lemon slices evenly. Cover with top crust. Cut several slits near center to permit steam to escape. Bake at 450 degrees for 15 minutes. Reduce heat to 375 degrees and bake for about 20 minutes or until a silver knife inserted near edge of pie comes out clean. Cool before serving. Serves 6.

## Lemon Chess Pie

*Mildred Warren*

1 unbaked 8-inch pie shell with upstanding rim
4 eggs
1/2 cup (1 stick) butter or margarine
2 cups sugar
1 tablespoon cornstarch
1/4 cup lemon juice
2 tablespoons grated lemon rind

Cream butter until fluffy, add sugar mixed with cornstarch, and cream together until light and fluffy. Add eggs, one at a time, beating well after each addition. Add lemon juice, grated rind, and blend. (Mixture will look curdly). Pour into the unbaked pie shell and bake at 350 degrees for about 35 to 45 minutes. Filling will be soft. Remove from the oven and cool on a wire rack. Serve with a garnish of slightly sweetened whipped cream.

## Almond Cream Pie

*Gil McArthur*

Almond Pastry Shell

1 cup sifted plain flour
1/2 teaspoon salt
1/3 cup shortening
3/4 cup finely chopped toasted almonds
2 tablespoons ice water

Almond Cream Pie

1 baked almond pastry shell
4 tablespoons cornstarch
3/4 cup sugar
1/2 teaspoon salt
2 1/2 cups milk
3 egg yolks, slightly beaten
1 tablespoon butter or margarine
1 teaspoon almond extract
1 teaspoon vanilla extract

Meringue

3 egg whites
1/4 teaspoon cream of tartar
6 tablespoons sugar

*Pastry shell:* Sift flour and salt into medium bowl. Cut in shortening until mixture is like coarse cornmeal. Stir in almonds. Sprinkle ice water gradually over mixture, tossing with a fork. Shape into a ball; roll between sheets of waxed paper, into an 11-inch circle. Refrigerate until ready to use. Fit pastry into 9-inch pie pan. Form neat rim around edge of pan; do not crimp.

*Filling:* Combine cornstarch, sugar and salt in saucepan. Stir in milk gradually. Cook over medium heat, stirring constantly until mixture thickens and comes to a boil. Boil one minute. Blend one-half the mixture into egg yolks; stir into mixture in saucepan; cook 1 minute, stirring constantly. Remove from heat; stir in butter and extracts; cool slightly. Pour filling into pastry shell.

*Meringue:* Beat egg whites and cream of tartar until foamy. Add sugar gradually. Continue beating until meringue forms stiff, glossy peaks. Spread meringue over pie filling, making sure it touches crust all the way around. Bake at 350 degrees for 15 to 20 minutes or until meringue is tipped with brown. Cool at room temperature.

## Frozen Lemon Pie

*Pirates' House*

cracker crumb crust (almond flavored)
1 can condensed milk
4 eggs, separated
1 can frozen lemonade (6 ounces), or juice of 4 lemons
1 cup whipped cream

Beat egg yolks. Add milk then lemonade (not diluted) and set in refrigerator while beating egg whites. Blend whipped cream into lemon mixture and fold into egg whites. Freeze overnight. Serve with whipped cream on top and a twirl of fresh lemon and a cherry.

## Lemon-Lime Sky High Pie

1 envelope unflavored gelatine
1 1/4 cups sugar, divided
1/4 teaspoon salt
6 eggs, separated
1/3 cup water
1/3 cup lemon juice
1/3 cup lime juice
1 teaspoon grated lemon rind
1 teaspoon grated lime rind
1/2 teaspoon cream of tartar
1 9-inch baked pastry shell or crumb crust

Mix together gelatine, 1/2 cup sugar and salt in top of double boiler. Beat egg yolks with water, lemon and lime juice; stir into gelatine mixture. Place over boiling water and cook, stirring constantly, until gelatine dissolves and mixture thickens slightly, about 6 minutes. Add lemon and lime rind. Chill, stirring occasionally, until mixture mounds slightly when dropped from spoon. Beat egg whites with cream of tartar until stiff but not dry; gradually add remaining 3/4 cup sugar and beat until very stiff. Fold in gelatine mixture. If necessary chill until mixture will pile. Turn into pastry shell, piling high in center. Chill until firm, several hours or overnight. Garnish with whipped cream and a lime twist. Makes 1 9-inch pie.

## Black Bottom Pie

*Pirate's House, Savannah*

1 envelope unflavored gelatin
1/4 cup water
1 cup sugar
1 1/2 tablespoons cornstarch
dash salt
2 eggs, separated
2 cups milk, scalded
1 teaspoon vanilla extract
2 squares unsweetened chocolate, melted
baked pie shell
1/4 teaspoon rum extract
1 teaspoon cream of tartar
1 cup whipping cream
1 tablespoon confectioners sugar
1 teaspoon chocolate decors

Soak gelatin in water; mix 3/4 cup sugar, cornstarch and salt; add egg yolks and beat well. Slowly add milk, stirring constantly; cook over low heat, stirring constantly, until mixture coats spoon.

Remove from heat and to 1 cup of custard add the melted chocolate and vanilla; mix well and spoon into baked crust; allow to cool.

To remaining custard, add gelatin, stirring until dissolved; cool, then stir in rum extract. Beat egg whites until foamy; add cream of tartar and continue beating until stiff; gradually add remaining 1/4 cup sugar, then fold into gelatin mixture. Spread over chocolate mixture in pie shell and chill; before serving, whip cream until stiff, sweeten with sugar and spread over pie; garnish with chocolate decors.

## Tropical Pie

Crust

1 cup corn flake crumbs
1/3 cup melted butter
2 tablespoons sugar
9-inch pie shell

Filling

1 cup milk, or half and half
1 pint vanilla ice cream, slightly softened
1 package (3 3/4 ounces) vanilla instant pudding mix

Glaze

1 1/2 cups (1 pound, 4 ounces) drained pineapple, crushed
1/2 cup pineapple syrup
1 tablespoon cornstarch

*Crust:* Blend ingredients together and press into pie shell. Chill.

*Filling:* Pour milk or half and half into mixing bowl; add pudding mix and ice cream. Beat slowly until well blended (one to two minutes). Pour into cereal crust. Refrigerate while making glaze.

*Glaze:* Drain pineapple. Measure syrup and add to cornstarch, gradually, stirring to keep mixture smooth. Cook over low heat, stirring constantly until thickened and clear. Add pineapple and cool. Spoon over pie. Chill at least an hour.

## Easy Cookies

1 egg white
1 cup chopped pecans
1 cup light brown sugar, firmly packed

Beat egg until stiff and add sugar and nuts. Drop onto greased cookie sheet. Bake 12 minutes at 325 degrees.

## Peppermint Candy Ice Cream

1 1/2 cups crushed peppermint stick candy
vanilla ice cream recipe

Prepare any vanilla ice cream recipe. Churn for about 15 minutes or until the ice cream has frozen to a mushy consistency. Add 1 1/2 cups crushed candy and continue freezing as directed.

## Burgundy Cherry Pie

1 baked pie shell
1 can Bing cherries
water
1 package cherry gelatin
1/2 cup Burgundy wine
2 teaspoons lemon juice

Drain and pit cherries, adding sufficient water to juice to make 1 1/4 cups. Add wine to liquid and heat. Add gelatin and stir until dissolved. Remove from heat and add lemon juice and cherries. Chill. When it begins to set, stir and pour into pie shell. Keep refrigerated until ready to serve.

## Peanut Brittle

*Mrs. Jimmy (Rosalynn) Carter*

3 cups sugar
1 cup white Karo
2 teaspoons soda
1 teaspoon vanilla
1 1/2 cups water
3 cups peanuts, raw
1/2 stick butter

Boil sugar, water and Karo until mixture spins thread; add peanuts. After adding peanuts, stir continuously until syrup turns a golden brown. Remove from heat and add remaining ingredients. Stir until butter melts. Pour quickly onto 2 cookie sheets with sides. As mixture begins to harden around edges, pull until thin.

## Chess Pie

1 cup sugar
1 cup butter
3 egg yolks
1 egg white
3 tablespoons water
1 teaspoon vanilla
pastry for 9-inch pie

Preheat oven to 350 degrees. Cream sugar and butter as for making cake. Add egg yolks and white, beat well. Add water and vanilla and beat again. Pour into a pie pan lined with pastry and bake until filling sets, about 35 minutes. Serves 6 to 8.

## Coffee Cloud Pie

*Glenn McCullough*

1 cup black walnuts, chopped (pecans may be substituted but the black walnut taste has no match)
1 can Eagle Brand milk
1 cup ultra black coffee
1 1/2 cups whipping cream

Blend condensed milk with cold coffee and add cream which has been whipped stiff. Pour into meringue shell and sprinkle with nuts. Place in freezer at least eight hours prior to serving.

## Meringue Shells

3 egg whites
1/4 teaspoon cream of tartar
3/4 cup sugar

Preheat oven to 275 degrees. Butter 9-inch pie pan. Have the egg whites room temperature. Beat egg whites and cream of tartar in small bowl of mixer at speed 7 for 1 minute. Continuing at same speed, gradually add sugar, beating for 5 minutes, or until the egg whites are stiff. Spread on bottom and sides of prepared pan. Bake 1 hour. Cool.

## Christmas Egg Nog Pie

1 envelope unflavored gelatin
1/2 cup sugar
1/8 teaspoon salt
3 eggs, separated
3/4 cup milk
1 tablespoon rum extract
1/4 teaspoon nutmeg
1 9-inch baked pie shell

In saucepan, combine gelatin, 1/4 cup of the sugar and salt. Beat egg yolks and milk together; add to gelatin mixture. Cook over low heat, stirring constantly, until gelatin is dissolved. Turn off heat; stir in extract and nutmeg. Chill until mixture mounds when dropped from spoon. Beat egg whites until foamy. Add remaining sugar a little at a time, beating until stiff. Carefully fold gelatin mixture into egg whites. Turn into pie shell. Chill until firm. Garnish rim with whipped cream and pieces of red maraschino cherries and citron to resemble a holly wreath. For a milder flavor use 1 1/2 teaspoons rum extract.

## White Fruit Cake

*Mrs. Belmont Dennis*

8 egg whites
2 cups sugar
1/2 cup butter
3 cups flour
3 teaspoons baking powder
3/4 cup sweet milk
pinch salt
1 pound cherries, chopped
1 pound pineapple, chopped
1 teaspoon vanilla
4 cups pecans, finely chopped

Cream butter and sugar. Flour fruits and nuts. Add salt and baking powder to flour. Set oven at 275 degrees. Add milk and flour alternately to butter and sugar mixture. Add vanilla and mix well. Lightly fold in fruits and nuts. Whip egg whites well and fold lightly into mixture. Place in tube cake pan and turn heat up to 300 degrees. Bake for 2 hours.

### Easy Mincemeat Pie

1 jar (1 pound, 12 ounces) prepared mincemeat
1 can (1 pound, 4 ounces) sliced apples, drained
1/2 cup molasses
pastry for 2-crust, 10-inch pie

Combine mincemeat, sliced apples and molasses. Line 10-inch pie plate with half the pastry. Turn in mincemeat mixture. Top with remaining pastry; seal and flute edges. Cut several slits in top of pie to allow steam to escape. Bake in 425-degree oven for 45 minutes. Makes 1 10-inch pie.

### Grandma's Plum Pudding

1/2 cup molasses
1/2 cup orange juice
1 cup raisins
1 cup chopped, mixed, candied fruit
1 apple, pared and chopped
1 tablespoon grated orange rind
2 eggs, slightly beaten
1 cup chopped nuts
1/2 cup (2 ounces) ground suet
3/4 cup fine dry bread crumbs
1/2 cup sifted all-purpose flour
1 teaspoon baking powder
1/2 teaspoon soda
1/4 cup sugar
1/2 teaspoon salt
1/2 teaspoon cinnamon
1/4 teaspoon allspice
1/4 teaspoon ground cloves

Combine molasses and orange juice. Pour over raisins, candied fruit, apple and orange rind; let stand one hour. Combine beaten eggs, nuts, suet and bread crumbs. Sift in remaining ingredients; blend well. Add fruit mixture; mix well. Turn into a greased 2-quart pudding mold with tight-fitting cover, or cover with aluminum foil and tie securely. Place on rack in deep kettle; pour in boiling water to half the depth of the mold. Cover; steam five hours, adding more boiling water during steaming if necessary. Serve warm with softened ice cream or pudding sauce. Makes 12 servings. If desired, mixture may be turned into 4 1 1/2-cup molds and steamed 2 1/2 hours. Makes 3 servings per mold.

## Honey Pecan Pie

2 tablespoons soft butter
1/4 cup brown sugar
1/2 cup flour
1 1/2 cups light corn syrup
1 1/2 cups honey
salt
vanilla
3 eggs, beaten
1 plain uncooked pie shell
1 cup pecan halves

Cream butter and brown sugar. Stir in flour, syrup, honey and salt. Add vanilla and eggs. Mix well. Pour into uncooked pie shell. Sprinkle nuts over top. Bake at 350 degrees for 1 hour and 10 minutes, or until knife inserted comes out clean. Cool before serving. Serves 8.

## Cherries Emily

*Mrs. N. S. (Elaine) Hayden*

Crust

1 1/2 cups graham cracker crumbs
1 stick margarine

Filling

1 large (8 ounce) package cream cheese
2 tablespoons milk
1 cup sugar
1 cup chopped pecans
1/2 pint cream
1 teaspoon vanilla
1 number-3 can cherry pie filling

*Crust:* Combine crumbs and soft margarine and press into 1 1/2 quart oblong pyrex dish. Bake at 325 degrees for 15 minutes. Chill.

*Filling:* Cream milk and cream cheese in bowl with mixer. Add sugar and mix well. Spread mixture on crust. Sprinkle pecans over creamed cheese. Whip cream, add vanilla and spread over layer of pecans. Chill 2 or 3 hours. Then add cherry pie filling on whipped cream. Chill overnight before cutting into squares and lifting out with spatula. Serves 8 to 10.

## Sweet Sue

*Mrs. Edna Pfaender*

Crust

18 chocolate wafers
1/3 cup margarine, melted

Filling

1/2 gallon coffee ice cream
1 small can evaporated milk
2 squares chocolate
1/2 cup sugar
1 tablespoon butter
chopped nuts
whipped cream
vanilla

*Crust:* Combine crumbled wafers and margarine; spread in pan. Bake 10 minutes. Cool.

*Filling:* Spread ice cream over cracker crust and freeze. Combine milk, chocolate, sugar and butter in double boiler. Stir until thick. When cool, spread over ice cream and freeze. Sprinkle chopped nuts over mixture.

Before serving, cover with whipped cream seasoned with sugar and vanilla. Decorate with chocolate shavings.

## Rum Torte

*Julia Dyar*

lady fingers, split
  and unfilled
3 eggs, separated
3/4 cup sugar
3 tablespoons rum
1 pint whipped cream
grated German chocolate

Line bottom of 8 x 12-inch pyrex pan with lady fingers. Beat egg yolks, add sugar and beat until creamy. Add rum. Beat egg whites until stiff; fold in whipped cream then egg yolk mixture. Pour over lady fingers, and sprinkle with grated chocolate. Refrigerate 8 to 10 hours, covered.

## Baked Custard

*Mary S. Mallard*

1 quart sweet milk
3/4 cup sugar
4 eggs
salt (to taste)
nutmeg
1 tablespoon vanilla

Beat eggs at medium speed. Add sugar gradually until well beaten. Add salt, milk and vanilla. Pour into 1 1/2 quart container. Sprinkle generously with nutmeg.

Place container in pan in 1 inch of water. Bake at 400 degrees for approximately 30 minutes, or until inserted knife comes out clean. Cool thoroughly before serving.

## Boiled Custard

*Mrs. Ralph (Frances) Owen*

1 quart milk
4 eggs
1 cup sugar
dash salt
1 teaspoon vanilla
1/2 teaspoon almond

Heat milk in top of double boiler. In the meantime, beat eggs until light, add sugar and salt, mixing well.

Pour hot milk over egg and sugar mixture and return to double boiler, cooking until it coats spoon. (Keep water in bottom of boiler boiling very gently over moderate heat and stir custard almost constantly until it thickens.) Remove from heat immediately when custard becomes thick and add flavoring. Pour into jars, cover, cool and refrigerate.

## Cherry Cobbler

*Julia Dyar*

1 can sour pitted cherries
2/3 cup sugar
2 teaspoons flour
1 tablespoon water
1 cup flour
1 teaspoon baking powder
1/4 teaspoon salt
1 tablespoon sugar
2 tablespoons butter
6 tablespoons milk

Blend 2/3 cup sugar and 2 teaspoons flour and mix with cherries. Allow to stand five minutes, then add water. Pour mix into deep glass or china baking dish. Mix and sift remaining flour, baking powder, salt and sugar. Cut in butter with knife. Add milk, mixing until soft dough is formed. Shape dough with hands to fit over cherries. Make 3 slits in dough to allow steam to escape. Place in 350-degree oven and bake 30 minutes. Serve in baking dish. (To make peach cobbler, use about 3 to 4 cups of peaches, and double the amount of dough).

## Apple Cheese Crisp

*Mrs. Belmont Dennis*

3 cups apples, chopped
  and peeled
4 tablespoons butter
3/4 cup sugar
1/2 cup flour
2 teaspoons lemon juice
1/8 teaspoon cinnamon
1/4 teaspoon salt
3/4 cup grated cheese
1/4 cup water

Place apples in shallow baking dish. Sprinkle with cinnamon. Add water and lemon juice. Combine sugar, flour and water and work in butter to form a crumbly mixture. Stir in grated cheese.

Pour mixture over apples and bake in 350 degree oven about 35 minutes until crust is brown and crisp. Serves 6.

## French Type Apple Pastry Strip

*Mrs. Belmont Dennis*

1/2 cup apple cider
1/4 cup sherry
1 tablespoon lemon juice
1/2 teaspoon cinnamon
1/4 teaspoon nutmeg
1/8 teaspoon salt
2 tablespoons sugar
3 tablespoons milk
1 cup seedless raisins
1 can (about 1 pound) apple slices
pastry for 1 crust pie or little more
1 tablespoon butter
3 tablespoons pecan halves

Combine first 7 ingredients. Bring to boiling in enamel or glass saucepan. Boil 5 minutes to reduce liquid. Lower heat, add raisins and simmer 5 minutes. Add drained apple slices.

Roll pastry into oblong about 13 X 9 inches. Place on greased, floured baking sheet. Edges may be scalloped, if desired.

Spoon filling down center of pastry strip. Dot with butter; sprinkle with pecans. Bring edges of pastry up and over filling toward center, leaving a center strip exposed. Turn narrow ends up to enclose end filling.

Brush pastry with milk. Bake at 425 degrees for 25 to 30 minutes until golden brown. Let cool. Slice crosswise to serve. Makes 6 or more servings.

## Date Nut Bread

*Mrs. Ralph (Frances) Owen*

1 cup chopped dates
1 cup sugar
2 tablespoons shortening
1 cup boiling water
2 1/2 cups flour
1 teaspoon baking powder
1 teaspoon salt
1 teaspoon soda
1 egg
1 teaspoon vanilla
1 cup chopped pecans

Pour boiling water over dates, sugar and shortening; let stand until cool. Sift soda, salt, baking powder with flour; add nuts and mix well.

Pour the first mixture into the flour mix, and blend until free of lumps. Add beaten egg and flavoring. Bake in greased loaf pan in moderate oven (350 degrees) until done.

## Banana Pudding

1/2 cup sugar
pinch of salt
3 tablespoons flour
4 eggs
2 cups milk
vanilla wafers
bananas
6 tablespoons sugar

Blend sugar, salt and flour. Add 1 whole egg and 3 yolks and mix together. Stir in milk. Cook over boiling water, stirring, until thickened. Remove from heat and cool.

In a baking dish, arrange a layer of whole vanilla wafers, a layer of sliced bananas and a layer of custard. Continue, making 3 layers of each.

Make a meringue of remaining 3 egg whites and 6 tablespoons sugar. Spread over banana mixture and brown in 375-degree oven. Makes 8 servings. Serve cold, not chilled.

### Tipsy Pudding

4 eggs
1/2 cup sugar
1 cup sifted flour
3/4 cup rum

Beat the eggs in a bowl. Gradually add the sugar, beating until thick and light. Add the flour, mixing lightly until well blended. Preheat oven to 350 degrees. Butter 6 custard cups and dust lightly with sugar. Divide the mixture evenly among the cups. Bake at 350 degrees for 20 minutes or until set and lightly browned. Pour 2 tablespoons of rum on each pudding. Serve cold.

### Sugared Walnuts

*Julia Dyar*

1 cup sugar
1 teaspoon lemon extract
2 tablespoons butter
1/3 cup concentrated orange juice, frozen
2 1/2 cups English walnuts

Combine sugar and orange juice and cook to soft ball stage (234 degrees on candy thermometer). Add extract and butter. Beat well until creamy in appearance and mixture begins to thicken. Add walnut halves and stir with 2 forks until nuts are covered. Pour out quickly on waxed paper or aluminum foil. Pull apart to form small clusters.

### Fudge

5 tablespoons butter
5 cups sugar
1 teaspoon vanilla extract
2 cups cream
5 ounces chocolate
chopped nuts, if desired

Melt butter in saucepan and add cream, sugar and chocolate. Stir gently until chocolate melts. Boil without stirring to 236 degrees, or until sample forms soft ball in cold water. Allow to cool, add vanilla extract and chopped nuts, if desired, and beat with a wooden spoon until it begins to stiffen. Pour onto buttered marble or into buttered pan and mark into squares at once.

## Whiskey Pecans

1 cup sugar
3 cups pecan halves
1/2 cup evaporated milk
2 tablespoons whiskey
pinch of salt

Put sugar and milk on slow fire and cook until soft-ball stage is reached. Add salt, nuts and whiskey, stirring until nuts are thoroughly covered. Pour out on waxed paper.

## Coconut Macaroons

3 egg whites
1/2 pound coconut
1/4 cup sugar

Beat egg whites until very stiff. Add sugar gradually, beating well. Fold in coconut. Drop by spoonfuls on well greased cookie sheet. Bake 30 minutes at 325 degrees.

## Boiled Custard

*Julia Dyar*

1 quart milk
1 heaping teaspoon flour
1 teaspoon vanilla
4 eggs
1 scant cup sugar

Mix flour and sugar. Beat eggs and add flour mixture. Put milk in double boiler and heat. Do not boil. Add 2 cups of hot milk to egg mixture in bowl; beat. Pour mixture back into remaining milk in double boiler; beat well. Cook until mixture coats a spoon, then strain. Add vanilla. After mixture cools, refrigerate.

## Apricot Balls

*Julia Dyar*

3 boxes dried apricots
1 cup nuts
2 tablespoons lemon juice
3 tablespoons powdered sugar (not sifted)

Put apricots and nuts through meat chopper, then combine. Mix sugar and lemon juice and add to apricots. Roll into balls and then into additional powdered sugar. Makes 125 very small balls.

## Peanut Brittle

*Carolyn McLeod*

2 cups sugar
1/4 cup cold water
3/4 cup Karo syrup
1/2 teaspoon salt
2 rounded teaspoons soda
1/2 stick margarine
1 pound shelled peanuts

In large iron skillet put sugar, water, salt and syrup and let it come to full boil. Add the peanuts and cook at medium heat for six minutes. Add margarine and cook two minutes more. Remove from heat and add soda. Stir well and pour onto greased hard surface, spreading one way. Wait about five minutes and stretch.

## Rice Pudding

2 eggs
2 cups milk
1 1/2 cups cold, cooked rice
1 cup raisins
1/2 cup sugar
1/8 teaspoon salt
1 teaspoon vanilla
dash nutmeg (optional)

Preheat oven to 350 degrees. Beat eggs until light. Add to milk and rice. Add other ingredients lightly. Place in 2-quart buttered casserole or baking dish. Bake uncovered in shallow pan of water for about an hour. Serves 6. If desired, pudding may be covered with meringue.

## Sugared Nuts

*Laura Conway*

1/2 cup Pet or
  Carnation milk
4 teaspoons water
4 cups pecans
2 cups sugar
1 teaspoon cinnamon (or
  1/2 cup chocolate chips)
1 teaspoon vanilla

If using cinnamon instead of chocolate chips, mix with sugar and then combine with other ingredients. Heat to soft ball stage (240 degrees) and add vanilla and pecans. If using chocolate chips, heat ingredients as directed and add chips after removing from heat. Do not add vanilla. Place on buttered cookie sheet or waxed paper. Separate nuts with 2 forks or fingers.

## Favorite Fudge

2 cups sugar
3 tablespoons butter
1/2 teaspoon salt
1 cup evaporated milk
1 teaspoon vanilla
1/2 cup miniature
  marshmallows
1 1/2 cups semi-sweet
  chocolate chips
2/3 cup chopped nuts

In 2-quart saucepan, combine sugar, butter, salt and evaporated milk. Bring to a rolling boil over medium heat; stir constantly. Continue boiling and stirring for 5 minutes. Turn off heat, add marshmallows, chocolate, vanilla and nuts. Stir until marshmallows and chocolate are melted and smoothly blended. Turn into buttered 8-inch square pan. Mark soft candy in squares. When cold, cut into pieces. Makes about 2 pounds.

## Mexican Pecan Candy

*Harriet Aldridge*
*Food Editor, Arkansas Gazette*

1 box light brown sugar
1/2 pint whipping cream
1 tablespoon butter
2 cups pecan halves
1 teaspoon vanilla

Place sugar and cream in heavy saucepan over medium heat. Stir until sugar is thoroughly dissolved, then simmer until it reaches soft ball stage (240 degrees). (Before this, it will boil up, then subside.) When a soft ball forms in cool water, remove the candy from heat; add butter. When almost lukewarm, dump in pecans and vanilla. Beat with wooden spoon. (The stopping point is difficult to describe, but the mass takes on a slightly opaque, creamy appearance. At this stage, stop beating immediately.)

Have sheets of wax paper on flat surface. With small tablespoon, drop candy onto wax paper. (A teaspoon to push the candy off the tablespoon helps. Work fast – the candy hardens quickly in the saucepan.)

## Divinity

2 cups white sugar
1/3 cup white Karo syrup
2/3 cup water
2 egg whites, beaten stiff
pecan halves (5 dozen)

Boil sugar, Karo and water until mixture forms a hard ball in cold water that will crack on cup. (Do not stir while cooking or candy might be grainy.) Add this syrup slowly to the egg whites, beating constantly until hard enough to drop from spoon. Arrange on waxed paper and press 1/2 pecan on top of each piece. Makes 5 dozen pieces.

## Pecan Balls

*Mrs. Belmont Dennis*

1 stick butter
2 tablespoons sugar
1 teaspoon vanilla
1 cup plain flour
1 cup chopped pecans

Combine ingredients and roll into tiny balls. Bake at 325 degrees for 45 minutes. Roll in powdered sugar.

## Date Balls

*Mary Waldrip*

2 sticks margarine
2 cups sugar
2 eggs (beaten)
1 pack dates (chopped)
1 1/2 cups chopped nuts
1 1/2 teaspoons vanilla
2 cups Rice Krispies
flaked coconut

Mix margarine, sugar, eggs and dates and boil 10 minutes. Cool. Add the chopped nuts, vanilla and Rice Krispies. Form into balls and roll in flaked coconut.

## Date Nut Balls

*Mrs. Belmont Dennis*

2 sticks margarine, melted
2 cups sugar
1 pound chopped dates
1/2 teaspoon salt
1 can angel flake coconut
2 cups nuts, chopped
1 teaspoon vanilla
4 cups Rice Krispies
2 tablespoons water
powdered sugar

Combine sugar, salt, dates and water with melted margarine. Cook 6 minutes, stirring to keep from sticking. Stir in coconut and remove from heat. Add vanilla and chopped nuts. Cool a little, then pour over Rice Krispies. Form into small balls and roll in powdered sugar.

## Rum (or Bourbon) Cookies

*Lois Grimes*

1 big box vanilla wafers
1 cup chopped nuts
1 cup powdered sugar
2 1/2 tablespoons cocoa
2 tablespoons white Karo syrup
10 tablespoons rum (or bourbon)

Mix all dry ingredients. Add liquid and syrup, mix well and roll into small balls. Roll in powdered sugar (this is in addition to the other sugar.)

## Quick Mix Oatmeal Cookies

*Lois Grimes*

2 cups flour
1 teaspoon salt
1 teaspoon baking powder
1 teaspoon soda
1 cup brown sugar
1 cup plain sugar
2 eggs
1 cup shortening (may be oil)
2 tablespoons water
2 teaspoons vanilla
3 cups oatmeal
1 package chocolate chips

Mix sugar and shortening. Add eggs. Sift dry ingredients and add to mixture. Stir in oatmeal. Drop in small balls on greased cookie sheet. Bake at 350 degrees 12 to 15 minutes. Makes about 6 dozen.

## Delicious Cookies

*Mrs. Belmont Dennis*

1/2 cup butter or margarine
1/4 cup confectioners sugar
1/2 teaspoon vanilla
1 cup chopped pecans
1 cup flour

Cream butter, sugar and vanilla until fluffy. Add one-half the chopped nuts. Blend in flour and remaining nuts. Shape into small balls and bake on ungreased cookie sheet in slow oven (325 degrees) for 10 to 15 minutes. Roll in confectioners sugar when cool.

### Fruit Whip

1 cup fruit pulp
1/8 teaspoon salt
1/2 cup sugar
2 egg whites, beaten
1 tablespoon lemon juice

Heat fruit pulp, salt and sugar together until sugar is dissolved. Beating constantly, slowly pour hot syrup over stiffly beaten egg whites. Add lemon juice. Pile into parfait glasses and serve immediately. Serves 4.

If desired, place mixture in greased baking dish. Place in pan of hot water and bake in slow oven (300 degrees) about 1 hour. Serve hot or cold.

### Tropical Freeze

2 cups water
3 cups sugar
1/2 teaspoon salt
3 cups water
1 cup orange juice
1/2 cup lemon juice
3 cups mashed bananas
(about 8 bananas)

Combine 2 cups water, sugar and salt in saucepan; bring to a boil. Cool. Add additional water, orange and lemon juice, and mashed bananas. Freeze as directed.

### Ambrosia

15 to 18 medium-size oranges
1 1/2 cups fresh or frozen
grated coconut
1 13 1/2-ounce can pineapple
chunks, drained (optional)
3/4 cup sugar or to taste

Peel oranges, being careful to remove all white membrane. Cut into small slices or pieces. Mix oranges and juice with sugar. Add coconut and pineapple chunks. Place in refrigator to chill. Serves 10 to 12.

## Syllabub

*Julia Dyar*

2 cups port or white wine
1/2 cup granulated sugar
1/2 teaspoon ground nutmeg
2 quarts cold milk

In a serving bowl, blend wine with sugar and nutmeg. Place milk in blender, 2 cups at a time, and beat until frothy. Pour into serving bowl. Stir and serve in punch cups. Makes about 20 4-ounce servings. Top each serving with whipped cream made with 1 cup heavy cream to which 1 tablespoon granulated sugar and 1 teaspoon cinnamon have been gradually added.

## Eggnog

12 egg yolks
1 1/2 cups bourbon
3/4 cup sugar
2 quarts milk
12 egg whites
1 quart whipping cream
nutmeg

Beat egg yolks until lemon colored. Add bourbon slowly, a jigger at a time. Add sugar slowly; then add milk and beat well.

Cover bowl and set in refrigerator overnight. Just before serving, beat egg whites until stiff and fold into yolk-milk mixture. Beat cream until stiff and add nutmeg. Pour over mixture. Ladle into cups so that each cup is topped with a layer of whipped cream and nutmeg. Yield: 30 servings.

## Lemon Ice

2 cups water
3 cups sugar
1 1/4 cups lemon juice
2 teaspoons lemon rind
1/4 teaspoon salt
8 cups water

Combine 2 cups of water and sugar in a saucepan. Bring to a boil. Chill in refrigerator before adding remainder of ingredients. Freeze as directed.

## President Polk's Eggnog

1 quart bourbon whiskey
1 quart cream, heavy
13 eggs
13 tablespoons sugar

Beat egg yolks with sugar until lemon colored, using electric beater. Add whiskey and let stand overnight (or even three or four days). When ready to serve, add whipped cream and fold in the beaten egg whites.

## Milk Punch

1 egg, well beaten
1 tablespoon sugar
1 tablespoon brandy
milk

Beat egg well. Pour the brandy over the sugar. Mix the egg, sugar and brandy well in a glass, and fill with milk.

## Coast Artillery Punch

*Jere N. Moore*

3 quarts champagne
1 gallon sweet Catawba wine
6 oranges
1/2 can pineapple
sugar to taste
1 quart sour mash bourbon
1 quart light rum
1 quart black tea
12 lemons
1/2 can Malaga grapes or cherries

Cut fruit into very small pieces. Spread sugar on top and let it soak in rum and tea for 2 hours. One hour before serving, put in Catawba wine with a large lump of ice. Add bourbon. When ready to serve, pour in champagne. Strawberries may be used instead of grapes and brandy instead of wine. This is a potent punch but very excellent.

## Holiday Punch

6 ounces lemon juice
2 6-ounce cans frozen
orange juice, prepared
1 fifth of vodka
1 quart club soda
1 1/2 quarts ginger ale
fruits

Combine ingredients and pour into punch bowl with chunks of ice. Garnish with fruit. Makes 41 3-ounce servings.

## Congealed Eggnog

1 quart whipping cream
1 cup milk
1 1/2 cups sugar
1 cup whiskey, or to taste
1 or 2 envelopes gelatin,
plain
4 eggs, separated

Soak gelatin in a little cold water. Heat milk to boiling point and pour over well dissolved gelatin; cool until lukewarm. Beat egg yolks well, add sugar and beat again. Add whiskey slowly. Add cooled gelatin to egg mixture, mix well and let stand until slightly congealed. Add stiffly beaten egg whites and cream, stiffly whipped. Let stand in refrigerator a while and serve with nutmeg sprinkled on top.

## Inexpensive Punch

2 ounces citric acid
crystals
1 can pineapple juice, tall
5 quarts cold water
2 quarts boiling water
1 can frozen orange juice
5 1/2 cups sugar

Dissolve citric acid crystals in boiling water. Let stand 24 hours in enamel or earthenware vessel. Add pineapple juice, orange juice, sugar and cold water. Serves 50.

## Sassafras Tea

red sassafras roots
water
cream
sugar

Use only red sassafras roots for this beverage. Scrub them and break into convenient size pieces. Cover with water and simmer for 20 minutes. If the tea is a dark red color, add water to make it clear red, about the strength of China tea. Strain and serve hot with cream and sugar.

## Melon Ball Cocktail

1 cup watermelon balls
1 cup honeydew melon balls
3 tablespoons sugar
2 cups canteloupe balls
2 tablespoons lemon juice
2 tablespoons sherry

Mix ingredients and chill. Serve in sherbet glasses. Garnish with a sprig of mint. The sherry may be omitted and ginger ale poured over the balls in the glass just before serving. Sprinkle with powdered sugar and garnish with mint leaves.

## Punch

*Julia Dyar*

2 cups sugar
juice of 6 oranges
1 can pineapple juice
4 cups water
juice of 6 lemons
2 quarts ginger ale

Boil sugar and water for 10 minutes. Cool and add orange and lemon juice. Add can pineapple juice. Before serving add ginger ale.

## Delicious Punch

1 quart grape juice
1/2 pint lemon juice
2 cups sugar
2 quarts orange juice
6 quarts water
3 cups ginger ale

Mix grape, orange and lemon juices with water. Add sugar; stir well. Add ginger ale before serving. Yields 40 servings.

## Mint Julep

12 sprigs fresh mint
6 lumps sugar
6 tablespoons water
cracked ice
12 jiggers bourbon

Use a 12- or 16-ounce silver goblet or a tall glass for each individual drink. Crush a sprig of mint against each glass or goblet, then discard the mint. Dissolve a lump of sugar in a tablespoon of water in each glass. Half fill each glass with cracked ice. Add 2 jiggers of bourbon and stir gently. Garnish with sprig of fresh mint.

## Hot Russian Tea

2 cups instant tea
2 cups orange concentrate, powdered
1 teaspoon cloves
2 1/2 cups sugar
2 small packages lemonade mix
2 teaspoons cinnamon

Mix all ingredients together. Store in covered container. Use 2 teaspoonsful of mixture to 1 cup hot water when serving. Makes 1 quart.

# JAMS & JELLIES.

## Jelly Test

*Spoon or Sheet Test:* Dip a metal spoon into the boiling mixture. Tilt the spoon until the syrup runs over the side. When the jellying stage is reached, the liquid will stop flowing in a stream and divide into distinct drops that run together and flake or sheet fróm the edge of the spoon.

*Thermometer Test:* The temperature should register 220 degrees (8 degrees higher than the boiling point of water).

## Applesauce

6 pounds apples
1 to 1 1/2 cups sugar
2 cups water

Select tart apples at the peak of their season from varieties which cook to a mush easily.

Wash the apples thoroughly, peel thin, quarter and core. Add water and simmer until fruit is soft. Shake the pan occasionally to prevent scorching. Add sugar to taste and stir to dissolve. Pour hot sauce into preheated jars, leaving 1/2 inch head space. Remove air bubbles. Wipe sealing edge of jar with a clean, damp cloth and adjust lid. Process pint and quart jars 10 minutes in a boiling water bath canner.

## Plum Jelly

3 1/2 pounds plums
3 cups sugar
1 1/2 cups water

Select about one-fourth under-ripe and three-fourths fully ripe plums. Sort, wash and cut into pieces. Do not peel or pit. Add water, cover and bring to a boil on high heat. Reduce heat and simmer 15 to 20 minutes or until the fruit is soft. Extract juice.

Measure juice into a saucepan and bring to a boil. Add sugar slowly, stirring constantly. Boil over high heat to 220 degrees or until mixture sheets from spoon. Remove from heat and skim off foam quickly. Pour jelly immediately into preheated containers and seal. Makes 3 to 4 1/2-pints.

### Plum Sauce or Spiced Plums

2 1/2 pounds plums
1 1/2 cups cold water
1 tablespoon cloves, whole
2 1/2 cups sugar
2 sticks cinnamon
1/2 cup cider vinegar

Select vine-ripened, firm, sound plums. Wash in several changes of cold water and drain.

Measure water into a saucepan and add plums. Place a tight-fitting lid on the saucepan. When the water begins to boil, reduce the heat and simmer until plums are tender (about 10-15 minutes).

Select standard, clear glass jars. Be sure jars are free from chips, cracks or breaks. Wash them in hot, soapy water and rinse in clear hot water. Put the jars, mouth downward, on a rack in 2 inches of water. Boil the water 5 minutes. Leave jars in the hot water until ready to use. Prepare the lids according to directions on the lid box.

Press the plums and liquid through a food mill, colander or coarse sieve to remove seed. Return the plum mixture to the saucepan. Add sugar, vinegar and spices (tied loosely in a coarse cloth, such as cheese cloth). Cook rapidly until thick and clear and mixture gives a very light jell test (218 degrees). Remove spice bag.

Pour mixture into the preheated jars, leaving 1/4 inch head space. Wipe mouth of jar with a clean, wet cloth. Adjust lid and seal the jar. Process pint jars at simmering temperature for 15 minutes in boiling water bath canner. Remove jars and set on cooling rack to cool.

### Strawberry and Pineapple Jam

2 cups strawberries, mashed
2 cups pineapple, canned and crushed
4 cups sugar
1 tablespoon lemon juice

Combine mashed strawberries and crushed pineapple with sugar. Cook rapidly until thick (about 20 minutes). Add lemon juice a few minutes before cooking is complete. Pour into preheated jars and seal while hot.

### Plum Jam

1 pound plums
1 1/2 cups sugar
1 cup water

Sort and wash the plums and cut them into pieces; do not peel or pit. Add water and cook plums until soft. Press the plums through a food mill or sieve. Return the de-seeded mixture to the saucepan. Stir in sugar and cook until the mixture is thick. Pour mixture into preheated jars and seal. Process 10 minutes in a boiling water bath canner.

### Damson Plum Preserves

1 1/2 quarts damson plums, prepared
5 1/2 cups sugar
1 cup water

Dissolve the sugar in the water and bring to a boil. Add the plums and boil, stirring gently, to 221 degrees, or until the fruit is translucent and the syrup is thick. Remove from heat and skim. Pour into preheated jars and seal immediately. Makes about 6 half-pints.

### Strawberry Jam

6 cups strawberries
5 cups sugar
2 tablespoons lemon juice

Sort and wash fully ripe strawberries; remove stems and caps. Crush the berries.

Mix crushed berries with sugar. Cook rapidly until thick (about 20 minutes). Add lemon juice a few minutes before cooking is complete. Pour into preheated jars and seal while hot.

### Strawberry Preserves Deluxe

1 1/2 quarts firm, red-ripe strawberries, stemmed
5 cups sugar
1/3 cup lemon juice

To prepare fruit, sort and wash fully ripe strawberries; remove stems and caps. Drain the berries. Do not use berries with hollow cores.

Combine strawberries and sugar; let stand 3 to 4 hours. Bring slowly to boiling, stirring occasionally until sugar dissolves. Add lemon juice. Cook rapidly until berries are clear and syrup is thick, about 10 to 12 minutes. Pour into a shallow pan. Let stand uncovered 12 to 24 hours in a cool place. Shake pan occasionally to distribute berries through syrup.

Bring the preserves to a rolling boil; pack in preheated jars and seal immediately. Store in a dark place to keep berries from fading. Makes 4 half-pints.

### Strawberry Nectar

1 pint strawberries
1 teaspoon lemon juice
4 tablespoons sugar

Place strawberries, sugar and lemon juice in a food blender; turn on low speed and convert to a liquid (15 to 30 seconds). Pour the liquid into a pint glass freezer jar or plastic container, leaving 1/2 inch of head space. Fasten lid on air-tight.

### Velva Strawberry

6 cups strawberry nectar
2 cups sugar
2 tablespoons lemon juice
1/2 teaspoon salt
2 tablespoons gelatin
1/2 cup water

Combine strawberry nectar, sugar, lemon juice and salt. Soak the gelatin in the water for 5 minutes and dissolve by heating over hot water for 10 minutes. Add the fruit mixture slowly to the gelatin, stirring continuously and vigorously. Freeze the mixture in an ice cream freezer or in refrigerator trays. The flavor and texture are better if frozen in an ice cream freezer.

### Blackberry Jelly

6 quarts blackberries (part
1/2 ripe or slightly green)
1 pint water
sugar

Wash berries and boil berries and water together for 15 minutes. Strain through jelly bag. Use 4 cups of juice to 3 cups sugar. Cook until jelly flakes off spoon, skim and pour into glasses. Cover with paraffin.

### Pear Preserves

4 pounds pears
4 cups water

3 pounds sugar
2 lemons, sliced

Select firm, slightly under-ripe pears. Peel and cut into quarters or eighths, depending on size of pear. If Pineapple or Kieffer pears are used, they should be boiled in clear water until they can be pierced with a fork (about 20 minutes). Make syrup with water pears were boiled in. Add sliced lemon and bring to boil. Place pears in syrup and cook until the fruit has a clear, transparent appearance and syrup gives the jelly test. Pour mixture into a shallow pan and let fruit plump overnight. Heat to boiling and pack in preheated jars. Seal and process 15 minutes in hot water bath at simmering temperature.

### Blueberry Preserves

2 quarts blueberries,
  well washed and drained

6 cups sugar
1/2 cup water

Mix the sugar in the water, heat and stir until all sugar is dissolved. Add berries to the boiling syrup and boil with frequent shaking of saucepan until the berries are translucent when lifted from syrup (about 10 minutes). Pour into a flat pan to change the position of the berries and promote taking up of syrup.

Pack berries in preheated jars while still warm, leaving 1/2 inch head space. Remove air bubbles and seal jars. Process in a boiling water bath canner at simmering temperature for 15 minutes.

## Muscadine Jam

5 pounds grapes, chopped and deseeded
5 pounds sugar

Cook deseeded grapes slowly until the hulls are tender. This will be about 15 minutes, but the time will vary with the variety of grapes. Add the sugar directly to the simmering hulls and pulp. Cook until the mixture reaches 220 degrees. Pack hot in preheated jars and seal. Makes 8 to 9 pints.

## Apple Preserves

2 pounds apples
2 1/2 cups water
1 tablespoon ginger root, or mixed whole spices or 12 cloves
4 cups sugar
1 tablespoon lemon juice
salt-vinegar or ascorbic acid water

Use apples that will hold their shape while cooking.

Dissolve sugar in water and bring to rolling boil. Set aside to cool. Meanwhile, peel and core apples. Cut large ones in sixths; leave small ones whole. Peel but do not core crab apples. To prevent discoloration, drop apple pieces into salt-vinegar or ascorbic acid water. Rinse the apple pieces in cold water and drain. Add the drained apple pieces and lemon juice to the cool syrup. Allow them to stand 10 minutes, then place on unit and cook gently until transparent.

Lift apples out and place in a shallow pan. For spiced apple preserves, tie ginger root, spices or cloves in a cheesecloth bag and put the bag in the syrup. Continue to boil until syrup registers 222 degrees on a candy thermometer or reaches the jell stage. Discard the spice bag and pour the hot syrup over the apples. Allow to cool, then heat to boiling and pack in preheated jars. Process at simmering temperature for 15 minutes. Yields 2 1/2 pints.

### Spiced Muscadine

5 pounds muscadine grapes
3 pounds sugar
1 tablespoon allspice
1 pint cider vinegar
1 tablespoon cinnamon

Pulp the grapes and cook pulp in small amount of water; cook until mushy. Put through coarse strainer to remove seeds. Add just enough water to the hulls to cover and boil until tender. Put hulls and pulp together, add sugar and seasonings and cook until thick. Pour into hot sterile glasses and seal with wax. Good with hot breads and as a condiment for meats and poultry.

### Strawberry Preserves

1 pound large ripe strawberries, prepared
1 pound sugar

Use large ripe strawberries. Wash, drain and remove the caps. To every pound of strawberries use one pound of sugar. Arrange the sugar and berries in layers and let stand overnight. Boil rapidly for 20 minutes, stirring occasionally, until the preserves are thick. Let the preserves become cold. Several hours later, bring to a boil again, skim and fill hot jars. Seal at once.

### Orange Marmalade

*Ben Green Cooper*
*The Jefferson Davis Receipt Book*

12 Seville oranges, thinly shredded and seeded
juice of 2 lemons
4 quarts water
8 cups loaf sugar

Shred oranges as thin as possible, taking out seeds, and pour water over them. Let boil very slowly for 2 1/2 hours. Then add sugar and let boil again for 1 1/2 hours. Take off fire and add juice from 2 lemons. Pour into jars or glasses and seal while hot.

## Spiced Grapes

5 pounds grapes, deseeded
1 cup vinegar
4 teaspoons mace, powdered
4 1/2 pounds sugar
1 1/2 teaspoons cinnamon, powdered

Boil grapes for 15 minutes or until hulls are tender. Add sugar and cook until thick. Add spices and vinegar and cook to 220 degrees. Pack hot in preheated jars and seal. Makes 9 to 10 pints.

## Sherry Jelly

1 package gelatin, raspberry flavored
1 tablespoon claret
1 cup hot water
1 cup sherry
2 tablespoons brandy

Dissolve gelatin in hot water; cool. Add sherry, claret and brandy (if desired). Pour into small mold, rinsed in cold water. Chill until set. Unmold. Serve with cold meat. Makes 6 to 8 servings.

## Grape Marmalade

5 pounds grape pulp and ground hulls
2 1/2 pounds sugar
2 1/2 cups pecans, chopped

Heat grape pulp with juice and put through a colander to remove seed. Grind hulls in a food chopper, using a fine blade. Cook until hulls are tender. Add sugar and cook very slowly, stirring repeatedly. Approximately 5 minutes before mixture reaches jelly-like consistency, add pecans. Cook until mixture is very thick. Pack in preheated jars and seal. Makes about 8 pints.

## Apple Butter

6 quarts apples, sliced
2 tablespoons cinnamon
1 gallon cider (reduced 1/2)
8 cups sugar

Use tart apples. Wash and remove cores. It is not necessary to peel them unless desired. Place apples in a preserving kettle with just enough water to cover and cook slowly until tender. Press through a colander or sieve. Measure the strained pulp. Add sugar, cider (boiled to reduce 1 gallon to 1/2) and cinnamon, and cook until thick. When butter is thick enough, pack hot in preheated jars. Process 15 minutes in hot water bath canner.

## Apple Jelly

apples, sliced or chopped
sugar
water

Select and wash fresh, sound, tart apples. Cut out and discard blossom and stem ends. Do not pare or core. Slice or chop apples into a saucepan and just barely cover with water. After the boiling point is reached, cook at simmering temperature 25 to 40 minutes. Immediately pour into cheesecloth or a thin sack and allow juice to drain. When the bag is cool enough to handle, squeeze to remove all juice possible. Then restrain the juice through a jelly bag or flannel bag (do not squeeze this bag).

Measure juice and place it in a large saucepan (not over 6 cups). Set on a hot unit and bring rapidly to a boil. Gradually stir in the sugar (usually 3/4 cup per cup of juice) and cook to the jell stage. Remove from heat, skim off foam and immediately pour into preheated jars. Either seal the jar or cover with a 1/8-inch coat of melted paraffin.

# KITCHEN ADVICES.

**Oven Heats**

| | | |
|---|---|---|
| 250 degrees | - | Very slow |
| 300 degrees | - | Slow |
| 325 degrees | - | Moderately slow |
| 350 degrees | - | Moderate |
| 375 degrees | - | Moderately hot |
| 400 degrees | - | Hot |
| 450 degrees to 500 degrees | - | Very hot |

Occasionally have your oven regulator tested for accuracy.

## Weights and Measures

In adapting a foreign recipe it may be necessary to experiment a little, since the ingredients may be slightly different from American ones.

| | | |
|---|---|---|
| Few grains, pinch, dash (dry) | = | less than 1/8 teaspoon |
| A dash (liquid) | = | a few drops |
| 3 teaspoons | = | 1 Tablespoon |
| 2 Tablespoons | = | 1/8 cup (1 ounce) |
| 4 Tablespoons | = | 1/4 cup |
| 5 1/3 Tablespoons | = | 1/3 cup |
| 8 Tablespoons | = | 1/2 cup |
| 8 ounces | = | 1/2 pint or 1 cup |
| 2 cups | = | 1 pint |
| 2 pints | = | 1 quart |
| 4 quarts (liquid) | = | 1 gallon |
| 8 quarts (dry) | = | 1 peck |
| 4 pecks (dry) | = | 1 bushel |
| 1 jigger | = | 1 1/2 fluid ounces (3 Tablespoons) |
| 1 large jigger | = | 2 fluid ounces (1/4 cup) |

## Temperature Definitions

| | | |
|---|---|---|
| 180 degrees | - | Simmering point of water |
| 212 degrees | - | Boiling point of water |
| 234 degrees to 240 degrees | - | Soft ball stage for syrups |
| 255 degrees | - | Hard crack stage for syrups |
| 320 degrees | - | Caramel stage for syrups |
| 220 degrees | - | Jellying point for jams and jellies |

At altitudes above 3000 feet, lower air pressure causes differences in the boiling point of water and syrups. Consult government bulletins for details.

## Equivalents

Bread crumbs

| | | |
|---|---|---|
| 4 ounces | = | 3/4 cup less 1 Tablespoon |

Butter, lard, other fats and cheese

| | | |
|---|---|---|
| 1 pound | = | 2 cups |
| 1 ounce | = | 2 Tablespoons |
| 1 stick | = | 1/2 cup |

Currants and raisins

| | | |
|---|---|---|
| 1 pound | = | 2 3/8 cups |

Flour

| | | |
|---|---|---|
| 1 pound | = | 3 1/2 to 4 cups |
| 1 ounce | = | 3 Tablespoons |

Nut meats

| | | |
|---|---|---|
| 4 ounces | = | 2/3 cup (chopped) |

Rice (uncooked)

| | | |
|---|---|---|
| 1 pound | = | 2 1/2 cups (8 cups cooked) |

Brown sugar

| | | |
|---|---|---|
| 1 pound | = | 2 1/4 cups (about) |

Confectioners' sugar

| | | |
|---|---|---|
| 1 pound | = | 3 3/4 cups (about) |

Granulated sugar

| | | |
|---|---|---|
| 1 pound | = | 2 cups |

Egg whites (approximately)

| | | |
|---|---|---|
| 1 | = | 1 1/2 Tablespoons |
| 4 to 6 | = | 1/2 cup |

Egg yolks (approximately)

| | | |
|---|---|---|
| 1 | = | 1 Tablespoon |
| 6 to 7 | = | 1/2 cup |

## Approximate Can Sizes

| Can size | Weight | Contents |
|---|---|---|
| 6 ounces | 6 ounces | 3/4 cup |
| 8 ounces | 8 ounces | 1 cup |
| Number 1 | 11 ounces | 1 1/3 cups |
| 12 ounces | 12 ounces | 1 1/2 cups |
| Number 303 | 16 ounces | 2 cups |
| Number 2 | 20 ounces | 2 1/2 cups |
| Number 2 1/2 | 28 ounces | 3 1/2 cups |

## Substitutions

Arrowroot

1 Tablespoon = 2 Tablespoons flour (as thickening).

Baking powder (tartrate or phosphate)

1 teaspoon = 2/3 teaspoon double-action type or 1/4 teaspoon baking soda plus 1/2 teaspoon cream of tartar.

Chocolate

1 ounce (1 square) = 3 Tablespoons cocoa plus 1 teaspoon to 1 Tablespoon shortening (less for Dutch cocoa).

Cornstarch

1 Tablespoon = 2 Tablespoons flour (as thickening).

Flour

Pastry flour. 1 cup = 1 cup all-purpose or bread flour less 2 Tablespoons

Potato flour. 1 Tablespoon = 2 Tablespoons flour (as thickening).

Milk

Fresh, whole. 1 cup = 1/2 cup evaporated milk plus 1/2 cup water or 1/2 cup condensed milk plus 1/2 cup water (reduce the sugar in the recipe) or 1/4 cup powdered whole milk plus 1 cup water or 1/4 cup powdered skim milk plus 2 Tablespoons butter and 1 cup water.

Fresh, skim. 1 cup = 1/4 cup powdered skim milk plus 1 cup water.

Sour. 1 cup = 1 cup lukewarm fresh milk (less 1 Tablespoon) plus 1 Tablespoon vinegar. Let stand 5 minutes.

## White Sauce

| Ingredients | Thin | Medium | Thick |
|---|---|---|---|
| Butter or shortening | 1 Tablespoon | 2 Tablespoons | 3 Tablespoons |
| Flour | 1 Tablespoon | 2 Tablespoons | 3 Tablespoons |
| Milk | 1 cup | 1 cup | 1 cup |

Melt butter or shortening, remove from heat and blend in flour until smooth. Slowly stir in milk. Cook until thick, stirring constantly. Season to taste with salt and pepper.

## Directions for Freezing Prepared Foods

| Food | To Prepare and Package | To Prepare for Table | Maximum Storage |
|---|---|---|---|
| Apples, baked | Bake as usual, until barely done. Cool quickly. Package in rigid containers. | Thaw in container or heat in oven at 325 degrees for 15 to 20 minutes. | 2 months |
| Breads, baked – biscuits, muffins, waffles | Prepare and bake as usual. Wrap in freezer paper or put into plastic bags. | Heat biscuits and muffins, unthawed at 300 degrees for 15 to 20 minutes; heat waffles in toaster. | 4 months |
| Cakes – baked layer, loaf and cup-cakes, angel, etc. | Prepare as usual. Cool. Wrap in freezer paper, or put in freezer bags. May be frozen in different portions. | Thaw in package at room temperature. If packaged in heat-proof wrapping, can thaw in oven at 375° for 10 minutes. | 6 months |
| Cookies, baked | Bake and cool quickly on rack. Use cartons or cellophane bags to freeze, with paper between layers and in spaces. | Thaw, wrapped, for 1/2 to 1 hour, if crisp type. Soft cookies may be placed on serving plate. | 6 months |

| Food | To Prepare and Package | To Prepare for Table | Maximum Storage |
|---|---|---|---|
| Cookies, unbaked | For bars or refrigerator, form into long roll. Wrap in freezer paper. | Process same as if fresh. | 4 months |
| Combination dishes – Creamed meat, poultry, fish | Add 1/4 teaspoon gelatin to each quart white sauce; cool rapidly by setting pan in ice water; stir but do not beat. Work with small quantities, use little fat. Use rigid container, cover with freezer paper, leave 1/2 - 1 inch head space. | Heat from frozen state in top of double boiler for 25 to 30 minutes. Caution: do not let stand at room temperature. | 6 months |
| Meats, roast | Cook as usual; cover with broth; keep in large chunks; put in rigid container, cover with sheet material to fit. | Thaw in refrigerator or at room temperature Slice cold or heat chunks in broth or gravy. | 3 months |
| ham | Bake or broil, cool and bone. Keep large pieces. Package in freezer paper or rigid containers. | Thaw in wrappings to slice cold, or heat in oven. | 1 month |

# INDEX.


**APPETIZERS**

**Cheeses**
- Brandied Cheese Balls .... 9
- Cheese and Tomato Curry . 29
- Cheese Balls .......... 29
- Cheese Blintzes ........ 7
- Cheese Diable ......... 8
- Cheese Fondue ........ 9
- Cheese Puffs .......... 46
- Cheese Roll .......... 8, 12
- Chili Cheese Roll ....... 8
- Chutney Cheese Spread ... 27
- Date Cheese Balls ....... 9
- Tequenos ............ 20

**Dips**
- Avocado Dip .......... 23
- Cocktail Dip .......... 27
- Dill Dip ............ 27
- Easy Crab Meat Dip ..... 58
- Guacomole ........... 13
- Smoky Egg Dip ........ 13

**Dressings**
- Chef's Salad Dressing for Fruit ............ 49
- Chef's Special Dressing ... 41
- Creamy Celery Seed Dressing .......... 38
- Dressing ............ 51
- Dressing for Tossed Salad .. 54
- Fluffy Honey Dressing ... 41
- Honey Dressing ........ 49
- Kitty's Salad Dressing .... 55
- Lemon Dressing ........ 42
- Nasturtium French Dressing 56
- Roquefort Cheese Dressing . 46
- Sour Cream Dressing ..... 53
- Spinach Dressing ....... 48
- Thousand Island Dressing .. 53
- Tomato Soup French Dressing .......... 55

**Eggs**
- Bacon-Mushroom Rarebit . 31
- Burgundy Poached Eggs ... 32
- Egg Roll ............ 12
- Eggs Benedict ......... 33
- Mushroom Eggs ........ 32
- Onion-Almond Omelet ... 32
- Quiche Lorraine ........ 30
- Tomato-Cheese Eggs ..... 31
- Welsh Rarebit ....... 31, 44

**Relishes**
- Beet Chutney ......... 24
- Kraut Relish .......... 35
- Pear Relish ........... 28
- Pepper Relish ......... 18

**Salads**
- Apricot Salad ......... 37
- Asheville Salad ......... 53
- Black Cherry Salad ...... 44
- Broccoli Congealed Salad .. 50
- Caesar Salad .......... 52
- Cheese Slaw .......... 17
- Cherry Pineapple Salad ... 51
- Chicken Salad ......... 39
- Cole Slaw ............ 47
- Compote of Fruit with Champagne ......... 47
- Congealed Salad ........ 43
- Crab Salad Parfait ....... 40
- Cranberry Salad ........ 23
- Cucumber Salad ........ 41
- English Pea Salad ....... 50
- Fresh Spinach Salad ..... 42
- Frozen Cranberry Cream Salad ............. 45
- Frozen Fruit Salad .... 38, 43
- Frozen Salad .......... 39
- Fruit Salad ........... 43
- Fruit Salad Loaf ........ 45
- Full a Beans Salad ...... 34
- Ginger Ale Salad ....... 48
- Green Pea Salad ........ 57
- Hot Potato Salad ....... 40
- Molded Three-Fruit Salad . 36
- Mushroom Salad ....... 34
- Pickle, Pineapple Nut Salad . 35
- Pineapple Salad ........ 49
- Sam's Salad ........... 54
- Shrimp Aspic Salad ...... 22
- Sour Cream Salad ....... 37
- Spiced Peach Salad ...... 48
- Tomato Aspic ......... 17
- Tossed Salad .......... 54
- Tuna Loaf Salad ........ 39
- Waldorf Salad ......... 38
- White Cherry Salad ...... 14
- White Fruit Salad ....... 36
- Wilted Spinach Salad ..... 42
- Yum Yum Salad ........ 47

**Sauces**
Barbecue Sauce . . . . . . 25, 28
Bearnaise Sauce . . . . . . . . 26
Creamy Dill Sauce . . . . . . 26
Hollandaise Sauce . . . . . 25, 33
Remoulade Sauce . . . . . . . 28
Souffle Sauce . . . . . . . . . 25
Tartar Cream Sauce . . . . . 21
**Snacks**
Baby Pizzas . . . . . . . . . . . 20
Bacon-Blanketed Appetizers 16
Canape Bases . . . . . . . . . . 16
Canape Lorenzo . . . . . . . . 21
Chicken Toasties . . . . . . . 10
Clam Canape . . . . . . . . . . 23
Curried Tuna Toasties . . . . 11
Deviled Ham Canapes . . . . 16
Fried Artichoke . . . . . . . . 17
Ham & Sweet Rolls . . . . . . 18
Marinated Vegetables . . . . 35
Mushroom Tempters . . . . . 15
Pickled Shrimp . . . . . . . . 24
Pickled Watermelon Rind . . 14
Rumaki . . . . . . . . . . . . . 59
Sausage Pineapple Kabob . . 52
Sherry Cheese Stuffed Celery . . . . . . . . . . . 18
Spiced Pickled Shrimp . . . . 22
Stuffed Cucumber . . . . . . 16
Super Stuffed Celery . . . . . 19
Tiny Tim Appetizers . . . . . 15
Water Chestnut Snack . . . . 60
**Soups**
Cream of Peanut Soup . . . . 55
Creme Vichyssoise . . . . . . 11
Cucumber Soup . . . . . . . . 15
Egg Drop Soup . . . . . . . . 61
Gazpacho . . . . . . . . . . . 57
Jajoukh . . . . . . . . . . . . . 61
Japanese Egg Yolk Soup . . 59
Peasant Soup . . . . . . . . . 60
President Eisenhower's Nasturtium-Vegetable Soup . 56
She-Crab Soup a la William Deas . . . . . . . . . . . . . 58
**Spreads**
Avocado Cream . . . . . . . . 30
Anchovy Spread . . . . . . . . 29
Newberg Spread . . . . . . . . 46
Shrimp Paste . . . . . . . . . 10

**BREADS**

Almond Bread . . . . . . . . . . . 197
Angel Biscuits . . . . . . . .206, 217
Applesauce Nut Bread . . . . . . 204
Baking Powder Sally Lunn . . . 210
Banana Bread . . . . . . . . . . . 203
Batter Bread . . . . . . . . . . . . 204
Blueberry Streusel Muffins . . . 196
Bran Rolls . . . . . . . . . . . . . . 216
Coastal Rice Bread . . . . . . . . 208
Coconut Bread . . . . . . . . . . . 201
Corn Fritters . . . . . . . . . . . . 214
Corn Meal Bread . . . . . . . . . 218
Corn Meal Muffins . . . . . . . . 206
Corn Sticks . . . . . . . . . . . . . 217
Country Breakfast Muffins . . . 220
Cracklin' Corn Bread . . . . . . . 215
Cream Biscuits . . . . . . . . . . . 216
Crumpets . . . . . . . . . . . . . . 212
Dilly Bread . . . . . . . . . . . . . 221
Doughnuts . . . . . . . . . . . . . 203
Easy Banana Bread . . . . . . . . 205
Easy Icebox Rolls . . . . . . . . . 219
Echota Hard Bread . . . . . . . . 213
Foolproof Waffles . . . . . . . . 200
Fruit Bars . . . . . . . . . . . . . . 211
Glazed Pineapple Fingers . . . . 195
Grandma's Buttermilk Rolls . . 219
Griddle Cakes . . . . . . . . . . . 202
Honey Twist Bread . . . . . . . . 199
Hot Cross Buns . . . . . . . . . . 198
Hush Puppies . . . . . . . . . . . . 215
Lemon Frosting . . . . . . . . . . 195
Mama's Favorite Corn Bread . . 207
Mexican Corn Bread . . . . . . . 214
Muffins with Cranberries . . . . 215
Never Fail Dumplings . . . . . . 218
Olivia Risberg's Pizza . . . . . . 222
Orange French Toast . . . . . . . 203
Orange Muffins . . . . . . . . . . 197
Orange Nut Bread . . . . . . . . . 200
Orange Pecan Bread . . . . . . . 205
Parmesan Casserole Bread . . . 220
Party Cheese Biscuits . . . . . . 208
Popovers . . . . . . . . . . . . . . 202
Potato Bread . . . . . . . . . . . . 221
Refrigerator Rolls . . . . . . . . . 211
Sara's Cheese Wafers . . . . . . . 213
Scones . . . . . . . . . . . . . . . . 212
Soul Food Corn Bread . . . . . . 208
Sourdough Bread . . . . . . . . . 209
Sourdough Starter . . . . . . . . 209
Southern Corn Bread for Two . 216
Spoon Bread . . . . . . . . . . . . 207
Sweet Potato Biscuits . . . . . . 200
Yeast Sally Lunn . . . . . . . . . 210
Yorkshire Muffins . . . . . . . . . 202
Yorkshire Pudding. . . . . . . . . 222

**DESSERTS**

**Beverages**
Coast Artillery Punch . . . . 287
Congealed Eggnog . . . . . . 288
Delicious Punch . . . . . . . . 290
Eggnog . . . . . . . . . . . . . . 286
Holiday Punch . . . . . . . . . 288
Hot Russian Tea . . . . . . . . 290
Inexpensive Punch . . . . . . 288

Melon Ball Cocktail . . . . . 289
Milk Punch . . . . . . . . . . . . 287
Mint Julep . . . . . . . . . . . . 290
President Polk's Eggnog . . . 287
Punch . . . . . . . . . . . . . . 289
Sassafras Tea . . . . . . . . . . 289
Syllabub . . . . . . . . . . . . . 286

**Cakes**
Apple Cake . . . . . . . . . . . 226
Banana Nut Cake . . . . . . . 249
Brown Sugar Pound Cake . . . . . . . . . .230, 240
Carrot Cake . . . . . . . . . . . 231
Cheeseless Cheese Cake . . . 244
Chocolate Delight Cake . . . 248
Cocoa and Cola Cake . . . . 239
Coffee-Coffee Cake . . . . . . 243
Colorful Sherbet Cake . . . . 253
Dark Beauty Fruit Cake . . . 257
Dark Fruit Cake . . . . . . . . 254
Famous Orange Chiffon Cake . . . . . . . . . . . . . 242
Foolproof Layer Cake . . . . 236
Franklin Cake . . . . . . . . . 231
Fruited Cheese Cake . . . . . 232
Fudge Cake . . . . . . . . . . . 235
Funny Cake . . . . . . . . . . 237
German Chocolate Cake . . 247
Gingerbread . . . . . . . . . . 238
Grandma's Applesauce Cake . . . . . . . . . . . . 227
Holiday Pound Cake . . . . . 257
Japanese Fruit Cake . . . . . 255
Lemonade Cake . . . . . . . . 233
Lemon Cheesecake . . .241, 246
Mocha Torte . . . . . . . . . . 245
Oatmeal Cake . . . . . . . . . .227
Old Fashioned Pound Cake . 228
Pecan Cake . . . . . . . . . . . 228
Perfect Chocolate Frosting . 236
Plum Cake . . . . . . . . . . . 229
Pound Cake (Variation) . . . 251
Praline Cake . . . . . . . . . . 252
Pumpkin Cake . . . . . . . . . 256
Red Velvet Cake . . . . . . . 229
Rum Torte . . . . . . . . . . . 273
Sour Cream Cake . . . . . . . 239
Sour Cream Coffee Cake . . 244
Sour Cream Pound Cake . . 240
Sunny Coffee Cake . . . . . . 230
"Sweet to Your Heart" Cake . . . . . . . . . . . . . 233
Walnut Glory Cake . . . . . . 250
White Fruit Cake . . . . . . . 270
Zwieback Cake . . . . . . . . . 234

**Candy**
Divinity . . . . . . . . . . . . . 282
Favorite Fudge . . . . . . . . 281
Fudge . . . . . . . . . . . . . . 278
Mexican Pecan Candy . . . . 282
Peanut Brittle . . . . . .268, 280
Sugared Nuts . . . . . . . . . . 281
Sugared Walnuts . . . . . . . . 278
Whiskey Pecans . . . . . . . . 279

**Cookies**
Apricot Balls . . . . . . . . . . 280
Coconut Macaroons . . . . . 279
Date Balls . . . . . . . . . . . . 283
Date Nut Balls . . . . . . . . . .283
Delicious Cookies . . . . . . . 284
Easy Cookies . . . . . . . . . . 267
Pecan Balls . . . . . . . . . . . 283
Quick Mix Oatmeal Cookies 284
Rum (or Bourbon) Cookies . 284

**Fruits**
Ambrosia . . . . . . . . . . . . 285
Apple Cheese Crisp . . . . . . 275
Baked Pears Elegante . . . . 251
Cherries Emily . . . . . . . . . 272
Cherry Cobbler . . . . . . . . 275
French Type Apple Pastry Strip . . . . . . . . . . . . . 276
Fresh Peach Cobbler . . . . . 252
Fruit Whip . . . . . . . . . . . 285

**Ice Cream**
Chocolate Chip-Mint Ice Cream . . . . . . . . . . 248
Chocolate Ice Cream . . . . . 247
Fabulous Vanilla Ice Cream . . . . . . . . . . . . 253
Lemon Ice . . . . . . . . . . . 286
Nut Brittle Ice Cream . . . . 249
Peppermint Candy Ice Cream . . . . . . . . . . . . 268
Strawberry Sherbet . . . . . . 250
Tropical Freeze . . . . . . . . 285

**Jams & Jellies**
Apple Butter . . . . . . . . . . 301
Apple Jelly . . . . . . . . . . . 301
Apple Preserves . . . . . . . . 298
Applesauce . . . . . . . . . . . 292
Blackberry Jelly . . . . . . . . 296
Blueberry Preserves . . . . . . 297
Damson Plum Preserves . . . 294
Grape Marmalade . . . . . . . 300
Jelly Test . . . . . . . . . . . . 291
Muscadine Jam . . . . . . . . 298
Orange Marmalade . . . . . . 299
Pear Preserves . . . . . . . . . 297
Plum Jam . . . . . . . . . . . . 294
Plum Jelly . . . . . . . . . . . . 292
Plum Sauce or Spiced Plums . . . . . . . . . . . . 293
Sherry Jelly . . . . . . . . . . . 300
Spiced Grapes . . . . . . . . . 300
Spiced Muscadine . . . . . . . 299
Strawberry and Pineapple Jam . . . . . . . . . . . . . 294
Strawberry Jam . . . . . . . . 295
Strawberry Nectar . . . . . . 296

Strawberry Preserves . . . . . 299
Strawberry Preserves Deluxe . . . . . . . . . . . . 295
Velva Strawberry . . . . . . . 296

**Pies**
Almond Cream Pie . . . . . . 264
Black Bottom Pie . . . . . . . 266
Blueberry Pie . . . . . . . . . . 261
Burgundy Cherry Pie . . . . . 268
Butter Pecan Pie Crust . . . . 261
Cherry Cream Pie . . . . . . . 260
Chess Pie . . . . . . . . . . . 269
Christmas Eggnog Pie . . . . 270
Coffee Cloud Pie . . . . . . . 269
The Cracker Crumble . . . . 224
Crumble Pie . . . . . . . . . . 225
Easy Mincemeat Pie . . . . . 271
Frozen Lemon Pie . . .259, 265
Georgia Lemon Pie . . . . . . 263
Honey Pecan Pie . . . . . . . 272
Lemon Chess Pie . . . . . . . 263
Lemon Chiffon Pie . . . . . . 259
Lemon Coconut Pie . . . . . 260
Lemon-Lime Sky High Pie . 265
Lemon Pie . . . . . . . . . . . 258
Meringue Shells . . . . . . . . 269
Mile High Lime Pie . . . . . . 262
Pecan Pie . . . . . . . . . . . 262
Pineapple Chiffon Pie . . . . 262
Rum Cream Pie . . . . . . . . 258
Tropical Pie . . . . . . . . . . . 267

**Other Desserts**
Baked Custard . . . . . . . . . 274
Banana Pudding . . . . . . . . 277
Boiled Custard . . . . . .274, 279
Charlotte Russe . . . . . . . . 243
English Trifle . . . . . . . . . . 232
Grandma's Plum Pudding . . 271
Rice Pudding . . . . . . . . . . 280
Sweet Sue . . . . . . . . . . . . 273
Tipsy Pudding . . . . . . . . . 278

**FOWL**
Char-broiled Chicken Halves . . 143
Charcoal Broiled Chicken . . . . 135
Chicken Bourguinone . . . . . . 138
Chicken Breasts with Rice . . . 141
Chicken Casserole . . . . . . . . . 140
Chicken Champignon . . . . . . 135
Chicken Curry . . . . . . . . . . . 137
Chicken-in-a-Beerpot . . . . . . . 141
Chicken in Wine . . . . . . . . . . 131
Chicken Kiev . . . . . . . . . . . . 143
Chicken Newburg . . . . . . . . . 146
Chicken Ravioli . . . . . . . . . . 138
Chicken Roll with Mushroom Sauce . . . . . . . . . . . . . . . 131
Chicken Salad Casserole . . . . . 132
Chicken-Sausage Casserole. . . . .137
Chinese Style Chicken Livers . 145
Country Captain Chicken . . . . 139
Delicious Patio Chicken . . . . . 134
Duck Stuffing . . . . . . . . . . . 149
Gourmet Broiled Chicken . . . 137
Grace's Sourdough Chicken Pie 133
Greek Chicken and Rice . . . . 140
Hawaiian Duck . . . . . . . . . . 148
Liver Stuffed Chicken Breasts with Sauce . . . . . . . . . . . 144
Low Country Fowl Bog . . . . . 130
Parsley Dumplings . . . . . . . . 139
Party Chicken . . . . . . . . . . . 132
Plantation Fried Chicken 'n Gravy . . . . . . . . . . . . . 142
Potted Doves . . . . . . . . . . . . 149
Pressed Chicken . . . . . . . . . . 136
Quail Continental . . . . . . . . . 147
Roast Duck . . . . . . . . . . . . . 148
Sauteed Chicken Livers . . . . . 145
Smothered Marsh Hens . . . . . 146
Southern Smothered Pheasant 150
Soy Squabs . . . . . . . . . . . . . 150
Steamed Chicken Mold . . . . . 134
Turkey Carving . . . . . . .128, 129
Wild Duck . . . . . . . . . . . . . 147

**MEATS**
Backbone . . . . . . . . . . . . 190
Baked Country Cured Ham 186
Baked Country Ham . . . . . 163
Baked Picnic Ham . . . . . 185
Barbecued Spareribs . . . . . 190
Barbecue Hamburgers . . . . 183
Batter Fried Chitterlings . . 159
Beef Ribs a la Griff . . . . . . 153
Beef Stew . . . . . . . . . . . 157
Beef Stew a-Eloise . . . . . . 161
Beef Stroganoff Casserole . 175
Blue Cheese Steaks . . . . . . 181
Braised Sirloin . . . . . . . . . 167
Broiled Lamb Chops . . . . . 171
Brunswick Stew . . . . . . . . 177
Burgundy Beef Tips with Mushrooms . . . . . . . . . 172
Calf's Liver in Wine . . . . . . 164
Chili con Carne . . . . . . . . 158
Chuckwagon Braised Liver . 165
Company Casserole . . . . . . 175
Corned Beef . . . . . . . . . . 179
Country Fried Steak . . . . . 163
Creole Spareribs . . . . . . . . 179
Crown Pork Roast with Corn Bread Stuffing . . . . . . . 188
Deviled Lamb Chops . . . . . 171
Diet Meat Loaf . . . . . . . . 183
Dixie Pork Chops . . . . . . . 191
Easy Pot Roast . . . . . . . . 162
Fabulous Hawaiian Marinated Steak . . . . . . . . . . . . . 182

French Chop Suey . . . . . . 178
Green Peppersteak . . . . . . 157
Ham and Asparagus
Casserole . . . . . . . . . . 187
Ham Mousse . . . . . . . . . . 187
Huberto's Own Spaghetti . . 176
Island Ham Rolls . . . . . . . 179
Lamb Chops with Mint Jelly 191
Lamb In The Ground . 169-170
Lasagna . . . . . . . . . . . . 177
Liver and Onions . . . . . . . 162
London Broil . . . . . . . . . . 164
Marinated Steak . . . . . . . . 158
Meat Loaf . . . . . . . . . . . . 180
Meat Loaf O'Brien . . . . . . 189
Me Jane Steak . . . . . . . . . 156
Mexican Eggplant Skillet . . 174
Moist Meat Loaf . . . . . . . . 181
Pepper Steak . . . . . . . . . . 160
Pineapple Ham Loaf . . . . . 185
Pork Chops in Wine Sauce . 189
Pork Tenderloin . . . . . . . . 191
Quick Stroganoff . . . . . . . 174
Rabbit Bourguignonne . . . 166
Rabbit Pie . . . . . . . . . . . . 167
Roasted Lamb . . . . . . . . . 168
Roast Venison . . . . . . . . . 162
Round Steak Supreme . . . . 161
Sauerbraten . . . . . . . . . . . 178
Sausage Casserole . . . . . . . 154
Scotch Steak and Kidney
Pie . . . . . . . . . . . . . . 159
Shepherd's Pie . . . . . . . . . 192
Sherry Roast Pork . . . . . . 192
Skillet Stroganoff . . . . . . . 173
South Georgia Brunswick
Stew . . . . . . . . . . . . 173
Spaghetti Meat Dish . . . . . 172
Steak Casserole . . . . . . . . 154
Steak with Rice . . . . . . . . 156
Summer Meat Loaf . . . . . . 182
Swedish Meat Ball Gravy . . 184
Swedish Meat Balls . . . . . . 184
Swiss Steak . . . . . . . . . . . 160
Talmadge Country
Fried Ham . . . . . . . . . . 166
Thursday Pot Roast . . . . . 165
Tortilla Flats . . . . . . . . . . 180
Tournedos . . . . . . . . . . . 155
Venison Steaks . . . . . . . . 163
Venison with Sour Cream . 168

**SEAFOOD**

Artichoke – Lobster
Newburg . . . . . . . . . . . 112
Baked Fish . . . . . . . . . . . . 118
Baked Flounder with Sauce . . 124
Baked Oysters . . . . . . . . . . 101
Baked Stuffed Pompano . . . . 101
Bayou Pie . . . . . . . . . . . . . 125
Beer-Batter Shrimp . . . . . . . . 116
Boiled Trout . . . . . . . . . . . . 122
Boneless Baked Shad . . . . . . . 97
Brook Trout Almondine . . . . 123
Chicken with Oysters . . . . . . 98
Clam Chowder . . . . . . . . . . . 125
Crab Cakes . . . . . . . . . . . . . 104
Crab Imperial . . . . . . . . . . . 102
Crab Louis . . . . . . . . . . . . . 120
Crabmeat Au Gratin . . . . . . . 103
Crab Mornay . . . . . . . . . . . . 105
Creole Shrimp . . . . . . . .118, 124
Deviled Crab . . . . . . . . .107, 108
Deviled Crab Casserole . . . . . 105
Deviled Salmon . . . . . . . . . . 117
Deviled Shrimp . . . . . . . . . . 121
Easy Shrimp Curry . . . . . . . . 114
Fish Chowder . . . . . . . . . . . 105
Fish Mulligan . . . . . . . . . . . . 110
Fried Bass Filets . . . . . . . . . . 124
Fried Catfish . . . . . . . . . . . . 104
Frog Legs Provencal . . . . . . . 111
Jiffy Creamed Eggs and
Seafood . . . . . . . . . . . . . 103
Lobster a la Newburg . . . . . . 110
Lobster Newburg . . . . . . . . . 111
Lobster Salad Supreme . . . . . 113
Oysters a la Poulette . . . . . . . 100
Oysters Rockefeller . . . . . . . 97
Oyster Stew . . . . . . . . . . . . 98
Quick Seafood Bisque . . . . . . 112
Salmon and Mushroom Stuffed
Potatoes . . . . . . . . . . . . . 100
Savannah Shrimp . . . . . . . . . 122
Scalloped Oysters . . . . . . . 98, 99
Scalloped Shad Roe . . . . . . . 121
Scallops au Gratin . . . . . . . . 102
Seafood a la King . . . . . . . . . 108
Seafood Chowder, Pilau,
Gumbo . . . . . . . . . . . . . 106
Seafood in Tomato Shells . . . 99
Shad Roe Spread . . . . . . . . . 117
Shrimp and Crabmeat
Casserole . . . . . . . . . . . 119
Shrimp de Jonghe . . . . . . . . . 114
Shrimp Remoulade . . . . . . . . 117
Shrimp & Rice . . . . . . . . . . . 115
Shrimp Rice – Jambalaya . . . 115
Shrimp Sea Island . . . . . . . . . 120
Shrimp Stuffed in Bell Peppers 119
Sole in Wine Sauce . . . . . . . . 123
Stuffed Avocados . . . . . . . . . 116
Stuffed Lobster, Jamaica
Style . . . . . . . . . . . . . . 109
Trout Almondine . . . . . . . . . 109
Tuna and Ripe – Olive Loaf . . 107
Tuna Bake with Cheese Swirls . 113

**VEGETABLES**


Artichoke & Asparagus Casserole . . . . . . . . . . . . . 90
Asparagus Casserole . . . . . . . . 93
Asparagus Pie . . . . . . . . . . . 94
Aunt Doveye's Stuffed Onions. 69
Baked Acorn Squash . . . . . . . 91
Baked and Stuffed Fluffy White Potatoes . . . . . . . . . . 87
Baked Eggplant . . . . . . . . . . 76
Baked Squash . . . . . . . . . . . 89
Broccoli Ring . . . . . . . . . . . 81
Broccoli Souffle . . . . . . . . . . 92
Broiled Tomatoes . . . . . . . . . 89
Brown Rice . . . . . . . . . . . . . 92
Brussels Sprouts with Pecan Sauce . . . . . . . . . . 66
Butternut Squash Souffle . . . . 67
Cabbage au Gratin . . . . . . . . 89
Candied Acorn Squash . . . . . 88
Candied Sweet Potatoes . . . . . 88
Carrot Casserole . . . . . . . . . . 90
Carrots and Cheese . . . . . . . . 91
Cheese Pudding . . . . . . . . . . 67
Cheese – Rice Casserole . . . . 85
Cheese Souffle . . . . . . . . . . . 79
Corn Pudding . . . . . . . . . . . 68
Crab and Mushroom Stuffed Potatoes . . . . . . . . . . . . . 86
Creamed Corn . . . . . . . . . . . 66
Creamed Chestnuts . . . . . . . . 72
Eggplant Casserole . . . . . . 73, 74
French Fried Toombs County Onions . . . . . . . . . . . . . . 68
Fresh Asparagus with Vinagrette Sauce . . . . . . . . . . . . . . . 94
Fried Rice and Shrimp . . . . . 77
Glazed Carrots . . . . . . . . . . . 88
Green Bean Casserole . . . . . . 80
Hopping John . . . . . . . . . . . 93
Italian Rice . . . . . . . . . . . . . 78
Lemon-Wild Rice with Shrimp. 82
Macaroni and Cheese Deluxe . 79
Macaroni Pie . . . . . . . . . . . . 71
Marinated Cauliflower . . . . . . 67
Never Fail Cheese Souffle . . . 81
Okra, Rice and Tomatoes . . . . 70
Onions in Cheese Sauce . . . . . 65
Pecan – Squash Souffle . . . . . 65
Pickled Beets . . . . . . . . . . . . 94
Potato Pancakes . . . . . . . . . . 84
Potatoes O'Glenn . . . . . . . . . 83
Rice Casserole . . . . . . . . . . . 83
Savannah Red Rice . . . . . . . . 91
Savory Red Cabbage . . . . . . . 70
Scalloped Corn . . . . . . . . . . . 66
Scalloped Onions . . . . . . . . . 75
Scalloped Sweet Potatoes . . . . 87
Scalloped Tomatoes . . . . . . . 70
Sour Cream Cabbage . . . . . . . 69
Spanish Omelet . . . . . . . . 71, 76
Spanish Rice . . . . . . . . . . 76, 77
Spinach Souffle . . . . . . . . . . 92
Squash Casserole . . . . . . . 68, 73
Stewed Corn . . . . . . . . . . . . 78
Stuffed Eggplant . . . . . . . 75, 77
Stuffed Green Peppers . . . . . . 72
Stuffed Zucchini . . . . . . . . . 82
Sweet Potato Balls . . . . . . . . 86
Sweet Potato Delight . . . . . . 85
Sweet Potato Souffle . . . . . . 84
Tuna Beans . . . . . . . . . . . . . 80
Turnip Greens . . . . . . . . . . . 85
Vegetable Pilaf . . . . . . . . . . 74
Woodchuck . . . . . . . . . . . . . 73


---

**APPLES**


Apple Butter . . . . . . . . . . . 301
Apple Cake . . . . . . . . . . . . 226
Apple Cheese Crisp . . . . . . . 275
Apple Jelly . . . . . . . . . . . . 301
Apple Preserves . . . . . . . . . 298
Applesauce . . . . . . . . . . . . 292
Applesauce Nut Bread . . . . . 204
French Type Apple Pastry Strip . . . . . . . . . 276
Grandma's Applesauce Cake . . . . . . . . . . . . . 227
Waldorf Salad . . . . . . . . . . 38


**ASPARAGUS**


Asparagus Casserole . . . . . 93
Asparagus Pie . . . . . . . . . 94
Fresh Asparagus with Vinagrette Sauce . . . . . 94
Ham and Asparagus Casserole . . . . . . . . . . . 187


**AVOCADO**


Avocado Cream . . . . . . . . 30
Avocado Dip . . . . . . . . . . 23
Guacomole . . . . . . . . . . . 13
Stuffed Avocados . . . . . . . 116


**BANANAS**


Banana Bread . . . . . . . . . 203
Banana Nut Cake . . . . . . . 249
Banana Pudding . . . . . . . . 277
Easy Banana Bread . . . . . . 205


**BEEF**


Barbecue Hamburgers . . . . 183
Beef Ribs A La Griff . . . . . 153
Beef Stew . . . . . . . . . . . . 157
Beef Stew a-Eloise . . . . . . 161

Beef Stroganoff Casserole . . . . . . . . . . 175
Burgundy Beef Tips with Mushrooms . . . . . . . . . 172
Corned Beef . . . . . . . . . . 179
Easy Pot Roast . . . . . . . . 162
Mexican Eggplant Skillet . . . . . . . . . . . . 174
Shepherd's Pie . . . . . . . . . . 192
Thursday Pot Roast . . . . . 165
Tournedos . . . . . . . . . . . 155

**BERRIES**
Blackberry Jelly . . . . . . . . 296
Blueberry Pie . . . . . . . . . . 261
Blueberry Preserves . . . . . . 297
Blueberry Streusel Muffins . . . . . . . . . . . 196
Strawberry Jam . . . . . . . . 295
Strawberry Nectar . . . . . . 296
Strawberry Preserves . . . . . 299
Strawberry Preserves Deluxe . . . . . . . . . . . . 295
Strawberry Sherbet . . . . . . 250
Velva Strawberry . . . . . . . 296

**BREADS**
Applesauce Nut Bread . . . . . . . . . . . . . 204
Baking Powder Sally Lunn . . . . . . . . . . . . . 210
Banana Bread . . . . . . . . . 203
Batter Bread . . . . . . . . . . 204
Coastal Rice Bread . . . . . . 208
Coconut Bread . . . . . . . . . 201
Corn Meal Bread . . . . . . . 218
Corn Sticks . . . . . . . . . . . 217
Cracklin' Corn Bread . . . . . . . . . . . . 215
Dilly Bread . . . . . . . . . . . 221
Echota Hard Bread . . . . . . 213
Gingerbread . . . . . . . . . . 238
Glazed Pineapple Fingers . . . . . . . . . . . . 195
Honey Twist Bread . . . . . . 199
Hot Cross Buns . . . . . . . . 198
Hush Puppies . . . . . . . . . . 215
Mama's Favorite Corn Bread . . . . . . . . . . . . 207
Mexican Corn Bread . . . . . 214
Orange Nut Bread . . . . . . . 200
Parmesan Casserole Bread . . . . . . . . . . . . 220
Potato Bread . . . . . . . . . . 221
Sourdough Bread . . . . . . . 209
Sourdough Starter . . . . . . 209
Southern Corn Bread for Two . . . . . . . . . . 216
Spoon Bread . . . . . . . . . . 207
Yeast Sally Lunn . . . . . . . 210

**CABBAGE**
Cabbage au Gratin . . . . . . 89
Cheese Slaw . . . . . . . . . . 17
Cole Slaw . . . . . . . . . . . . 47
Savory Red Cabbage . . . . . 70
Sour Cream Cabbage . . . . . 69

**CARROTS**
Carrot Cake . . . . . . . . . . . 231
Carrot Casserole . . . . . . . . 90
Carrots and Cheese . . . . . . 91
Glazed Carrots . . . . . . . . . 88

**CASSEROLES**
Beef Stroganoff Casserole . . . . . . . . . . 175
Carrot Casserole . . . . . . . . 90
Chicken Casserole . . . . . . . 140
Chicken Salad Casserole . . . . . . . . . . 132
Chicken-Sausage Casserole . . . . . . . . . . 137
Deviled Crab Casserole . . . . . . . . . . 105
Eggplant Casserole . . . . 73, 74
Green Bean Casserole . . . . 80
Ham and Asparagus Casserole . . . . . . . . . . 187
Parmesan Casserole Bread . . . . . . . . . . . . . 220
Rice Casserole . . . . . . . . . 83
Sausage Casserole . . . . . . . 154
Shrimp and Crabmeat Casserole . . . . . . . . . . 119
Squash Casserole . . . . . 68, 73
Steak Casserole . . . . . . . . 154

**CHEESE**
Asheville Salad . . . . . . . . . 53
Blue Cheese Steaks . . . . . . 181
Brandied Cheese Balls . . . . 9
Carrots and Cheese . . . . . . 91
Cheese and Tomato Curry . . . . . . . . . . . . 29
Cheese Balls . . . . . . . . . . 29
Cheese Blintzes . . . . . . . . 7
Cheese Diable . . . . . . . . . 8
Cheese Fondue . . . . . . . . 9
Cheeseless Cheese Cake . . . . . . . . . . . . 244
Cheese Pudding . . . . . . . . 67
Cheese Puffs . . . . . . . . . . 46
Cheese-Rice Casserole . . . . 85
Cheese Roll . . . . . . . . . . 8, 12
Cheese Slaw . . . . . . . . . . 17
Cheese Souffle . . . . . . . . . 79
Chili Cheese Roll . . . . . . . 8
Chutney Cheese Spread . . . . . . . . . . . . 27
Cocktail Dip . . . . . . . . . . 27
Date Cheese Balls . . . . . . . 9

Dill Dip . . . . . . . . . . . . . 27
Easy Crab Meat Dip . . . . . 58
Macaroni and Cheese
Deluxe . . . . . . . . . . . . 79
Never Fail Cheese
Souffle . . . . . . . . . . . . 81
Onions in Cheese
Sauce . . . . . . . . . . . . . 65
Parmesan Casserole
Bread . . . . . . . . . . . . . 220
Party Cheese
Biscuits . . . . . . . . . . . 208
Quiche Lorraine . . . . . . . . . 30
Roquefort Cheese
Dressing . . . . . . . . . . . 46
Sara's Cheese
Wafers . . . . . . . . . . . . 213
Sherry Cheese Stuffed
Celery . . . . . . . . . . . . 18
Tequenos . . . . . . . . . . . . 20
Tomato-Cheese Eggs . . . . . 31
Welsh Rarebit . . . . . . . . . 31

**CHERRIES**
Black Cherry Salad . . . . . . 44
Burgundy Cherry Pie . . . . . 268
Charlotte Russe . . . . . . . . 243
Cherries Emily . . . . . . . . . 272
Cherry Cobbler . . . . . . . . 275
Cherry Cream Pie . . . . . . . 260
Cherry Pineapple
Salad . . . . . . . . . . . . . 51
Crumble Pie . . . . . . . . . . 225
White Cherry Salad . . . . . . 14

**CHOWDER**
Clam Chowder . . . . . . . . . 125
Fish Chowder . . . . . . . . . 105
Fish Mulligan . . . . . . . . . . 110
Seafood Chowder,
Pilau, Gumbo . . . . . . . 106

**CORN**
Corn Meal Bread . . . . . . . 218
Corn Meal Muffins . . . . . . 206
Corn Pudding . . . . . . . . . 68
Corn Sticks . . . . . . . . . . . 217
Cracklin' Corn
Bread . . . . . . . . . . . . . 215
Creamed Corn . . . . . . . . . 66
Mama's Favorite
Corn Bread . . . . . . . . . 207
Mexican Corn
Bread . . . . . . . . . . . . . 214
Scalloped Corn . . . . . . . . . 66
Soul Food Corn Bread . . . . 208
Southern Corn Bread
for Two . . . . . . . . . . . 216
Stewed Corn . . . . . . . . . . 78

**CRAB**
Canape Lorenzo . . . . . . . . . 21
Crab Cakes . . . . . . . . . . . 104
Crab Imperial . . . . . . . . . 102
Crab Louis . . . . . . . . . . . 120
Crabmeat au Gratin . . . . . 103
Crab Mornay . . . . . . . . . . 105
Crab and Mushroom
Stuffed Potatoes . . . . . 86
Crab Salad
Parfait . . . . . . . . . . . . 40
Deviled Crab . . . . . . .107, 108
Deviled Crab
Casserole . . . . . . . . . . 105
Easy Crab Meat
Dip . . . . . . . . . . . . . . 58
She-Crab Soup a la
William Deas . . . . . . . . 58
Shrimp and Crabmeat
Casserole . . . . . . . . . . 119
Stuffed Avocados . . . . . . . 116

**CUCUMBERS**
Cucumber Salad . . . . . . . . 41
Cucumber Soup . . . . . . . . 15
Jajoukh . . . . . . . . . . . . . 61
Stuffed Cucumber . . . . . . 16

**DATES**
Date Balls . . . . . . . . . . . . 283
Date Cheese Balls . . . . . . . 9
Date Nut Balls . . . . . . . . . 283

**DUCK**
Duck Stuffing . . . . . . . . . 149
Hawaiian Duck . . . . . . . . 148
Roast Duck . . . . . . . . . . . 148
Wild Duck . . . . . . . . . . . . 147

**EGGS**
Bacon-Mushroom
Rarebit . . . . . . . . . . . . 31
Burgundy Poached
Eggs . . . . . . . . . . . . . 32
Egg Drop Soup . . . . . . . . 61
Egg Roll . . . . . . . . . . . . . 12
Eggs Benedict . . . . . . . . . 33
Japanese Egg Yolk
Soup . . . . . . . . . . . . . 59
Jiffy Creamed Eggs
and Seafood . . . . . . . . 103
Mexican Eggplant
Skillet . . . . . . . . . . . . 174
Mushroom Eggs . . . . . . . . 32
Onion-Almond Omelet . . . 32
Quiche Lorraine . . . . . . . . 30
Smoky Egg Dip . . . . . . . . 13
Spanish Omelet . . . . . . 71, 76
Tomato-Cheese Eggs . . . . . 31

**FISH**
Anchovy Spread . . . . . . . . 29
Baked Fish . . . . . . . . . . . 118
Baked Flounder with Sauce . . . . . . . . . 124
Baked Stuffed Pompano . . . . . . . . . . 101
Boiled Trout . . . . . . . . . . 122
Boneless Baked Shad . . . . . . . . . . . . 97
Brook Trout Almondine . . . . . . . . . 123
Curried Tuna Toasties . . . . . . . . . . . 11
Deviled Salmon . . . . . . . . 117
Fish Chowder . . . . . . . . . 105
Fish Mulligan . . . . . . . . . . 110
Fried Bass Filets . . . . . . . . 124
Fried Catfish . . . . . . . . . . 104
Japanese Egg Yolk Soup . . . . . . . . . . . . 59
Salmon and Mushroom Stuffed Potatoes . . . . . 100
Scalloped Shad Roe . . . . . 121
Shad Roe Spread . . . . . . . 117
Sole in Wine Sauce . . . . . . 123
Trout Almondine . . . . . . . 109
Tuna Bake with Cheese Swirls . . . . . . . . 113
Tuna Beans . . . . . . . . . . . 80
Tuna Loaf Salad . . . . . . . . 39
Tuna and Ripe-Olive Loaf . . . . . . . . . . . . 107

**FRUIT**
Ambrosia . . . . . . . . . . . . 285
Applesauce Nut Bread . . . . 204
Apricot Salad . . . . . . . . . 37
Banana Bread . . . . . . . . . 203
Black Cherry Salad . . . . . . . . . . . . . 44
Blueberry Streusel Muffins . . . . . . . . . . . 196
Chef's Salad Dressing for Fruit . . . . . . . . . . . 49
Cherry Pineapple Salad . . . . . . . . . . . . . 51
Compote of Fruit with Champagne . . . . . 47
Congealed Salad . . . . . . . . 43
Cranberry Salad . . . . . . . . 43
Dark Beauty Fruit Cake . . . . . . . . . 257
Dark Fruit Cake . . . . . . . . 254
Dressing . . . . . . . . . . . . . 51
English Trifle . . . . . . . . . . 232
Fluffy Honey Dressing . . . . . . . . . . . 41
Franklin Cake . . . . . . . . . 231
Frozen Cranberry Cream Salad . . . . . . . . . . . . . 45
Frozen Fruit Salad . . . . 38, 43
Frozen Salad . . . . . . . . . . 39
Fruit Bars . . . . . . . . . . . . 211
Fruit Salad . . . . . . . . . . . 43
Fruit Salad Loaf . . . . . . . . 45
Fruited Cheese Cake . . . . . 232
Fruit Whip . . . . . . . . . . . 285
Japanese Fruit Cake . . . . . 255
Melon Ball Cocktail . . . . . 289
Molded Three-Fruit Salad . . . . . . . . . . . . . 36
Muscadine Jam . . . . . . . . 298
Pickle, Pineapple Nut Salad . . . . . . . . . . . . . 35
Pineapple Salad . . . . . . . . 49
Sausage Pineapple Kabob . . . . . . . . . . . . 52
Spiced Muscadine . . . . . . . 299
Spiced Peach Salad . . . . . . 48
Strawberry and Pineapple Jam . . . . . . . 294
Tropical Freeze . . . . . . . . 285
Waldorf Salad . . . . . . . . . 38
White Cherry Salad . . . . . . 14
White Fruit Cake . . . . . . . 270
White Fruit Salad . . . . . . . 36
Yum Yum Salad . . . . . . . . 47

**HAM**
Baked Country Cured Ham . . . . . . . . . . . . . 186
Baked Country Ham . . . . . 163
Baked Picnic Ham . . . . . . 185
Deviled Ham Canapes . . . . 16
Eggs Benedict . . . . . . . . . 33
Ham and Asparagus Casserole . . . . . . . . . . 187
Ham Mousse . . . . . . . . . . 187
Ham & Sweet Rolls . . . . . . 18
Island Ham Rolls . . . . . . . 179
Pineapple Ham Loaf . . . . . 185
Talmadge Country Fried Ham . . . . . . . . . 166

**LAMB**
Broiled Lamb Chops . . . . . 171
Deviled Lamb Chops . . . . . 171
Lamb Chops with Mint Jelly . . . . . . . . . . 191
Lamb In The Ground . 169-170
Peasant Soup . . . . . . . . . . 60
Roasted Lamb . . . . . . . . . 168

**LEMON**
Frozen Lemon Pie . . .259, 265
Georgia Lemon Pie . . . . . . 263
Lemonade Cake . . . . . . . . 233
Lemon Cheesecake . . .241, 246
Lemon Chess Pie . . . . . . . 263
Lemon Chiffon Pie . . . . . . 259
Lemon Coconut Pie . . . . . 260

Lemon Dressing . . . . . . . . 42
Lemon Frosting . . . . . . . . 195
Lemon Ice . . . . . . . . . . . 286
Lemon-Lime Sky
High Pie . . . . . . . . . . . 265
Lemon Pie . . . . . . . . . . . 258

**LIVER, CALF'S**
Calf's Liver
in Wine . . . . . . . . . . . . 164
Chuckwagon Braised
Liver . . . . . . . . . . . . . . . .165
Liver and Onions . . . . . . . 162

**LIVER, CHICKEN**
Chinese Style
Chicken Livers . . . . . . . 145
Liver Stuffed Chicken
Breasts with Sauce . . . . 144
Rumaki . . . . . . . . . . . . . 59

**LOBSTER**
Artichoke-Lobster
Newberg . . . . . . . . . . . 112
Lobster a la
Newberg . . . . . . . . . . . 110
Lobster Newberg . . . . . . . 111
Lobster Salad
Supreme . . . . . . . . . . . 113
Newberg Spread . . . . . . . . 46
Stuffed Lobster,
Jamaica Style . . . . . . . 109

**MEAT LOAF**
Diet Meat Loaf . . . . . . . . 183
Meat Loaf . . . . . . . . . . . 180
Meat Loaf O'Brien . . . . . . 189
Moist Meat Loaf . . . . . . . . 181
Summer Meat Loaf . . . . . . 182

**MUFFINS**
Blueberry Streusel
Muffins . . . . . . . . . . . 196
Corn Meal Muffins . . . . . . 206
Country Breakfast
Muffins . . . . . . . . . . . 220
Muffins with
Cranberries . . . . . . . . . 215
Orange Muffins . . . . . . . . 197
Yorkshire Muffins . . . . . . 202

**MUSHROOMS**
Bacon-Mushroom
Rarebit . . . . . . . . . . . . 31
Crab and Mushroom
Stuffed Potatoes . . . . . 86
Mushroom Eggs . . . . . . . . 32
Mushroom Salad . . . . . . . 34
Mushroom Tempters . . . . . 15

**NUTS**
Butter Pecan Pie
Crust . . . . . . . . . . . . . 261
Cream of Peanut
Soup . . . . . . . . . . . . . 55
Date Nut Balls . . . . . . . . . 283
Honey Pecan Pie . . . . . . . 272
Mexican Pecan Candy . . . . 282
Nut Brittle Ice
Cream . . . . . . . . . . . . 249
Orange Nut Bread . . . . . . . 200
Peanut Brittle . . . . . .268, 280
Pecan Balls . . . . . . . . . . . 283
Pecan Cake . . . . . . . . . . . 228
Pecan Pie . . . . . . . . . . . . 262
Pickle, Pineapple
Nut Salad . . . . . . . . . . 35
Sugared Nuts . . . . . . . . . . 281
Sugared Walnuts . . . . . . . . 278
Walnut Glory Cake . . . . . . 250
Whiskey Pecans . . . . . . . . 279

**ONIONS**
Aunt Doveye's
Stuffed Onions . . . . . . 69
French Fried Toombs
County Onions . . . . . . 68
Onion-Almond Omelet . . . 32
Onions in Cheese
Sauce . . . . . . . . . . . . . 65
Scalloped Onions . . . . . . . 75

**ORANGES**
Famous Orange Chiffon
Cake . . . . . . . . . . . . . 242
Orange French
Toast . . . . . . . . . . . . . 203
Orange Marmalade . . . . . . 299
Orange Muffins . . . . . . . . 197
Orange Nut Bread . . . . . . . 200
Orange Pecan Bread . . . . . 205

**OYSTERS**
Baked Oysters . . . . . . . . . 101
Chicken with
Oysters . . . . . . . . . . . 98
Oysters a la
Poulette . . . . . . . . . . . 100
Oysters Rockefeller . . . . . 97
Oyster Stew . . . . . . . . . . 98
Scalloped Oysters . . . . . 98, 99

**PEARS**
Baked Pears Elegante . . . . 251
Pear Preserves . . . . . . . . . 297
Pear Relish . . . . . . . . . . . 28

**PEAS**
English Pea Salad . . . . . . . 50
Green Pea Salad . . . . . . . . 57
Hopping John . . . . . . . . . 98

Vegetable Pilaf . . . . . . . . . 74

**PIES**
Asparagus Pie . . . . . . . . . . 94
Black Bottom Pie . . . . . . . 266
Chess Pie . . . . . . . . . . . . 269
Christmas Egg Nog Pie . . . . . . . . . . . . . . . 270
Coffee Cloud Pie . . . . . . . 269
Easy Mincemeat Pie . . . . . 271
Mile High Lime Pie . . . . . . . . . . . . . . . 262
Rum Cream Pie . . . . . . . . 258
Shepherd's Pie . . . . . . . . . 192
Scotch Steak and Kidney Pie . . . . . . . . . 159

**PINEAPPLES**
Cherry Pineapple Salad . . . . . . . . . . . . . 51
Glazed Pineapple Fingers . . . . . . . . . . . . 195
Pickle, Pineapple Nut Salad . . . . . . . . . . 35
Pineapple Chiffon Pie . . . . . . . . . . . . . . . 262
Pineapple Ham Loaf . . . . . 185
Pineapple Salad . . . . . . . . 49
Sausage Pineapple Kabob . . . . . . . . . . . . 52
Tropical Pie . . . . . . . . . . . 267
Yum Yum Salad . . . . . . . . 47

**PLUMS**
Damson Plum Preserves . . . . . . . . . . . 294
Grandma's Plum Pudding . . . . . . . . . . . 271
Plum Cake . . . . . . . . . . . 229
Plum Jam . . . . . . . . . . . . 294
Plum Jelly . . . . . . . . . . . . 292
Plum Sauce or Spiced Plums . . . . . . . . 293

**PORK**
Barbecued Spareribs . . . . . 190
Creole Spareribs . . . . . . . . 179
Crown Pork Roast with Corn Bread Stuffing . . . 188
Dixie Pork Chops . . . . . . . 191
Pork Chops in Wine Sauce . . . . . . . . . 189
Pork Tenderloin . . . . . . . . 191
Sherry Roast Pork . . . . . . 192

**POTATOES**
Baked and Stuffed Fluffy White Potatoes . . . . . . . 87
Crab and Mushroom Stuffed Potatoes . . . . . 86
Creme Vichyssoise . . . . . . 11
Hot Potato Salad . . . . . . . 40
Potato Bread . . . . . . . . . . 221
Potatoes O'Glenn . . . . . . . 83
Potato Pancakes . . . . . . . . 84
Salmon and Mushroom Stuffed Potatoes . . . . . 100

**RICE**
Brown Rice . . . . . . . . . . . 92
Cheese-Rice Casserole . . . . 85
Coastal Rice Bread . . . . . . 208
Fried Rice and Shrimp . . . 77
Hopping John . . . . . . . . . 93
Italian Rice . . . . . . . . . . . 78
Lemon Wild Rice With Shrimp . . . . . . . . 82
Okra, Rice and Tomatoes . . . . . . . . . . 70
Rice Casserole . . . . . . . . . 83
Rice Pudding . . . . . . . . . . 280
Savannah Red Rice . . . . . . 91
Spanish Rice . . . . . . . . 76, 77
Steak with Rice . . . . . . . . 156

**ROLLS**
Easy Icebox Rolls . . . . . . . 219
Grandma's Buttermilk Rolls . . . . . . . . . . . . 219
Refrigerator Rolls . . . . . . . 211

**SAUSAGE**
Chicken-Sausage Casserole . . . . . . . . . . 137
Company Casserole . . . . . . 175
Sausage Casserole . . . . . . . 154
Sausage Pineapple Kabob . . . . . . . . . . . . 52

**SHRIMP**
Bayou Pie . . . . . . . . . . . . 125
Beer-Batter Shrimp . . . . . . 116
Creole Shrimp . . . . . .118, 124
Deviled Shrimp . . . . . . . . 121
Easy Shrimp Curry . . . . . . 114
Lemon-Wild Rice with Shrimp . . . . . . . . 82
Pickled Shrimp . . . . . . . . 24
Savannah Shrimp . . . . . . . 122
Shrimp Aspic Salad . . . . . . 22
Shrimp and Crabmeat Casserole . . . . . . . . . . 119
Shrimp de Jonghe . . . . . . . 114
Shrimp Paste . . . . . . . . . . 10
Shrimp Remoulade . . . . . . 117
Shrimp & Rice . . . . . . . . . 115
Shrimp Rice Jambalaya . . . . . . . . . . 115
Shrimp Sea Island . . . . . . . 120
Shrimp Stuffed in Bell Peppers . . . . . . . . 119

Spiced Pickled Shrimp . . . . . . . . . . . . 22
Stuffed Avocados . . . . . . . 111

**SOUFFLES**
Broccoli Souffle . . . . . . . . . 92
Butternut Squash Souffle . . . . . . . . . . . . 67
Cheese Souffle . . . . . . . . . 79
Never Fail Cheese Souffle . . . . . . . . . . . . 81
Pecan-Squash Souffle . . . . . . . . . . . . 65
Souffle Sauce . . . . . . . . . 25
Spinach Souffle . . . . . . . . 92
Sweet Potato Souffle . . . . . . . . . . . . 84

**SPINACH**
Fresh Spinach Salad . . . . . . . . . . . . . 42
Spinach Dressing . . . . . . . 48
Spinach Souffle . . . . . . . . 92
Wilted Spinach Salad . . . . . . . . . . . . . 42

**SQUASH**
Baked Acorn Squash . . . . . 91
Baked Squash . . . . . . . . . 89
Butternut Squash Souffle . . . . . . . . . . . . 67
Candied Acorn Squash . . . . . . . . . . . . 88
Pecan-Squash Souffle . . . . 65
Squash Casserole . . . . . 68, 73
Stuffed Zucchini . . . . . . . 82

**STEAK**
Blue Cheese Steaks . . . . . . 181
Braised Sirloin . . . . . . . . . 167
Country Fried Steak . . . . . 163
Fabulous Hawaiian Marinated Steak . . . . . . 183
Green Peppersteak . . . . . . 157
London Broil . . . . . . . . . . 164
Marinated Steak . . . . . . . . 158
Me Jane Steak . . . . . . . . . 157
Pepper Steak . . . . . . . . . . 160
Round Steak Supreme . . . . 161
Scotch Steak and Kidney Pie . . . . . . . . . 159
Steak Casserole . . . . . . . . 154
Steak with Rice . . . . . . . . 156
Swiss Steak . . . . . . . . . . . 160

**STEWS**
Beef Stew . . . . . . . . . . . . 157
Beef Stew a-Eloise . . . . . . 161
Brunswick Stew . . . . . . . . 177
Oyster Stew . . . . . . . . . . 98
South Georgia Brunswick Stew . . . . . . 173

**STROGANOFF**
Beef Stroganoff Casserole . . . . . . . . . . 175
Quick Stroganoff . . . . . . . 174
Skillet Stroganoff . . . . . . . 173

**SWEET POTATOES**
Candied Sweet Potatoes . . . . . . . . . . . 88
Scalloped Sweet Potatoes . . . . . . . . . . . 87
Sweet Potato Balls . . . . . . . . 87
Sweet Potato Biscuits . . . . 200
Sweet Potato Delight . . . . 85
Sweet Potato Souffle . . . . 84

**TOMATOES**
Asheville Salad . . . . . . . . . 53
Broiled Tomatoes . . . . . . . 89
Cheese & Tomato Curry . . . . . . . . . . . . 29
Okra, Rice and Tomatoes . . . . . . . . . . 70
Scalloped Tomatoes . . . . . 70
Seafood in Tomato Shells . . . . . . . . . . . . . 99
Tomato Aspic . . . . . . . . . 17
Tomato-Cheese Eggs . . . . . 31
Tomato Soup French Dressing . . . . . . . . . . . 55

**VENISON**
Roast Venison . . . . . . . . . 162
Venison with Sour Cream . . . . . . . . . . . . 168
Venison Steaks . . . . . . . . 163